Connectives of English Speech:
The Correct Usage of Prepositions, Conjunctions, Relative Pronouns and Adverbs Explained and Illustrated

James Champlin Fernald

CONNECTIVES OF ENGLISH SPEECH

Connectives Of English Speech

THE CORRECT USAGE OF PREPOSITIONS, CON-
JUNCTIONS, RELATIVE PRONOUNS AND
ADVERBS EXPLAINED AND
ILLUSTRATED

BY

JAMES C. FERNALD, L. H. D.

*Author of "Expressive English," "English Synonyms and
Antonyms," etc.*

FUNK & WAGNALLS COMPANY

NEW YORK AND LONDON

Copyright, 1904, by FUNK & WAGNALLS COMPANY:

(Printed in the United States of America)

2—32

PUBLISHED IN THE UNITED STATES

CONTENTS

(v)

INTRODUCTION

Thought-Connectives

There are certain words that express the great essentials of human thought, as objects, qualities, or actions; these are nouns, adjectives, and verbs. Such words must always make up the substance of language. Yet these are dependent for their full value and utility upon another class of words, the thought-connectives, that simply indicate relation; these are prepositions, conjunctions, relative pronouns and adverbs. If we compare words of the former class to the bricks that make up the substance of a wall, we may compare those of the latter class—the thought-connectives—to the mortar that binds the separate elements into the cohesion and unity of a single structure.

The value of these connectives may be clearly manifested by simply striking them out of any well-known paragraph and showing the barrenness and confusion that result.

Thus by the omission of the thought-connectives, the first sentence of the Declaration of Independence becomes a mere cipher, capable of many meanings, and needing a key for its interpretation, while by the restoration of the thought-connectives the meaning becomes luminous, as in the following:

"The course human events becomes necessary one people dissolve the political bands have connected them another, assume the powers the earth the separate equal station the laws nature nature's God entitle them, a decent respect the opinions mankind requires \they should declare the causes impel them the separation."

"*When, in the course of* human events, it* becomes necessary *for* one people *to* dissolve the political bands *which* have connected them *with* another, *and to* assume *among* the powers *of* the earth the separate *and* equal station *to which* the laws *of* nature *and of* nature's God entitle them, a decent respect *to* the opinions *of* mankind requires *that* they should declare the causes *which* impel them *to* the separation."

Such an example shows the great importance of prepositions and other connectives as the means of binding words into sentences. Without such helps all speech would be made up of brief, isolated, and fragmentary statements. The movement of thought would be constantly and abruptly broken. Much would need to be guessed at; much would, after all, be doubtful or obscure; while the mental difficulty involved in following such statements would render them practically valueless. For easy, effective, and pleasant reading or hearing, the mind needs to have the connections of thought clearly indicated from point to point. The path of discourse may be steep, winding, or even intricate, but should always clearly show enough of forward reach to leave the traveler in no doubt where to set his foot. Prepositions, conjunctions, relative pronouns and adverbs are the ever-recurring finger-boards that point the thought onward, or enable it on occasion to retrace its way, and make all clearer and surer by turning backward

* NOTE.—For the connective force of *it* in such use see INTRODUCTORY PARTICLES in the Addenda, pp. 315, 316.

for a new start. At the same time it should be said that the discourse in which these thought-connectives are most freely and wisely used is that in which it will be found least necessary to turn backward in order to make the meaning clear and sure.

As has been well said by Austin Phelps,* "The wrong use or the omission of connective words is often the occasion of looseness of style. The superior precision of the Greek tongue is said, by those who are experts in teaching it, to be in part due to the abundance of connectives in its vocabulary. For some of its connective particles our language has no equivalents; yet such as we have serve often to knit one's style together in exact and forcible collocations. Coleridge says that a master of our language may be known by his skilful use of connectives. This is one secret of the vigor of Coleridge's own style. His prolonged and involuted sentences derive from this source often a wonderful continuity, without which his profound conceptions could not find adequate expression. In order to represent some thoughts, style needs a certain sweep of sustained expression, like the sailing of an eagle on wings of scarcely visible vibration. Such, often, is Coleridge's style; and his command of it is often due to his precise use of connective words. It is still more abundantly and grandly illustrated in the prose style of Milton. Hence arises the independence of both of fragmentary expression, such as the majority of

---

* *English Style in Public Discourse* ch. 1, pp. 83, 84.

writers would think to be all that some thoughts admit of in human speech. Hence their freedom from that which Southey calls the 'Anglo-Gallican style, whose cementless periods are understood beforehand, they are so free from all the connections of logic.' Dr. Arnold, speaking of this feature in the thinking of Coleridge, says that he would have been more perfectly understood if he had written in classic Greek. . . . No man can be supremely eloquent in laconics. You can not express the rising and the expanding and the sweep and the circling of eloquent feeling, in a style resembling that which seamen call 'a chopping sea.' For such thinking, you must have at command a style of which an oceanic ground-swell, or the Gothic interweaving of forest-trees, is the more becoming symbol. . . . But you must have such a style for the most exact utterance of certain elevated and impassioned thoughts. . . . Yet, in the construction of such a style, you must use connective words, links elaborately forged, inserted in the right joints of style, to make them flexible without loss of compactness. One word of such exact connective force in the right place, with the right surroundings before and after, may make all the difference between a disjointed and a linked style."

The connective words, those "links elaborately forged" through centuries as the means of binding words and sentences together into a structural unity, are worthy of thorough and careful consideration such as they have scarcely yet received.

PART I

I—Prepositions: Their Office and Use

Among the connectives prepositions may be first considered, since they are used to connect words rather than clauses or sentences. The preposition usually precedes a noun or pronoun, to which circumstance it owes its name, *preposition* being derived from the Latin *pre*, before, and *pono*, place. The preposition is a word usually *placed before* another, which is called its object, and which it is said to "govern."*

Yet a little consideration will show that this so-called "government" is purely theoretical. In the usage with many pronouns, indeed, the control of the preposition over its object appears in the change of case of the following pronoun, as when we say "*to* him," "*of* her," "*by* us." But in the expressions "*to* it," "*of* this," "*by* that," there is absolutely no change in the form of the pronoun. The same is true of all nouns. In the statements "*Brutus* killed Cæsar" and "Cæsar was killed by *Brutus*," the noun *Brutus* is the same in both, whether it stands as the subject of the verb or the so-called object of the preposition. In the Latin a decided difference appears. In that language the first of the two statements above given would be "*Brutus* Cæsarem interfecit," while the latter would be "Cæsar a *Bruto* interfectus est," the nominative *Brutus* being changed to the ablative *Bruto* following the preposition *a*, which is here equivalent to the English *by*. English grammarians have found it convenient to follow this analogy, and to hold that a noun with no change of form is in the

---

* "We speak of both verbs and prepositions as governing in the objective the word that is their object, because it is compelled to be put in that case after them." W. D. WHITNEY *Essentials of English Grammar* ch. 5, p. 32.

(1)

objective (or object) case when it is construed with a preposition. We might often more fittingly speak of the *consequent* than of the *object* of an English preposition.

In one respect, indeed, the English usage of a noun with a preposition approximates to the Latin construction, viz.: in rendering the words less dependent upon position. For instance, in the sentence "Brutus killed Cæsar," the dependence of the meaning upon the order of the words is absolute. If we say "Cæsar killed Brutus" we have reversed the statement. If we say "Cæsar Brutus killed," or "Brutus Cæsar killed," the statement is hopelessly ambiguous, and no one by reading it could determine which was the slayer and which the slain. But in the Latin the meaning is not thus dependent upon the position of the words. Since the noun which is in the accusative case (corresponding to the English objective) really undergoes change of form, the words may be placed in any order which emphasis or euphony may require, and "Cæsarem Brutus interfecit," "Cæsarem interfecit Brutus," "Interfecit Brutus Cæsarem," etc., would all have the unvarying meaning "Brutus killed Cæsar."

By the use of the preposition in English, we approach the Latin freedom of construction. If the preposition directly precedes the noun or pronoun which is its object, then the phrase so constructed may be transposed to any position in the sentence without changing its essential meaning. The statements "Cæsar was killed by Brutus," "Cæsar by Brutus was killed," "By Brutus was Cæsar killed," are identical in signification.

The same is true if any modifier, as one or more adjectives or a noun in apposition, intervene between the preposition and its object, so long as the whole phrase is kept together. We may say "by the perfidious Brutus," by his professed friend Brutus," etc., and we shall find that the entire phrase may be transposed to any position in the sentence as freely as the preposition with the unmodified noun. Thus the use of prepositions is especially important in English as contributing to a freedom and variety of construction that in our language could not be otherwise attained, since we have sacrificed the case-endings which form so important an element of the construction in the Latin, the Greek, and various other languages.

The freedom of transposition of an English prepositional phrase referred to above is, however, subject to an important limitation. When such prepositional phrase directly limits a noun or adjective, it can not in many cases be separated from that noun or adjective without change of meaning. As Goold Brown observes, the statement "He rose *heavy at heart*" can not be made to read "*At* heart he rose heavy." "The man *of* learning spoke" is not the same as "The man spoke *of* learning."

The preposition is a word that looks backward as well as forward, and does not exhaust its effect upon the word that immediately follows it. The phrase "*to* John" conveys no intelligible idea. The mind instantly asks, "What happened *to* John?" To what act or fact does the "*to*" refer back? So of the phrase "*to* Richmond" we ask at once, "What *to* Richmond?" Is it "the train *to* Richmond," "the distance *to* Richmond," or did some one send or go "*to* Richmond"? If we say "*by* Henry," the question is, "What was done *by* Henry?" If we say "*of* the city," "*in* the house," "*against* the wind," the mind instantly inquires what is *of*, *in*, or *against*; and so in every other possible case. Thus it appears that its antecedent is as necessary to a preposition as its object or consequent, in order to express any completeness of thought. The preposition is as truly a connective as the conjunction. Its least office is to limit the use and relation of the word that follows it. Its chief value is in the connecting of that word with some preceding term, thus binding words together into that unity of thought which makes possible the coherent sentence.

"In one respect, the preposition is the simplest of all the parts of speech: in our common schemes of grammar, it has neither classes nor modifications. Every connective word that governs an object after it, is called a preposition, because it does so; and

in etymological parsing, to name the preposition as such, and
define the name, is, perhaps, all that is necessary. But in syntactical parsing, in which we are to omit the definitions, and state
the construction, we ought to explain what terms the preposition
connects, and to give a rule adapted to this office of the particle.
It is a palpable defect in nearly all our grammars, that their syntax contains *no such rule*. 'Prepositions govern the objective
case,' is a rule for the objective case, and not for the syntax of
prepositions. 'Prepositions show the relations of words, and of
the things or thoughts expressed by them,' is the principle for the
latter; a principle which we cannot neglect without a shameful
lameness in our interpretation—that is, when we pretend to parse
syntactically." *

Preposition Ending Sentence

Simply stated, a preposition is a word that shows the relation
between an antecedent and a consequent in the same sentence.

Oddly enough, the very name *preposition* is a misnomer in
English, since an English preposition may follow the noun or pronoun which it is said to "govern"; and, in fact, the *preposition*
or "word placed before" may be the very last word in the sentence, *placed after* everything else, while yet the meaning is perfectly clear; as, this is the gun *that* he was shot *with*. Many
grammarians have undertaken to fight this thoroughly live and
vernacular idiom, and force the *preposition* into conforming to
its name by always *standing before* its object. But the idiom is
stronger than the grammarians. The schoolboys have invented the
rebellious paraphrase, "Never use a preposition to end a sentence
with." The people go on using the prohibited idiom in conversation
every day, and an examination of our literature shows that this
idiom has the indorsement of the foremost writers of our language.

Ford. There is no better way than that they spoke *of*.
SHAKESPEARE *Merry Wives of Windsor* act iv, sc. 4, l. 22.

Fenton. . . . I have a letter from her
Of such contents as you will wonder *at*.
SHAKESPEARE *Merry Wives of Windsor* act iii, sc. 6, l. 18.

* GOOLD BROWN *Grammar of English Grammars* pt. iii, ch. 10, p. 455.

What a taking was he *in* when your husband asked what was in the basket!

> SHAKESPEARE *Merry Wives of Windsor* act iii, sc. 3, l. 188.

> All is but toys; renown and grace is dead;
> The wine of life is drawn, and the mere lees
> Is left this vault to brag *of*.

> SHAKESPEARE *Macbeth* act ii, sc. 3, l. 99.

> O melancholy!
> Who ever yet could sound thy bottom? find
> The ooze, to show what coast thy sluggish crare
> Might easiliest harbor *in!*

> SHAKESPEARE *Cymbeline* act iv, sc. 2, l. 205.

Such kindness as he knows he regards her *with*, I believe.

> DICKENS *Nicholas Nickleby* vol. ii, p. 220.

Hanging was the worst use a man could be put *to*. SIR HENRY WOTTON *The Disparity between Buckingham and Essex*.

Dost thou love life? Then do not squander time, for that is the stuff life is made *of*. FRANKLIN *Poor Richard's Almanac*.

Three things are men most likely to be cheated *in*—a horse, a wig, and a wife. FRANKLIN *Poor Richard's Almanac*.

The soil out of which such men as he are made is good to be born *on*, good to live *on*, good to die *for* and to be buried *in*.

> LOWELL *Among My Books, Second Series, Garfield*.

> Oh, for boyhood's time of June,
> Crowding years in one brief moon,
> When all things I heard or saw,
> Me, their master, waited *for*.

> WHITTIER *The Barefoot Boy* st. 8.

> I count life just a stuff
> To try the soul's strength *on*, educe the man.

> ROBERT BROWNING *In a Balcony* l. 642.

> *Faliero.*   Ay—
> If that which is not be, and that which is
> Be not, I shall be: this I doubt not *of*.

> SWINBURNE *Marino Faliero* act iii, sc. 1.

Faliero.   . . . But for men
The eternal fire hath no such pang to smite
As this their jests make nought *of.*

SWINBURNE *Marino Faliero* act ii, sc. 1.

The virility and vigor of our language are shown in the obstinate persistence of this forceful idiom. "The worst use a man could be put *to*" brings *use* and *man*, the two important terms, closely together, in a prominent place in the sentence, leaving the note of connection to be lightly appended at the end. "The worst use *to which* a man could be put" separates the important words by the uncared-for particles *to* and *which.* The mind hurries past the preposition and relative to reach the important thing referred to, finding the impediments of formal correctness very much in its way. Unfettered and vigorous speech brushes these formalities aside, gives first place to the words expressing the important thought, and then pays its grammatical scot at the end of the sentence. It is an element of power in the English language that it can thus march across technicalities to attain the great purpose of speech—the expression of thought—securing directness and emphasis without sacrifice of clearness.

The limitation to be put upon such use applies not to the preposition as such, but to the use of any small and unaccented word at the end of a sentence where special dignity, formality, or rhetorical fulness and resonance may be required. The question is one of style rather than of grammar, of emphasis rather than of correctness. See THAT under RELATIVE PRONOUNS, p. 277.

"When a preposition *begins* or *ends* a sentence or clause, the terms of relation, if both are given, are transposed; as, 'To a studious *man* action is a relief.'—*Burgh.* That is, 'Action is a relief *to* a studious man.' '*Science* they (the ladies) do not *pretend* to.' —*Id.* That is, 'They do not pretend *to* science.' 'Until I have done that *which* I *have spoken* to thee of.'—Gen. xxviii, 15. The word governed by the preposition is always the subsequent term of the relation, however it may be placed; and if this be a relative pronoun the transposition is permanent. The preposition, however, may be put before any relative, except *that* and *as;* and this is commonly thought to be its most appropriate place; as, 'Until I have done that *of which* I have spoken to thee.' Of the placing of it last Lowth says, 'This is an idiom *which* our language is strongly inclined *to*'; Murray and others, 'This is an idiom *to which* our language is strongly inclined'; while they all add, 'it prevails in common conversation and suits very well with the familiar style in writing; but the placing of the preposition before the relative is more graceful, as well as more perspicuous, and agrees much better with the solemn and elevated style.' "*

Prepositions and Adverbs

"The syntactical function of prepositions is of the greatest extent within the simple sentence, from which they in great part pass into the construction as conjunctions and undertake the connection of its members, as on the other hand they may appear in the sentence as independent adverbs—which they are originally in part."—MAETZNER *English Grammar* vol. ii, p. 218.

This suggestion that the prepositions were originally adverbs seems eminently reasonable, and is confirmed by the fact that most of the words used as prepositions have also adverbial use, as *about, above, around, beneath,* etc.

"To a preposition the prior or antecedent term may be a noun, an adjective, a pronoun, a verb, a participle, or an adverb; and the subsequent or governed term may be a noun, a pronoun, a pronominal adjective, an infinitive verb, or a participle. In some instances also, as in the phrases *in vain, on high, at once, till now, for ever, by how much, until then, from thence, from above,* we find adjectives used elliptically, and adverbs substantively, after the preposition. But in phrases of an adverbial character what is elsewhere a preposition often becomes an adverb."†

The following quotations illustrate the readiness with which a preposition takes for its object or consequent an adverb that in other use might itself be a preposition or adverbial phrase:

O let thy graces *without cease* Drop *from above.*
HERBERT *Grace* st. 1.

---

* GOOLD BROWN *Grammar of English Grammars* pt. iii, ch. 10, p. 663.
† GOOLD BROWN *Grammar of English Grammars* pt. iii, ch. 10, p. 435.

Her battlements and towers, *from off* their rocky steep,
Have cast their trembling shadows for ages o'er the deep.
> ADELAIDE PROCTER *Legend of Bregenz* st. 8.

When the loose mountain trembles *from on high*,
Shall gravitation cease, if you go by?
> POPE *Essay on Man* ep. iv, l. 128.

This world of natural men is staked off from the Spiritual World by barriers which have never yet been crossed *from within.*
> DRUMMOND *Natural Law, Biogenesis* p. 71.

In the following sentence the preposition evidently governs a prepositional phrase:

A huge wave lifted us high in the air, and, as it slipped *from under* the brig, down went her forefoot upon the ice.
> L. I. HAYES *Arctic Boat Journey* ch. 1, p. 4.

The wave did not slip *from* the brig, nor did it slip *under* the brig, but the two ideas must be combined to give the meaning, and the words *from under* have the effect of a compound preposition.

The first use of prepositions was undoubtedly in the designation of place or space. From this the transition was easy to the idea of time, or of various abstract relations. From the thought of what is *beyond* a certain limit in space, it is easy to pass to the idea of an event *beyond* a certain limit in time. The thing that is *above* another is easily thought of as superior, as it is at least in elevation. Hence we speak of a thing as *above* price, of a noble person as *above* a mean action, or of the law of God as *above* the laws of man. So, conversely, goods may be sold *under* price, or an action may be *beneath* contempt. Such extension of meaning is but a part of that system of unstudied metaphor that pervades all language, making words which at first expressed only material facts or relations to become the vehicles of mental and spiritual ideas.

"If our purpose were to give a learner his first idea of a preposition, we might say that it is a word which expresses the relation of one thing to another in respect of place or position. We might go on to illustrate by saying:

"'The house stands *upon* rising ground. There is a lawn *before* the door, a veranda *along* one side of the house, *behind* it an apple orchard bending *under* the weight *of* its ruddy fruit. *Below* the orchard the river flows *between* rocky banks, and *beyond* it rises a steep woody hill. A little *up* the stream there is a bridge *across* it, so high that boats can pass *beneath* it.'

"We might next explain what is so very common that a device found to serve well for one purpose is apt to be applied to many others. So many other relations besides those of place are expressed by prepositions. Thus there are relations of time— *before* noon; *between* dawn and sunrise; *during* the eclipse; *after* the Revolution. *Before* frost, *before* rain, *after* taking the oath, are but slight modifications of the same. Prepositions also express cause, instrumentality, manner, and purpose.

> "'The house was struck *by* lightning.'
> "'It was all *through* love of fame.'
> "'They fled *for* fear of discovery.'
> "'The letter was sealed *with* wax.'
> "'She prayed *with* zeal and fervor.'
> "'They were working *for* an education.'

"Prepositions thus take a variety of secondary meanings.
"*Through* has not the same signification in:

> "'I was walking *through* a wood'

and

> "'They betrayed him *through* envy.'

So one may walk *with* a lady, *with* difficulty, *with* a limp, *with* a cane, *with* a sprained ankle." [*]

"Now, if prepositions are concerned in expressing the various relations of so many of the different parts of speech, multiplied, as these relations must be, by that endless variety of combinations which may be given to the terms, and if the sense of the writer or speaker is necessarily mistaken as often as any of these relations are misunderstood or their terms misconceived, how shall we estimate the importance of a right explanation and a right use of this part of speech?" [†]

---

[*] SAMUEL RAMSEY *The English Language and English Grammar* ch. 8, p. 465.
[†] GOOLD BROWN *Grammar of English Grammars* pt. iii, ch. 10, p. 435.

How admirably has Byron, in his "Prisoner of Chillon," lit up his description of the 'little isle' by the fine choice of prepositions:

> "And then there was a little isle
> Which *in* my very face did smile,
>   The only one in view;
> A small green isle, it seemed no more,
> Scarce broader than my dungeon floor,
> But *in* it there were three tall trees,
> And *o'er* it blew the mountain breeze,
> And *by* it there were waters flowing,
> And *on* it there were young flowers growing,
>   Of gentle breath and hue."

II—Prepositions Defined and Illustrated

The principal English prepositions are the following:

abaft, aboard, about, above, across, after, against, along, amid or amidst, among or amongst, around (see also *round*), *aslant, at, athwart,*

Barring, bating, before, behind, below, beneath, beside or *besides, between, betwixt, beyond, but* (compare *except*), *by,*

Concerning, considering,

Down, during,

Ere, except, excepting (compare *but*),

For, from,

In, inside, into,

Mid, midst,

Notwithstanding,

Of, off, on (compare *upon*), *out, outside, over, overthwart,*

Past, pending, per,

Regarding, respecting, round (compare *around*),

Save, saving, since,

Through, throughout, till (compare *until*), *to* (compare *unto*), *touching, toward* or *towards,*

Under, underneath, until (compare *till*), *unto* (compare *to*), *up, upon* (compare *on*),

Via,

With, within, without.

In addition to these, there are many prepositional phrases, which, while they may be easily separated into their elements, are yet always used as phrases, and have all the effect of compound prepositions; as, *according to, in accordance with, on account of, because of, with* or *in respect to, in consideration of, in spite of, by means of, with* or *in regard to, in default of, in consequence of*, *with* or *in reference to*, *as to*, etc. The meaning of such phrases is usually evident from a knowledge of the separate words, and need not be particularly explained.

As this work is designed for popular utility and ready reference, it has been thought best to take up the prepositions and other words discussed in alphabetical order, rather than in the order of their importance or of any system of philosophical classification. The alphabetical is the simplest of all arrangements, and leaves the reader in no doubt where to turn. He has only to know how a word is spelled, when he may seek and find it as in a dictionary.

In the quotations, prominence is given to the Anglican or Authorized Version of the English Bible as an acknowledged authority of pure Elizabethan English. With this are especially associated Shakespeare and Milton, while numerous authors of eminence, both English and American, are appealed to as authority for the statements made.

ABAFT

This nautical preposition is very ancient, and is derived from *aft* or *æftan*, back, behind, after, first reinforced by the prefix *be-* or *bi-*, by, near, forming *baft*, which was in use as a separate word in the fourteenth century. This was further reinforced by the prefix *a-*, on or at, forming the word *abaft*. The most common application of this word is to denote that which is on the after part of a ship or other vessel, or which is farther aft than the object of the preposition; as:

The black cook . . . had a bunk just *abaft* the galley.
COFFIN *Old Sailor's Yarns* ch. 4, p. 81.

That is, the black cook's bunk was a little farther aft than the galley.

[This term (*abaft*) is not used with reference to things out of the ship. YOUNG *Naut. Dict.*]

Objects outside of and directly behind a ship are commonly spoken of as *astern* of the ship. But there is a broadly inclusive use of the word *abaft* in the phrase *abaft the beam*, which is prepositional in form, but adverbial in sense. If a line be drawn directly across a vessel at right angles to the keel till it intersects the horizon on each side, and if the line of the keel be prolonged directly astern till it, too, cuts the horizon, then any object between the cross-line and the stern-line on the right-hand side may be described as "to starboard *abaft the beam*," and any object in the corresponding place on the left as "to port *abaft the beam*."

The wind is aft through the northeast, just *abaft the beam*. MAURY *Physical Geography of the Sea* xv, 642.

MURRAY'S *New English Dictionary*.

ABOARD

Aboard, like *abaft*, is distinctly a nautical preposition. It is compounded of the prefix *a-*, on, plus the noun *board*, and is thus equivalent to the fuller prepositional phrase *on board of*.

Of place exclusively:

1. Upon the deck of, or within the boards or sides of (a ship or other vessel).

Aboard my galley I invite you all.
SHAKESPEARE *Antony and Cleopatra* act ii, sc. 6, l. 104.

He had ten carpenters with him, most of which were found *aboard* the prize they had taken.
DE FOE *Captain Singleton* ch. 18, p. 165.

The prepositional phrase *aboard of* is also often used:

He came *aboard of* my ship.
DE FOE *Captain Singleton* ch. 12, p. 151.

A boat went *aboard of* the Ayacucho and brought off a quarter of beef.   DANA *Two Years before the Mast* ch. 9, p. 45.

2. By extension on, upon, or in any conveyance; as, come *aboard* the car; we can talk when we get *aboard* the train.

3. Across or alongside of: a secondary nautical meaning; as, to lay the ship *aboard* the enemy.

ABOUT

About is derived from the Anglo-Saxon *ābūtan*, which is composed of *an-*, on, plus *būtan*, outside. *About* thus signifies directly and literally *on the outside of*.

I. Of place or space:

1. Surrounding (an object) on all sides, so as to encircle it, equivalent to *around* or *all around*.

Set bounds *about* the mount.   *Ex.* xix, 23.

He made a trench *about* the altar.   *1 Kings* xviii, 32.

The chain he drew was clasped *about* his middle.
      Dickens *Christmas Carol* st. 1, p. 22.

A chain of gold *about* his neck.   *Dan.* v, 7.

A leathern girdle *about* his loins.   *Matt.* iii, 4.

> Like one who wraps the drapery of his couch
> *About* him, and lies down to pleasant dreams.
>   Bryant *Thanatopsis* l. 81.

It was found necessary to erect a stockade *about* the town-hall and to plant caltrops and other obstructions in the squares and streets.   Motley *John of Barneveld* vol. ii, ch. 14, p. 185.

2. Here and there around; on various sides; encompassing.

When my children were *about* me.   *Job* xxix, 5.

The parts of Libya *about* Cyrene.   *Acts* ii, 10.

About the new-arrived, in multitudes, The ethereal people ran.
      Milton *Paradise Lost* bk. x, l. 28.

The heathen that were *about* us.   *Neh.* v, 17.

Getting into a beaked ship, he [Caius] sailed to and fro, striking and sinking the vessels which lay *about* the bridge.
      Keightley *Roman Empire* pt. i, ch. 4, p. 72.

Mere facts . . . are the stones heaped *about* the mouth of the well in whose depth truth reflects the sky.
      E. C. Stedman *Nature and Elements of Poetry* ch. 6, p. 196.

The solitary sandpipers . . . appear to have a special fondness for stagnant pools in and *about* the woods.
      B. H. Warren *Birds of Pennsylvania, Sandpiper* p. 90.

3. In motion around; moving so as to encircle or pass around; as, the movement of the earth *about* the sun.

The slingers went *about* it, and smote it.   *2 Kings* iii, 25.

> We count for poets . . . all
> Who wind the robes of ideality
> *About* the bareness of their lives.
>   JEAN INGELOW *Gladys* st. 44.

Men dance the carmagnole all night *about* the bonfire.
           CARLYLE *French Revolution* vol. iii, bk. v, ch. 4, p. 192.

Now wail low winds *about* the forest eaves.
           ELAINE GOODALE *Fringed Gentian* st. 4.

The choughs that call *about* the shining cliff.
           COVENTRY PATMORE *St. Valentine's Day* l. 28.

4. In motion on, upon, or over; to and fro upon; here and there around; to or toward all sides of; as, peddling goods *about* the country; wandering *about* the world; look *about* you.

Smite *about* it with a knife.   *Ezek.* v, 2.

The mourners go *about* the streets.   *Eccl.* xii, 5.

The watchmen that went *about* the city.   *Cant.* v, 7.

Walk *about* Zion and go round *about* her.   *Psalm* xlviii, 12.

In about ten days [the captain] was entirely well and *about* the ship.   DE FOE *Captain Singleton* ch. 11, p. 189.

Every glib and loquacious hireling who shows strangers *about* their picture-galleries, palaces, and ruins is called a 'cicerone,' or a Cicero.   TRENCH *On the Study of Words* lect. iii, p. 88.

Shopping *about* the city, ransacking entire depôts of splendid merchandise, and bringing home a ribbon.
           HAWTHORNE *House of Seven Gables* ch. 12, p. 188.

The tombs of the ancient Electors were broken open: the corpses, stripped of their cerecloths and ornaments, were dragged *about* the streets.   MACAULAY *England* vol. iv, ch. 20, p. 343.

Jesus saw great multitudes *about* him.   *Matt.* viii, 18.

Pure inspirations of morn Breathed *about* them.
           OWEN MEREDITH *Lucile* pt. i, can. 4, st. 6.

She saw the tattered banners falling   *About* the broken staffs.
R. W. GILDER Decoration Day st. 1.

5. Somewhere within a circle bounding; on some side of; beside; close to; somewhere near; at, in, or by; as, idlers hanging *about* the door; there is a man *about* the house.

There was no room to receive them, no, not so much as *about* the door.   *Mark* ii, 2.

They that were *about* him with the twelve.   *Mark* iv, 10.

6. Hence, specifically, on or near the person of; in possession of; attending; connected with; with; at hand; as, I have not the money *about* me.

If you have this about you,
(As I will give you when we go,) you may
Boldly assault the necromancer's hall.
MILTON Comus l. 647.

For besides the wasteness of the silence, motionless machines have a look of death *about* them.
MACDONALD Robert Falconer ch. 17, p. 182.

About his ordinary bearing there was a certain fling, . . . a confidence in his own powers.
GEORGE ELIOT Middlemarch vol. i, bk. ii, ch. 18, p. 187.

II. Of time: indefinitely near to; approximating to; near; close to; not far from: an extension into a kindred realm of the usage regarding place (I., 6); as, *about* noon; *about* a year ago.

He went out *about* the sixth and ninth hour.   *Matt.* xx, 5.

About the fourth watch of the night.   *Mark* vi, 48.

Be you in the park *about* midnight.
SHAKESPEARE Merry Wives of Windsor, act v, sc. 1, l. 12.

About that time, Herod the king stretched forth his hand to vex certain of the church.   *Acts* xii, 1.

About midnight the shipmen deemed that they drew near to some country.   *Acts* xxvii, 27.

And it was *about* the space of three hours after.   *Acts* v, 7.

About the year 180 of our era, we have from a great churchman [Irenæus] the most express testimony to the Four Gospels of our canon.   MATTHEW ARNOLD *God and the Bible* p. 191.

III. Of quantity, approximating to; approaching; not far from; not much more or less than; near; close to: an extension of the usage in reference to place, I., 5, 6, and to time, II.

They that had eaten were *about* four thousand men.

Mark viii, 9.

Jesus began to be *about* thirty years of age.   *Luke* iii, 23.

When they had rowed *about* five and twenty or thirty furlongs.

John vi, 19.

A number of men, *about* four hundred.   *Acts* v, 36.

And all the men were *about* twelve.   *Acts* xix, 7.

Sil. How tall was she? *Jul. About* my stature.
SHAKESPEARE *Two Gentlemen of Verona* act iv, sc. 4.

Camas, . . . a bulbous root *about* the size of a small onion, . . . when roasted and ground, is made into bread by the Indians, and has a taste somewhat like cooked chestnuts.

P. H. SHERIDAN *Memoirs* vol. i, ch. 4, p. 54.

IV. Of various relations:

1. In connection with; engaged in; occupied with; interfering with; concerned in; prosecuting; undertaking; endeavoring to do: compare I., 5, 6, and IV., 2.

I must be *about* my Father's business.   *Luke* ii, 49.

The prince himself is *about* a piece of iniquity.
SHAKESPEARE *Winter's Tale* act iv, sc. 4, l. 698.

Martha was cumbered *about* much serving, . . . careful and troubled *about* many things.   *Luke* x, 40, 41.

But why should I bother *about* my ancestors? I am sure they never bothered *about* me.

H. JAMES, JR. *The American* ch. 17, p. 298.

2. Having relation to; in reference to; concerning; touching; regarding; respecting; on account of; because of; as, to talk, think, or know *about*; to be angry *about*. (Compare AT.)

Then there arose a question between some of John's disciples and the Jews *about* purifying.   *John* iii, 25.

They determined that Paul and Barnabas . . . should go up to Jerusalem unto the apostles and elders *about* this question.

                        Acts xv, 2.

There arose no small stir *about* that way.   *Acts* xix, 23.

If the real climbers are ever to be differentiated from the crowd who write and talk *about* the mountains, it is only to be done by dispensing with professional assistance.

         TYNDALL *Hours of Exercise* ch. 22, p. 259.

A man's wife and his oldest friend generally know something *about* his real nature, its besetting temptations, . . . and its possibilities.   WM. BLACK *Princess of Thule* ch. 19, p. 309.

On Saturday she was in a terrible taking *about* the cholera; talked of nothing else.

     MACAULAY in Trevelyan's *T. B. Macaulay* vol. i, ch. 4, p. 214.

Some parts of Colonel Stephen's letter, *about* reinforcements, . . . were only meant as a finesse in case they should fall into the enemy's hands.   WASHINGTON in Sparks's *Writings of Washington* vol. ii, pt. i, p. 156.

They told me what a fine thing it was to be an Englishman, and *about* liberty and property, . . . and I find it is all a flam.

         W. GODWIN *Caleb Williams* vol. ii, ch. 5, p. 57.

How much more amiable is the American fidgetiness and anxiety *about* the opinion of other nations . . . than the John Bullism which affects to despise the sentiments of the rest of the world!

         COLERIDGE *Table Talk* Aug. 20, 1830.

About may be preceded by *from*, the phrase with *about* being viewed as a unity, a single designation of locality, time, etc.

Get you up *from about* the tabernacle of Korah, Dathan, and Abiram.   *Num.* xvi. 24.

In the denoting of locality, the combination *round about* was formerly very common, *round* intensifying the original idea of surrounding or encompassing contained in *about*.

The cities that were *round about* them.   *Gen.* xxv, 5.

The Egyptians digged *round about* the river.   *Ex.* vii, 24.

The Levites shall pitch *round about* the tabernacle. *Num.* i, 58.

And, behold, the mountain was full of horses and chariots of fire *round about* Elisha.   *2 Kings* vi, 17.

> Herne the hunter . . .
> Doth all the winter time, at still midnight,
> Walk *round about* an oak.
> SHAKESPEARE *Merry Wives of Windsor* act iv, sc. 4, l. 30.

> . . . Through a cloud,
> Drawn *round about* thee like a radiant shrine.
> MILTON *Paradise Lost* bk. iii, l. 378.

Verbs and Other Antecedents

Among the vast number of verbs that may be followed by *about*, its use in other than the local sense is especially worthy of notice in connection with the following verbs: *see, ask, seek, hear, talk, write, inquire, contend, consult, think, know, care, to disturb oneself, worry, fret, complain*, etc.

Adjectives and nouns allied to these verbs also freely take the preposition *about*; as, *inquisitive, contentious, thoughtful, informed* (well or ill), *anxious, solicitous, disturbed, worried, angry, interested*, etc. *Thoughtful* also takes *for*: thoughtful *about* the business, thoughtful *for* his friend. *Angry, disturbed, worried*, and the like also take *at*. *Interested* may be followed by *in*; *worried, disturbed*, etc., may take *by* with reference to agency; as, disturbed *by* callers. *Thought, anxiety, worry, inquiry, question, contention, quarrel, disturbance, complaint, anger*, etc., also readily take *about* before the object concerned. The noun *interest* is, however, commonly followed by *in*, as the verb and the participle *interested* may readily be.

Distinctions

About—around: As used of place, these prepositions are often interchangeable. We may speak of the earth's revolution *about* or *around* (or *round*) the sun. As far as a distinction can be drawn, it would seem to be that *around* keeps closer to the suggestion of surrounding, encircling movement, while *about* more readily applies to distributed activity touching here and there; to travel *around* the earth is to encircle it; to travel *about* the earth is to go in various directions here and there over it.

About—of—on: See ON.

III—Prepositions Defined and Illustrated

ABOVE

Above is from the Anglo-Saxon *ābufan*, which is compounded of *an*, on, plus *bufan*, above.

I. Of place or space:

1. Vertically over, without reference to distance; higher than; on the top of; over; as, the heaven *above* us; the boards are piled one *above* another.

Fowl that may fly *above* the earth. *Gen.* i, 20.

Above it stood the seraphim. *Isaiah* vi, 2

By the sky that hangs *above* our heads.
SHAKESPEARE *King John* act ii, sc. 2, l. 397.

The stars *above* us govern our conditions.
SHAKESPEARE *King Lear* act iv, sc. 8, l. 35

Hell opens and the heavens in vengeance crack
Above his head. WORDSWORTH *Sonnets* xxxii.

Above the tide, each broadsword bright
Was brandishing like beam of light.
SCOTT *Lady of the Lake* can. 6, st. 18.

2. Rising beyond the level of (though not vertically over); more elevated than; higher than; measured up from the level of; as said of a stream, nearer to the source; as, mountains rising *above* the plain; two thousand feet *above* the sea.

Seek not to crop *above* the heads of men
To be a better mark for envy's shafts.
JOAQUIN MILLER *Ina* act i, sc. 2.

My adventurous song,
That with no middle flight intends to soar
Above the Aonian mount.
MILTON *Paradise Lost* bk. i, l. 15.

> Still her gray rocks tower *above* the sea
> That crouches at their feet.
> > FITZ-GREENE HALLECK *Connecticut* st. 1.

Since the tertiary period two-thirds of Europe have been lifted *above* the sea.   DRAPER *Intell. Devel. Eur.* vol. i, ch. 2, p. 31.

Harar . . . is situated on a table-land, 5,500 feet *above* the sea, whence the climate is dry, temperate and healthy.
> > BAYARD TAYLOR *Lake Regions Cent. Afr.* ch. 2, p. 8.

A station which raises a man too eminently *above* the level of his fellow-creatures is not the most favorable to moral or to intellectual qualities.   DE QUINCEY *Opium-Eater* prelim., p. 55.

3. Farther north than: with indirect reference to position on a map; as, all the land *above* the fortieth parallel of north latitude.

The terminus of the 7th range falls upon that [the Ohio] river, 9 miles *above* the Muskingum.   MORSE *Am. Geography* I, p. 458.

II. Of time:

1. Exceeding (a specified period); more than; beyond; as, it lasted *above* three hours.

> It was never acted; or, if it was, not *above* once.
> > SHAKESPEARE *Hamlet* act ii, sc. 2, l. 440.

2. Rarely, more ancient than: with indirect reference to position in a tabulated list of dates; as, the period *above* the sixteenth century.

III. Of various relations:

1. Superior to; more than; in excess of; surpassing; exceeding; beyond; over:

(*a*) In number or quantity; as, blessings *above* measure; *above* 500 yards.

In person, the pedler was a man *above* the middle height.
> > COOPER *The Spy* ch. 8, p. 41.

The general direction is S. E. for *above* 400 miles.
> > *Lippincott's Gazetteer* 1908, p. 1592.

(*b*) Of sounds:

(1) Higher in pitch than; as, *above* concert pitch.

Above the hum of the multitude and the roll of the drums, rose the clear and ringing blasts of the cavalry bugles.

J. E. COOKE *Surry of Eagle's Nest* ch. 123, p. 444.

(2) Surpassing in volume, clearness, or intensity; audible beyond; as, the captain's voice rang out *above* the din; *above* all other sounds was heard the cannon's roar.

(c) In quality or excellence; as, virtue is *above* price.

> But mercy is *above* this sceptred sway,
> It is enthrond in the hearts of kings.
> SHAKESPEARE *Merchant of Venice* act iv, sc. 1, l. 193.

The instinct of the chivalrous gentleman asserted itself *above* the dread of death or the feeling of rank.

NICOLAY AND HAY *Abraham Lincoln* vol. ix, ch. 10, p. 282.

(d) In authority, rank, or power; as, the king is *above* the subject; the moral is *above* the civil law.

The law of self-defence is *above* every other law.

BURKE *Speeches, Impeachment of Hastings* vol. ii, p. 181.

Not now as a servant, but *above* a servant, a brother beloved.

Philemon 16.

2. Beyond the reach, power, or influence of; as, *above* reproach; *above* calumny; *above* suspicion; *above* a base suggestion.

> Thou hast a charmd cup, O Fame!
> A draught that mantles high,
> And seems to lift this earthly frame
> *Above* mortality.
> Away! to me—a woman—bring
> Sweet water from affection's spring.
> MRS. HEMANS *Woman and Fame.*

> —while I hear
> This, this is holy;
> These vespers of another year,
> This hymn of thanks and praise,
> My spirit seems to mount *above*
> The anxieties of human love,
> And earth's precarious days.
> WORDSWORTH *Poems of Sentiment and Reflection* xxvi, st. 4.

Cæsar's wife should be *above* suspicion.

PLUTARCH *Life of Cæsar* ch. x.

Distinctions

Above—on—over—up—upon: *Above* is the most inclusive of these prepositions. It can ordinarily be substituted for *on*, *upon*, or *over;* as, the boards were piled one *on* or *upon* another (one *above* another); the hawk flies *over* the wood (*above* the wood). But it will be seen that while *above* is more inclusive it is less definite; the boards laid one *on* another are in contact, but when laid one *above* another, they may not touch. *Over* contains often an intimation, though it may be slight, of extension or motion across, while *above* may simply imply greater elevation. If we say, the mountain towers *above* the plain, we think only of its height; but if we say, the mountain towers *over* the plain, we think of the plain as in the shadow of the mountain and dominated by it. So we say the mountain is 7,000 feet *above* the sea, where it would be impossible to say 7,000 feet *over* the sea. *Up* implies ascending motion; as, the ship sailed *up* the river, where *above* or *over* could not be used.

[*Above* has reference to a higher position in space.

Over relates to an extension along the superior surface of another object.

Upon relates to the contact of a body with the superior surface of another.

Beyond refers to the greater distance of a body.

Above does not carry the idea of contact with a body below it; *over* may or may not carry the idea.

Figuratively, *above* conveys the idea of superiority; as, "The prince is *above* the peasant"; *over*, the idea of authority; as, "The church has *over* her, bishops" (SOUTH).

Upon, the idea of immediate influence; as, "The effect of oratory *upon* an audience"; *beyond*, the idea of extent; as, "The power of Providence '*beyond* the stretch of human thought'" (THOMSON).

Above and *over* are sometimes used interchangeably; as, "The sky *above* us, or *over* us." "*Above* ten thousand men were in the army." "He was seen of *above* five hundred brethren at once" (*1 Cor.* xv, 6).

More than, *upwards of*, are also used by good writers.

FALLOWS *100.000 Synonyms and Antonyms.*]

For the contrasted prepositions *below—beneath—down—under —underneath*, see DISTINCTIONS under BENEATH.

Above—beyond : In the metaphorical use, we speak of a person as being *above* suspicion. We speak of an act or fact as being *beyond* controversy, dispute, doubt, or question. A thing may be said to be either *above* or *beyond* price.

ACROSS

Across is derived from the noun *cross* joined with the prefix *a-*, on, representing the Anglo-Saxon *an*, on; *i. e.*, on a cross, in the manner of a cross.

I. Of place or space:

1. Passing through or over the surface of, so as to cross it; crossing; in the direction of a crossing line or movement.

> When my good falcon made her flight *across*
> Thy father's ground.
> > SHAKESPEARE *Winter's Tale* act iv, sc. 3, l. 17.

> *Across* the brook like roebuck bound,
> And thread the brake like questing hound.
> > SCOTT *Lady of the Lake* can. 3, st. 18, l. 9.

> The musk-rat or the mink leads a long, silent, glittering trail *across* the glassy water.   GIBSON *Strolls* p. 55.

> The ball ricochetted completely *across* the broad surface of the lake . . . in continuous splashes.
> > BAKER *Rifle and Hound in Ceylon* ch. 3, p. 49.

> I have seen the clouds file as straight *across* the sky toward a growing storm . . . as soldiers hastening to the . . . attack or defense.   BURROUGHS *Locusts and Wild Honey* p. 94.

> But, at intervals, as the night-wind swept *across* the bastion, it bore sounds of fearful portent to the ear.
> > F. PARKMAN *Conspiracy of Pontiac* vol. i, ch. 10, p. 222.

2. On or from the other side of; over; beyond; as, the house is just *across* the street; we heard the chimes *across* the river.

> Ring out the old, ring in the new,
> Ring, happy bells, *across* the snow.
>
>   TENNYSON *In Memoriam* pt. cvi, st. 2.

> Yes, sweet it seems *across* some watery dell
> To catch the music of the pealing bell.
>
>   HEBER *Europe* st. 1.

> I throw a kiss *across* the sea,
>   I drink the winds as drinking wine,
> And dream they all are blown from thee,
>   I catch the whisper'd kiss of thine.
>
>   JOAQUIN MILLER *England.* 1871. *Introduction.*

II. Figuratively, passing over, as a movement or expression; over; as, a shadow comes *across* me; an expression of doubt flitted *across* his face.

All its associations and traditions swept at once *across* his memory.   G. O. TREVELYAN *Life and Lett. of Lord Macaulay* vol. ii, ch. 7, p. 22.

> *Across* the monarch's brow there came
> A cloud of ire, remorse, and shame.
>
>   SCOTT *Marmion* can. 5, st. 15.

Verbs and Other Antecedents

Verbs and nouns denoting or implying motion, as *walk, run, march, look, reach, flit, pass, passage, flight, glance,* etc., are commonly followed by *across.*

Distinctions

Across—along—over—through: Across signifies so as to cross, and indicates a direction at right angles to that denoted by *along.* We go *along* the river's bank; we sail, row, or swim *across* the river. Yet we speak of going *across* a bridge when we really go *along* it, *i. e.*, in the direction of its length. This is by transference of the idea of *crossing* the river to the traversing of the bridge by which the river is crossed. *Along* is used, though less frequently, in this connection :

> *Along* the bridge Lord Marmion rode.
> Proudly his red-roan charger trod.
>
>   SCOTT *Marmion* can. 1, st. 5.

Over is not confined to any specific direction; a man may ride *over* a field to and fro and in all directions, as in searching for something. If he rides *across* the field, it is from one side of the field to the other. One goes *through* something from outside to outside. To go *through* a wood is to start in from open ground on one side and to come out upon open ground on the other side. Only a bird, a cloud, a wind, or the like could go *across* or *over* the wood. A person is said to pass *through* an enclosure, as a room or a garden, when he passes from outside to outside of it; he may go *across* by passing from side to side within its bounds. One is said to walk *over* a stretch of turf or gravel, which is under his feet, but *through* a field of growing grain which he penetrates and separates as he passes.

ADOWN

See DOWN.

AFTER

After is derived from the Anglo-Saxon *æfter*, behind, or further off, from *af*, off, plus the comparative suffix *-ter*.

I. Of place, in the rear of; farther back than; following; behind: often implying a tendency to press toward; as, to follow *after* the troops.

And Abigail hasted . . . with five damsels of hers that went *after* her.   *1 Sam.* xxvi, 42.

And the king went forth and all the people *after* him.
           2 Sam. xv, 17.

York. Let us pursue them ere the writs go forth :—
        What says Lord Warwick? Shall we *after* them?
War. *After* them! nay, before them if we can.
        SHAKESPEARE *3 K. Henry VI.* act. v, sc. 3, l. 27.

II. Of time: following; succeeding.

1. Subsequently to; at a later period than: used of time following a specified period or event, whether such period or event be past, present, or future; as, *after* his death the property was divided; *after* this there can be no hesitation; wheat will be cheap *after* harvest.

It is easy enough, *after* the ramparts are carried, to find men to plant the flag on the highest tower.

> Macaulay *Essays, Mackintosh's History* p. 397.

After a few graceful wheels and curvets, we take our ground.

> Thackeray *Roundabout Papers, Ogres* p. 203.

After the Restoration there was a country party and a court party, and to these the names of Whig and Tory were applied in 1679, in the heat of the struggle which preceded the meeting of the first short parliament of Charles II.

> *Encyc. Brit.* 9th ed., vol. xxiv, p. 540.

A great many men cannot conceive of a personal continuance *after* the bodily functions are exhausted.

> J. Weiss *Immortal Life* ch. 1, p. 4.

Electricity has rendered [the exposition] viewable *after* dark.

> Julian Ralph in *Harper's Monthly* Jan., 1892, p. 207.

It was not until *after* the Revolution . . . that the censorship of the press was given up by the law of England.

> G. P. Fisher *Reformation* ch. 15, p. 529.

[Note.—*After* in this sense is used to govern an entire clause, as a preposition often does in Greek, and in such use has been by some classed as a conjunction: formerly in such use often followed by *that*, *after that*

But *after* I am risen again, I will go before you into Galilee.

> *Matt.* xxvi, 32.

Now *after that* John was put in prison, Jesus came into Galilee.

> *Mark* i, 14.]

2. In succession to; following successively or repeatedly: used of events that follow in some definite order, alternation, or series; as, time *after* time, day *after* day.

After the dance was concluded, the whole party was entertained with brawn and beef, and stout home-brewed.

> Irving *Sketch-Book, Christmas Day* p. 270.

He passed week *after* week in clambering the mountains.
JOHNSON *Rasselas* ch. 5, p. 27.

It was the custom, too, of these devout vagabonds, *after* leaving the chapel, to have a grand carouse.
IRVING *Astoria* ch. 13, p. 126.

After night day comes, and *after* turmoil peace.
EDWIN ARNOLD *Light of Asia* bk. v, st. 8.

3. Subsequently to and because of; because of; as the result of; as, *after* this explanation, one can not help understanding.

Dawson, *after* his announcement of the animal nature of the Eozoon, suggested the name Eozoic. DANA *Geology* pt. iii, p. 148.

After he had received the honor of knighthood from his sovereign, he assumed the heraldic device of three wiverns. AGNES STRICKLAND *Queens of Eng., Elizabeth* in vol. iii, ch. 8, p. 328.

4. Subsequently to, and in spite of; in spite of; notwithstanding; as, *after* the best endeavors, one may fail; *after* all concessions, reconciliation proved impossible: hence the phrase *after all*, equivalent to when everything has been done, considered, or the like; as, they failed *after all*.

For, *after all*, the object of religion is conversion, and to change people's behaviour.
MATTHEW ARNOLD *Last Essays, Bishop Butler* p. 92.

III. In derived or metaphorical use:

1. Behind or below in place or rank; inferior to.

What can the man do that cometh *after* the king? *Eccl.* ii, 12.

'I am content,' he answered, 'to be loved a little *after* Enoch.'
TENNYSON *Enoch Arden* st. 29, l. 425.

2. Pressing or tending toward; in search or pursuit of; in quest of; seeking or striving for; for: an extension of the idea of following in place; as, to strive *after* wisdom.

[As *after* with verbs of movement intimates in general the tendency of pressing to an object, it is associated with notions of an activity, substantives, etc., in connection with objects towards which a striving or desire is directed. In this manner it stands with such notions as *seek, search, ask, call, listen, hunt, endeavor, gape, hunger, thirst*, and others, so that *after* frequently coincides in effect with *for*. MAETZNER *English Grammar* vol. ii, p. 446.]

One thing have I desired of the Lord, that will I seek *after*.

Ps. xxvii, 4.

As the hart panteth *after* the water brooks.   Ps. xlii, 1.

> My servant, Travers, whom I sent
> On Tuesday last, to listen *after* news.
>> SHAKESPEARE *2 K. Henry IV.* act i, sc. 1, l. 77.

> The petty pesterers, with card and stamp,
> Who hunt for autographs, were *after* me.
>> HOLLAND *Kathrina, Labor* pt. iii, st. 60.

No man can fitly seek *after* truth who does not hold truth in the deepest reverence.   BUSHNELL *Sermons* sermon ix, p. 180.

St. Paul . . . showed them that they were feeling *after* God, but blindly, ignorantly, wrongly.

ROBERTSON Sermons fourth series, ser. xxiv, p. 802.

3. According to the nature, wishes, or customs of ; in accordance with ; in conformity to ; according to ; in proportion to ; as, you are a man *after* my own heart.

Ahithophel hath spoken *after* this manner : shall we do *after* his saying?   *2 Sam.* xvii, 6.

> Their clothes are *after* such a pagan cut too,
> That, sure, they've worn out Christendom.
>> SHAKESPEARE *K. Henry VIII.* act i, sc. 8, l. 14.

The floors are sometimes of wood, tessellated *after* the fashion of France.   MACAULAY *Eng.* vol. i, ch. 8, p. 275.

The Church Government is severely Presbyterian, *after* the discipline of Calvin.   EVELYN *Diary, Mar. 23, 1646.*

It is easy in the world to live *after* the world's opinion.
EMERSON Essays, Self-Reliance in first series, p. 49.

4. In imitation of ; in the manner of ; in obedience to ; in conformity to ; as, a picture *after* Titian.

And God said, Let us make man *after* our likeness.   *Gen.* i, 26.

In answer to Philip's desire to behold a theophany *after* the manner of the Old Testament, Jesus said, 'He that hath seen Me hath seen the Father.'

> J. P. THOMPSON *Theology of Christ* ch. 11, p. 147.

At least we might have a betrothment *after* the royal fashion.

> MARY R. MITFORD *Our Village, Outing* Sept. 26, 1824.

5. For the sake of; in remembrance or observance of; by the name of; as, the boy was named *after* Lincoln.

Our eldest son was named George *after* his uncle.

> GOLDSMITH *Vicar of Wakefield* ch. 1, p. 36.

6. In relation to; about; concerning; as, to look *after* my affairs; to inquire *after* one's health.

Take heed to thyself . . . that thou inquire not *after* their gods.

> *Deut.* xii, 30.

Verbs and Other Antecedents

[As *after* with verbs of movement intimates in general the tendency of pressing to an object, it is associated with notions of an activity, substantives, etc., in connection with objects towards which a striving or desire is directed. In this manner it stands with such notions as *seek, search, ask, call, listen, hunt, endeavor, gape, hunger, thirst,* and others, so that *after* frequently coincides in effect with *for*. MAETZNER *English Grammar* vol. ii, p. 445.]

Distinctions

After—behind:

[In a local meaning, *after,* in partial distinction from *behind,* is not so much used of the quiet abiding in the rear of an object as to suppose a progressive or striving movement in which although not absolutely there lies the tendency to press on to an object, and which is rarely conceived in its result.

> MAETZNER *English Grammar* vol. ii, p. 445.]

Thus, to *follow behind* would be tautological, since *follow* includes the meaning of *behind;* but to *follow after* is in approved use, since *after* adds the idea of seeking to overtake. So strong is this implication that it is felt in connection even with the neuter verb *be,* as when one says, "I am *after* you."

After—for: *After* and *for* are in certain uses equivalent and used interchangeably. One may be said to be named *after* or *for* Lincoln; one may seek *after* fame or seek *for* it. The fact that *after* carries the sense of seeking, reaching toward, or caring for (probably from the following or pursuing *after* something desired) disposes of the objection that of course one is named *after* any one who lived before him. *After* has other references than that to time, signifying *according to, in behalf of,* etc. *In behalf of* or *for the sake of* one loved or honored, we give a child or a place his name, thus naming the person or place *after* (in behalf of) him.

[*After—for* are often used interchangeably, especially after words expressing desire, striving, search, etc. To thirst *after* truth or *for* truth, to search *after,* or *for* knowledge, hunt *after,* or *for* riches, strive *after,* or *for* fame, eager *for,* or *after* position. Fallows *100,000 Synonyms and Antonyms.*]

After—since: *After* excludes while *since* includes reference to the present time. The statement "*After* the battle of Marathon the Greeks no longer feared the Persians" puts the whole matter far from the present. Greeks and Persians ceased to be competitors centuries ago. But the statement "*Since* the Reformation the principles of religious liberty have steadily advanced" brings the advance up to to-day. "*After* my departure I heard nothing from him" puts all expectancy or likelihood of hearing far into the past. It is so we should speak of one long dead. But "*Since* my departure I have heard nothing" keeps expectancy and possibility open to the very moment of utterance.

IV—Prepositions Defined and Illustrated

AGAINST

Against is derived from the Middle English *againest*, from *again* plus the adverbial ending *-es* plus the intensive ending *-t*, the idea of being opposite or opposed underlying all the meanings both of the adverb *again* and of the preposition *against*.

I. Of place or space: in a direct line toward; opposite to.

1. Of position:

(a) directly opposite; facing; in front of: often preceded by *over*; as, *against* the background of the sky; *over against* the temple.

Go into the village *over against* you.   *Matt.* xxi, 2.

> The ships' masts standing row by row
> Stark black *against* the stars.
> > MORRIS *Jason* bk. ix, st. 18.

> High in the topmost zenith a central spark,
> A luminous cloud that glow'd *against* the dark.
> > E. C. STEDMAN *Alice of Monmouth* div. xx, st. 4.

Above, *against* the clouds of twilight, ghostly on the gray precipice, stand, myriad by myriad, the shadowy armies of the Unterwalden pine.   RUSKIN *Mod. Paint.* vol. v, pt. vi, p. 98.

> *Against* the sheer, precipitous mountain-side
> Thorwaldsen carved his Lion at Lucerne.
> > ALDRICH *Thorwaldsen* l. 6.

(b) In contact with and pressing upon; bearing upon; as, to lean *against* a wall.

We fended the canoes off the sides, and assisted our progress by pushing *against* the rocks.
BAKER in Bayard Taylor's *Lake Regions Cent. Afr.* ch. 34, p. 377.

Putting his feet, now, *against* the wall, so as to get a good purchase, and pushing, . . . the trunk, with much difficulty, was slid out.   POE *Tales, Von Kempelen* in first series, p. 107

3

2. Of motion, into contact or collision with; so as to meet, strike, or the like; in movement toward: often implying force; as, the ship was dashed *against* the rocks.

> And heel *against* the pavement echoing, burst
> Their drowse.
>   TENNYSON *Idylls of the King. Geraint and Enid* l. 271.

The waves pounded like Titanic sledge-hammers *against* the vessel's quivering timbers.

>   KENNAN *Tent Life in Siberia* ch. 2, p. 14.

The linden, like a lover, stands   And taps *against* thy window pane.   T. B. READ *Arise* st. 2.

I brushed *against* a withered old man tottering down the street under a load of yarn.   J. M. BARRIE *Auld Licht Idylls* ch. 4, p. 97.

II. Of time, approximating to (a specified moment or event); in anticipation of; in preparation for; in view of; in time for; as, be ready *against* the third day.

[NOTE.—The object of the preposition in such use is often a clause or phrase, which has sometimes been improperly supposed to be a conjunctive use; as, be ready *against* visitors come.]

And they made ready the present *against* Joseph came at noon: for they heard that they should eat bread there.   *Gen.* xliii, 25.

III. Of various relations :

1. In opposition to, as in character, spirit, or purpose; opposite or contrary to; in hostility to; not in conformity with (compare I., 2); counter to; as, *against* my will; to set up your opinion *against* mine.

Thine eye be evil *against* thy poor brother, . . . and he cry unto the Lord *against* thee.   *Deut.* xv, 9.

Blame is safer than praise. . . . As long as all that is said is said *against* me, I feel a certain assurance of success.

>   EMERSON *Essays, Compensation* in first series, p. 98.

Eight of the older girls came forward, and preferred *against* her charges — alas, too well founded — of calumny and falsehood. MARGARET FULLER OSSOLI *Summer on the Lakes, Mariana* ch. 4, p. 89.

The stream of public opinion now sets *against* us; but it is about to turn, and the regurgitation will be tremendous.
    WHITTIER *Prose Works, William Leggett* in vol. i, p. 417.

I strove *against* the stream and all in vain.
  TENNYSON *Princess* pt. vi, *Song, Ask Me No More* st. 8, l. 2.

I hear him charge his saints that none . . .
Blaspheme *against* him with despair.
      E. B. BROWNING *De Profundis* st. 19.

A fault in respect to the settled forms of words, that is, an offense *against* the etymology of a language, is denominated a barbarism. DAY *Art of Discourse* div. ii, pt. i, ch. 8, p. 260.

2. In resistance to for protection; so as to protect or defend from; adversely concerning; as, to warn *against* a plot.

He declares to all nations that he will stand by his political creed *against* the world.
    A. GILMAN *Making of American Nation* ch. 21, p. 168.

Energy in government is essential to . . . security *against* external and internal dangers.
    MADISON in *The Federalist* No. xxxvii, p. 168.

The weak, *against* the sons of spoil and wrong,
Banded, and watched their hamlets, and grew strong.
      BRYANT *The Ages* st. 11.

The searching tenderness of her woman's tones seemed made for a defense *against* ready accusers.
    GEORGE ELIOT *Middlemarch* vol. ii, ch. 76, p. 578.

In Sweden sanitary amulets are made of mistletoe-twigs, and the plant is supposed to be a specific *against* epilepsy and an antidote for poisons. FISKE *Myths and Myth-Makers* ch. 2, p. 61.

So in human action, *against* the spasm of energy, we offset the continuity of drill. EMERSON *Conduct of Life, Power* p. 65.

Thy grave is shut *against* the lies Of this false world.
    G. H. BOKER *The Book of the Dead* pt. vi, st. 1.

At four different points have the vast towers been pushed to the walls, filled with soldiers, and defended *against* the fires of the besieged by a casing of skins.
    W. WARE *Zenobia* vol. ii, letter xiv, p. 181.

His soul was steeled *against* the grosser seductions of appetite.
     Prescott *Biog. and Crit. Miscell., C. B. Brown* p. 12.

3. To the debit of; as, to charge items *against* a customer.

Bene. Sir, I shall meet your wit in the career, an you charge
it *against* me.
     Shakespeare *Much Ado about Nothing* act v, sc. 1, l. 186.

4. Of comparison, as of objects weighed in opposite scales, or
placed opposite to each other for measurement or the like, commonly metaphorical: in comparison with; contrasted with; as an
offset to. (Compare I., 1 (a).)

     But in that crystal scales let there be weigh'd
     Your lady's love *against* some other maid.
     Shakespeare *Romeo and Juliet* act. i, sc. 2, l. 96.

Weighed *against* your lying ledgers must our manhood kick the
beam?
     Whittier *The Pine-tree* st. 2.

     And solid pudding *against* empty praise.
     Pope *The Dunciad* bk. i, l. 54.

5. In preparation for; as a resource for; so as to meet or be
ready for (compare II.); as, money laid up *against* old age; provision *against* famine.

It is the duty of parents to make a prudent provision for their
children, and *against* the accidents of life.
     Guthrie *Man and the Gospel, Riches* p. 185.

In the city is a public granary, an admirable resource *against*
scarcity.
     John Adams *Defence of Constitutions* vol. i, letter xv, p. 47.

Distinctions

Against—before—by—for : As referring to time these words
have kindred use. *For* distinctly denotes purpose. "Be ready
for the third day" means "be prepared to meet that day's
demands." *By* in the same sentence would mean "not later
than," so that the third day shall not come and not find you ready.
"*Before* the third day" would mean in advance of its coming, the
preparation to be all completed at some earlier time. *Against*

combines the senses of *by* and *for*, signifying both punctuality and purpose. *Against* the third day means not later than its coming and with distinct preparation for whatever it is to bring. *Against* in this sense is now, however, much less used than formerly, *by* being largely employed in its place.

[*Against—from* are often interchangeable; as, "Shelter *from* the blast or *against* the blast." Thus we may say, "Defend us *against*, or *from*, protect us *against*, or *from*, secure us *against*, or *from*, our enemies."

               FALLOWS *100,000 Synonyms and Antonyms.*]

Against—with :   See under WITH.

ALONG

Along is derived from the Anglo-Saxon *andlang*, from *and-*, against, plus *lang* = long, *i. e.*, against the length, in the direction of the length.

I. Of place or space: referring to movement, direction, or extension in the line of the length of some object; through or over the length of; at points distributed through or over the length of; in or by the course of; on the line of; in the direction of; beside; by; near; as, the ship sailed *along* the coast; an electric shock runs *along* the nerve; trees are planted *along* the road.

They robbed all that came *along* that way by them.

               Judges ix, 25.

Along the crowded path they bore her now, pure as the newly fallen snow.   DICKENS *Old Curiosity Shop* ch. 72, p. 329.

Along the road-side the elder-berry's cymes have been transformed to clusters of shining black berries.

       GEO. H. ELLWANGER *The Garden's Story* ch. 14, p. 307.

Flags and rushes grow *along* its plashy shore.

            HAWTHORNE *Mosses, The Old Manse* p. 15.

Along the forest-glade   The wild deer trip.

            THOMSON *Seasons, Summer* l. 59.

Then a cold and deathlike stupor slowly crept *along* my frame.

            T. B. READ *Christine* st. 9.

I cautiously coasted *along* shore, which was full of snags and sawyers.   ALEX. WILSON in Ord's *Life of Wilson* in *Am. Ornithology* vol. i, p. 88.

I passed *along* the narrow ridge of a reef . . . while a swash of some depth lay close within.
W. ELLIOTT *Carolina Sports, Bass Fishing* p. 141.

We flew away with bellying sail *along* the coast of Maheta.
STANLEY *Through the Dark Continent* vol. i, ch. 8, p. 168.

II. Of time, considered as having extension in length :

During the course or lapse of; during; through; throughout; as, *along* the track of centuries.

> The love that leads the willing spheres
> *Along* the unending track of years.
BRYANT *Song of the Sower* st. 10.

> Sprinkled *along* the waste of years.
KEBLE *Christian Year, Advent Sunday* st. 8, l. 8.

While we glide *along* the stream of time.
JOHNSON *Rasselas* ch. 34, p. 188.

Distinctions

Along—beside—by : *Along* has always the suggestion of extent or motion in the direction of the length. *Beside* and *by* with verbs of motion may convey the same idea. We may say "We walked *by* the river," or "We walked *beside* the river," or "We walked *along* the river's bank." In the last sentence it is necessary to use the word "bank" or other limiting term, because *along* might apply to the stream itself, as a light might be said to flash *along* the river; *beside* and *by* need no such limitation, because it is contained in the very meaning of the words.

On the other hand, we may speak of a man as living *beside* the river or *by* the river, with reference to a fixed location; to live *along* the river would suggest a wandering life. A house may stand *beside* or *by*, but not *along*, the river; the boat plies *along* the river.

AMID

Amid is derived from the Anglo-Saxon *on-middan*, composed of *on*, on, plus *middan*, middle, *i. e.*, on or *in the middle, in the midst*. The variant form *amidst* does not differ materially in meaning or use.

[The recent tendency seems to be to distinguish *amidst* from *amid* by using it especially of scattered things or of something moving in the midst of other things.   *Standard Dictionary*.]

Amid and *amidst* are often abbreviated, especially in poetry, to *mid* and *midst*. *Amidst* is more common in ordinary speech than *amid*.

I. Of place or space:

Surrounded or encompassed by; in the midst of; mingled with; among; not limited to the exact center.

> All *amid* them stood the tree of life.
> > MILTON *Paradise Lost* bk. iv, l. 218.

The villages peeped out *amid* the woodlands, the church bells were sounding pleasantly across the meadows.
> > H. S. CUNNINGHAM *The Heriots* ch. 34, p. 227.

> > He arose,
> Ethereal, flush'd, and like a throbbing star
> Seen '*mid* the sapphire heaven's deep repose.
> > KEATS *Eve of St. Agnes* st. 36.

Amid the throng in Elizabeth's antechamber the noblest form is that of the singer who lays the 'Faerie Queen' at her feet.
> > GREEN *Short Hist. Eng. People* ch, 7, § 7, p. 423.

> *Amid* its fair broad lands the abbey lay.
> > BRYANT *The Ages* st. 20.

The young imagination delights to dwell *amid* the bosky recesses of this little spot.
> > HUGH MILLER *Scenes and Legends of Scotland* ch. 9, p. 123.

As he advanced he was soon lost *amidst* the bayous and marshes which are found along the Red River and its tributaries.
> > BANCROFT *United States* vol. i, ch. 3, p. 49.

II. Of circumstances, acts, conditions, etc.:

Existing or acting in the midst of; affected by: often adding the implication of opposition or resistance; as, comfort *amid* life's sorrows; he stood firm *amid* temptations.

Agricultural life appears to have been his beau ideal of existence, which haunted his thoughts even *amid* the stern duties of the field.   IRVING *Washington* vol. i, ch. 26, p. 284.

Yet, *amid* vacillation, selfishness, weakness, treachery, one great man was like a tower of trust; this was Gaspar de Coligny.   F. PARKMAN *Pioneers of France* pt. i, ch. 2, p. 18.

Amidst the thickest carnage blazed the helmet of Navarre.   MACAULAY *Battle of Ivry* st. 4.

See, Sidney bleeds *amid* the martial strife.   POPE *Essay on Man* ep. 4, l. 101.

Half drowned *amid* the breakers' roar.   SCOTT *Marmion* can. ii, st. 11.

Distinctions

Amid—amidst—among—in the midst of: Following the etymology, *amid* denotes simply position, where one object (in the middle or midst) is surrounded by others, while *among* denotes a mingling, so that one object is intermingled (literally or figuratively) with others. That which is *amid* is thought of as separate from the things that surround it. This idea of separation or distinction may reach even to a latent implication of hostility. Thus we never say "*amid* friends," but we may say "*amid* enemies." *Among* always implies some direct relation, as of companionship, union, similarity, or perhaps even of active hostility. So one says "I found myself *among* friends," or, conversely, "I found myself *among* enemies" (*i. e.*, enemies to be met and dealt with directly, and not merely surrounding as would be denoted by *amid*). So we say "one instance *among* many" (*i. e.*, many of the same kind). We may say "The nest was hidden *amid* (or *among*) the leaves"; in using *amid* we think only of the position of the nest in relation to the leaves that are all around it; in using *among* we think of the leaves as factors that shut in and conceal the nest.

[*Amid* (a poetical form) and *amidst*, denote in the *midst* or the middle of, or surrounded by; as, "A tree *amidst* the garden." "A task performed *amidst* many interruptions." *Among* or *amongst*, as its etymology implies, denotes an intermixture or a mingling. It implies a collection of objects with which something is intermixed or mingled; as, "He was *among* his friends." "Pamphlets were found *among* the books." We may say *among* the schoolmen; *among* the philosophers, *among* the Americans, *among* the Orientals, *among* the ideas advanced, *among* the arguments used. In none of these cases could *amid*, or *amidst*, be used. So we may say *amidst* temptations, *amidst* sufferings, *amidst* difficulties, *amidst* the waves. *Among*, or *amongst*, could not be used in these cases. . . .

Milton says of the seraph Abdiel:

> "Faithful found
> *Among* the faithless, faithful only he,"

because he had been one of the number of the rebellious host before they had fallen, and was yet intermingled with them. But when he determined to leave them, Milton discriminatingly adds—

> "From.*amidst* them forth he passed."
> FALLOWS *100,000 Synonyms.*]

The distinction is also finely observed in the following sentence:

Amid the crowd and crush of life, each soul is in personal solitude with God. MARTINEAU *Studies of Christianity, Christ. Without Priest* p. 58.

The "crowd" is around without communion or sympathy; hence the soul is said to be "*amid* the crowd."

When the poet would picture the feeble old minstrel, depressed and confused, he writes:

> *Amid* the strings his fingers strayed
> And an uncertain warbling made.
> SCOTT *Lay of the Last Minstrel* int. st. 5, L. 1.

The minstrel's hand for the time was a stranger to the strings of his almost disused harp.   On the other hand, the Scripture says :

— *Among* them that are born of women there hath not risen a greater than John the Baptist.   *Matt.* xi, 11.

Here is indicated the prophet's full human participation and fellowship with the race to whom he ministered ; he was one *among* them.   Similarly we read :

All Israel . . . as well the stranger as he that was born *among* them.   *Josh.* viii, 33.

In neither of the last two instances would it be possible to say *amid*.   The prepositional phrase *in the midst of* is not subject to the limitations of *amid*, but may denote participation, companionship, or fellowship.   Thus one may be *in the midst of* friends, of engagements, or of pleasures.   But, on the other hand, the Scripture says :

Take me not away *in the midst of* my years.   *Ps.* cii, 24.

Here the reference is simply to the middle point of time.   Thus the phrase *in the midst of* seems to sweep the whole range of thought from *amid* to *among*.

Errors

In our (their) midst :   These expressions hold their own with singular obstinacy, considering that they are without recognized authority of any kind.   They are used chiefly in connection with religious matters, and yet the Scripture carefully avoids such phrases, using instead the preposition *of* with the objective following.

Where two or three are gathered together in my name, there am I *in the midst of them.*   *Matt.* xviii, 20.

AMONG, AMONGST

Among is derived from the Anglo-Saxon *onmang*, from *on*, in, plus *mang*, for *mange*, dative of *(ge)mang*, a mingling, crowd, literally *in the mingling, in the crowd*.

I. Of place or space:

Mingled with; having position or movement in the midst of; included within a mass or multitude of objects; in or into the midst of; surrounded by; as, *among* the crowd; to fall *among* thieves.

Among these fountains . . . the melon-seller erects his booth, swashing his boards constantly with water.
W. W. STORY *Roba di Roma* vol. ii, ch. 17, p. 481.

And, fairest of all streams, the Murga roves
Among Merou's bright palaces and groves.
MOORE *Lalla Rookh, Veiled Prophet* pt. i, st. 1.

Among all the buildings, the most noble objects were the steeples built upon the churches.   JOHN ADAMS *Works, Defence of the Constitution* in vol. v, ch. 6, p. 299.

It was sometimes ticklish steering *among* the rafts and arks with which the river was thronged.
N. P. WILLIS *Rural Letters, Under a Bridge* letter xv, p. 188.

Flow gently, sweet Afton, *among* thy green braes,
Flow gently, I'll sing thee a song in thy praise.
BURNS *Flow Gently, Sweet Afton* st. 1, l. 1.

From peak to peak, the rattling crags *among*,
Leaps the live thunder!
BYRON *Childe Harold* can. 3, st. 92.

II. Of various relations:

1. In the class or group of or with; in the number or company of; as, one example *among* many.

Nature does require
Her times of preservation, which, perforce,
I, her frail son, *amongst* my brethren mortal
Must give my tendance to.
SHAKESPEARE *K. Henry VIII.* act iii, sc. 2, l. 145.

Our British soil is over rank, and breeds
Among the noblest flowers a thousand pois'nous weeds.
>> SWIFT *Ode to Dr. William Sancroft* st. 5.

Few of us ever discover bigots *among* those who agree with us.
>> MARTYN *Wendell Phillips* bk. iii, ch. 4, p. 388.

We firmly believe History will rank Mr. Lincoln *among* the most prudent of statesmen and the most successful of rulers.
>> LOWELL *Political Essays, Abraham Lincoln* p. 184.

2. In association with (a number of persons or objects); having relation to; connected with; as, some truth may be found *among* many errors.

What news *among* the merchants?
>> SHAKESPEARE *Merchant of Venice* act iii, sc. 1, l. 24.

Whether it is possible to think without the aid of language, is a question which has been a constant source of dispute *amongst* logicians and psychologists.
>> T. FOWLER *Elements of Deductive Logic* int., ch. 3, p. 7.

Among the wakeful and normal states of the soul, reverie is the purest and the most perfect instance of phantasy.
>> PORTER *Human Intellect* pt. ii, ch. 5, p. 325.

His face wore that bland liveliness . . . which marks the companion popular alike *amongst* men and women.
>> GEORGE ELIOT *Romola* bk. i, ch. 3, p. 85.

Among unmitigated rogues mutual trust is impossible.
>> SPENCER *Essays, State-Tamperings* in vol. iii, p. 326.

There is, it seems to me, a terrible want of esprit de corps *among* women.
>> FRANCES P. COBBE *Duties of Women* lect. v, p. 156.

The small Italian hound of exquisite symmetry, was a parlor favorite and pet *among* the fashionable dames of ancient times.
>> IRVING *Sketch-Book, Royal Poet* p. 111.

3. With the notion of division or distribution, affecting all of; so as to be shared by; as, the money was divided *among* the poor of the town.

There is a lad here, which hath five barley loaves, and two small fishes: but what are they *among* so many?   *John* vi, 9.

The country was portioned *among* the captains of the invaders.
    Macaulay *England* vol. i, p. 84.

4. In the country or time of; according to the customs of; as, religious observances *among* the Greeks; the usage *among* educated people.

Among the Anglo-Saxons the free population was divided into eorl and ceorl, the men of noble and of ignoble descent.
    Lingard *England* vol. i, ch. 7, app. 1, p. 287.

The most solid walls and impregnable fortresses were said, *among* the ancients, to be the work of the Cyclops, to render them the more respectable.   Lemprière *Class. Dict.*

Nothing is more certain than the essential identity *among* all ancient nations of the professions—religion, law, and medicine, which the progress of civilization has separated into three.
    Kitto *Daily Bible Illust.*, *45th Week* in vol. iv, p. 195.

Among rude nations no profession is honourable but that of arms.   Russell *Modern Europe* vol. i, letter xxxv, p. 213.

Distinctions

Amid—among: See under amid.

V—Prepositions Defined and Illustrated

AROUND, ROUND

Around is simply the word *round* with the addition of the prefix *a-*, having the general sense "on," but here producing no change in the meaning. There is little if any difference, either in signification or usage, between the two forms *around* and *round*.

[The shorter form is not distinguished in meaning from *around*.   MAETZNER *English Grammar* vol. ii, p. 326.]

[*Round* has all the senses of *around*, and is hardly distinguished from it in common use, but lays, if anything, more stress on the strictly circular nature of the position or relation, *around* approaching nearer to *about*.   *Standard Dictionary*.]

I. Of place or space :

1. About the circuit of ; on all sides of ; on various sides of ; so as to encircle, encompass, or envelop ; encircling ; surrounding ; enclosing ; bounding ; about ; as, to sail *around* or *round* the world.

The determination of the solar motion *around* the ecliptic may be considered the birth of astronomical science.
S. NEWCOMB *Popular Astronomy* pt. i, ch. 1, p. 16.

The slack sail . . . flagg'd *around* the mast.
MOORE *Lalla Rookh, Fire-Worshippers* pt. iii, st. 9.

And the wild bee hears her, *around* them humming,
And booms about them, a joyous stir.
W. W. STORY *Spring* st. 4.

The convulsive quiver and grip
Of the muscles *around* her bloodless lip.
WHITTIER *Mogg Megone* pt. i, st. 17.

> Like those verdant spots that bloom
> *Around* the crater's burning lips,
> Sweetening the very edge of doom !
> MOORE *Lalla Rookh, Fire-Worshippers* pt. iv, st. 4.

> Again my trooping hounds their tongues shall loll
> *Around* the breathed boar.   KEATS *Endymion* bk. i, st. 19.

2. Of indefinite extension, in all or many directions about or from; as, the field of force *around* either pole of a magnet.

The worship of one's own will fumes out *around* the being an atmosphere of evil.
MACDONALD *Annals of a Quiet Neighbourhood* ch. 15, p. 320.

The Indian pea . . . grows on a long, villous flower-stalk, *around* which both blossoms and leaves are symmetrically arranged.   LUDLOW *Heart of the Continent* ch. 2, p. 85.

3. Encircling so as to avoid; as, to get *around* a difficulty: in conversational rather than literary use.

4. On the other side of ; to be reached or found by passing; as, the church *around* the corner.

5. In the region of; here and there in the parts of; in various parts of; about; as, to wander *around* the city.

> Look *around* the habitable world, how few
> Know their own good, or knowing it, pursue.
> DRYDEN *Juvenal* satire x.

Glorious indeed is the world of God *around* us, but more glorious the world of God within us.   LONGFELLOW *Hyperion* p. 79.

Distinctions

About—around: See under ABOUT.

ASLANT

Aslant, originally an adverb formed by adding to *slant* the prefix *a-*, has long been used as a preposition, signifying across or over in a slanting direction or position ; athwart.

> There is a willow grows *aslant* a brook.
> SHAKESPEARE *Hamlet* act iv, sc. 7, l. 167.

AT

At is the Anglo-Saxon *æt*, retaining its original sense.

[*At* primarily denotes simple occupancy of a point in space; whence arise numerous derived and figurative meanings, as of time, direction, etc., by which the word partakes of the meaning of numerous other prepositions and prepositional phrases.
Standard Dictionary.]

[In its fundamental meaning as to space it originally denotes the proximity to something, though it never gives prominence to the reference to the interior in the same manner as *in*.
MAETZNER *English Grammar* vol. ii, p. 874.]

[*At* is used to denote relations of so many kinds, and some of these so remote from its primary local sense, that a classification of its uses is very difficult. MURRAY *New English Dictionary.*]

I. Of place or space:

1. Denoting position:

(*a*) Occupying the exact position of; on; in: denoting a definite and precise point of contact; as, *at* the center of the circle.

At the termination of this bridge, one enters the Commune of Jurançon.   ELLIS *Summer in the Pyrenees* ch. 5, p. 108.

(*b*) In contact with; in; on; upon: without precise limitation of a point of contact; as, *at* the top of the ladder; *at* the bottom of the sea.

It was necessary, of course, that a considerable portion of the crews should be *at* the ropes in tacking ship.
J. F. DAVIS *The Chinese* vol. ii, ch. 11, p. 86.

(*c*) In proximity to; in the vicinity or region of; close to; by; near; as, he was seated *at* table; the carriage is *at* the door.

Boswell . . . was always laying himself *at* the feet of some eminent man, and begging to be spit upon and trampled upon.
MACAULAY *Essays, Boswell's Johnson* p. 141.

At our feet the brook took its rise in a green quagmire.
W. BESANT *For Faith and Freedom* ch. 24, p. 178.

The sight of a soldier *at* the poll has always been like a red rag to a bull among all English people.

> N. S. SHALER *Kentucky* ch. 18, p. 384.

Lo! all my soldiers camped upon the road;
And all my city waited *at* the gates.

> EDWIN ARNOLD *Light of Asia* bk. vii, st. 22.

At every turn, with dinning clang,
The armourer's anvil clashed and rang.

> SCOTT *Marmion* can. 5, st. 6.

Thus was Religion wounded sore
At her own altars, and among her friends.

> POLLOK *Course of Time* bk. ii, l. 601.

John Bull . . . would set up a chop-house *at* the very gates of paradise.

> IRVING *Washington* vol. i, ch. 6, p. 61.

The Imperial Guard had bivouacked *at* the great stone of Lützen.

> J. K. HOSMER *Short Hist. German Lit.* pt. i, p. 228.

(*d*) Within the limits of; in; within; present in; as, the Capitol *at* Washington; he is *at* the ball grounds.

She might not rank with those detestable
That let the bantling scald *at* home.

> TENNYSON *Princess* v, st. 16.

With his [Webster's] advent *at* Washington, a new school of oratory,—now known throughout the country as 'the Websterian,'—was formed . . . in its Demosthenian simplicity and strength.

> MATHEWS *Oratory and Orators* ch. 11, p. 324.

He was educated *at* Magdalen College, Oxford, and entered into public life at the age of twenty-eight, being returned member of Parliament for the county of Dorset, in April, 1640.

> C. A. GOODRICH *British Eloquence, Lord Digby* p. 15.

The best act of the marvellous genius of Greece was its first act . . . in the instinct which *at* Thermopylæ held Asia at bay.

> EMERSON *Society and Solitude, Courage* p. 217.

At the parish-church I doze against the high pew-backs as I listen to the seesaw tones of the drawling curate.

> D. G. MITCHELL *Reveries of a Bachelor, Father-Land* p. 180.

4

The mob was cantoned *at* home among an overawed and broken-spirited people.   EVERETT *Orations, July 4, '26* p. 107.

(e) Denoting measurement or interval more or less definitely expressed: viewed or considered from; with an interval of; as, pistols *at* thirty paces.

Even in the most violent storms the water is probably calm *at* the depth of ninety or a hundred feet.
    MARY SOMERVILLE *Connection of Phys. Sciences* § 13, p. 91.

     All round a hedge upshoots, and shows
     At distance like a little wood.
      TENNYSON *The Day-Dream, Sleeping Palace* st. 6.

But alas! the halls of old philosophy have been so long deserted, that we circle them *at* shy distance as the haunt of phantoms and chimæras.
    COLERIDGE *Works, Lay Sermon* vol. i, p. 445.

2. Denoting or implying motion and direction:

(a) In the direction of; in reference to; in pursuit of; in quest of; applying to; to; toward; after; as, to look *at* the moon; to shoot *at* a mark; to aim *at* the sun; to catch *at* a straw; to strike *at* a ball.

Thus, intellect is ever pointing in derision *at* the fogyism of faith; and faith retaliates with scorn *at* the irreverence of intellect.   WINCHELL *Sci. and Religion* ch. 8, p. 212.

They aim *at* it, And botch the words up fit to their own thoughts.   SHAKESPEARE *Hamlet* act iv, sc. 5.

For getting a strong impression that a skein is tangled, there is nothing like snatching hastily *at* a single thread.
    GEORGE ELIOT *Mill on the Floss* ch. 8, p. 69.

Apollyon . . . made *at* him, throwing darts as thick as hail.
    BUNYAN *Works, Pil. Prog.* pt. i, ch. 9, p. 116.

The Jewish mind, so far forth as it was monotheistic, aimed *at* catholicity.   J. F. CLARKE *Ten Great Religions* ch. 12, p. 508.

The idea of resistance, by force, was nowhere glanced *at* in the most distant manner.   WIRT *Patrick Henry* ch. 2, p. 61.

We but catch *at* the skirts of the thing we would be.
>>> OWEN MEREDITH *Lucile* pt. i, can. 5, st. 1.

A slouching laborer . . . came out to look *at* the unusual scene with a slow bovine gaze.
>>> GEORGE ELIOT *Adam Bede* ch. 2, p. 18.

Dogs do always bark *at* those they know not.
>>> RALEIGH *Hist. World* vol. i, pref., p. 2.

(*b*) In or into contact with; upon; on; against; as, to knock *at* the door.

He batter'd *at* the doors; none came.
>>> TENNYSON *Princess* v, st. 11.

He knocked *at* another door, using for the purpose the thick end of his shillelagh, with which he beat a rousing tattoo.
>>> CHARLOTTE BRONTÉ *Shirley* ch. 2, p. 10.

(*c*) By way of; through, as in entrance or exit; as, smoke came out *at* the windows.

My master, Sir John, is come in *at* your backdoor, Mistress Ford, and requests your company.
>>> SHAKESPEARE *Merry Wives of Windsor* act iii, sc. 3.

They pushed us down the steps and through the court,
And with grim laughter thrust us out *at* gates.
>>> TENNYSON *Princess* iv, st. 35.

'Tis some visitor entreating entrance *at* my chamber door.
>>> POE *The Raven* st. 3.

Honesty shines in the face, but villainy peeps out *at* the eyes.
>>> SPURGEON *Treas. David* vol. i, p. 125.

Coachman: As I was coming in *at* the gate, a strange gentleman whisk'd by me.   ADDISON *The Drummer* act. v.

II. Of time:

1. On or upon the point or stroke of; upon the coming of; as, the train will leave *at* 2 P. M.

Rom.: Have you an army ready, say you?
Vols.: A most royal one; the centurions and their charges . . . to be on foot *at* an hour's warning.
>>> SHAKESPEARE *Coriolanus* act iv, sc. 3.

> In the deep nook, where once
> Thou call'dst me up *at* midnight.
> > SHAKESPEARE *The Tempest* act i, sc. 2.

Sleep—and *at* break of day   I will come to thee again!
> > WORDSWORTH *Pet Lamb* st. 15.

> *At* midnight, in the forest shades,
> Bozzaris ranged his Suliote band.
> > HALLECK *Marco Bozzaris* st. 2.

> We buried him darkly *at* dead of night,
> The sods with our bayonets turning.
> > WOLFE *Burial of Sir John Moore* st. 2.

At this distance of time it is not easy to catch him tripping, and if we refuse to be guided by the opinion of his contemporaries, we almost inevitably fall victims to his incomparable plausibility.   W. MINTO *Daniel Defoe* ch. 6, p. 85.

Even *at* the present day the arms of the craft-guild may often be seen blazoned in cathedrals.
> > GREEN *Short Hist. Eng. People* ch. 4, § 4, p. 218.

2. During the course or lapse of; during; in; by; as, to lie awake *at* night; the matter is *at* present uncertain.

> Men *at* some time are masters of their fates.
> > SHAKESPEARE *Julius Cæsar* act i, sc. 2, l. 138.

> His listless length *at* noontide would he stretch.
> > GRAY *Elegy* st. 26.

I often sent small squads *at* night to attack and run in the pickets along a line of several miles.
> > J. S. MOSBY *War Reminiscences* ch. 4, p. 45.

Thinking of the nests of birds, the dams of beavers, the tree-platforms of apes, it can scarcely be supposed that man *at* any time was unable to build himself a shelter.
> > E. B. TYLOR *Anthropology* ch. 10, p. 229.

III. Of various relations:

1. Of occasion, cause, or instrument; on the happening of; on the instant of; on the utterance of; in response to; because of; by means of; through the agency of; on; upon; by; through; as, *at* the signal the attack was made; pleased or angry *at* something.

> Thousands *at* his bidding speed.
>
> MILTON *Sonnet, On His Blindness* 1. 12.

I determined, *at* every hazard, to lift up the standard of emancipation in the eyes of the nation, within sight of Bunker Hill, and in the birth-place of Liberty. GARRISON in O. Johnson's *Wm. Lloyd Garrison* vol. ii, ch. 2, p. 42.

I replied, that we, having assisted in the conquest of Canada, *at* a great expense of blood and treasure, had some right to be considered in the settlement of it.

> B. FRANKLIN *Autobiography* vol. ii, ch. 10, p. 276.

At the triumph of Aurelian . . . eight hundred pairs of gladiators fought. STORRS *Divine Origin* lect. viii, p. 258.

Athelwold was thunderstruck *at* the proposal.

> W. RUSSELL *Modern Europe* vol. i, letter xvii, p. 99.

Every man alone is sincere. *At* the entrance of a second person, hypocrisy begins.

> EMERSON *Essays, Friendship* in first series, p. 163.

Peter saw the bulk of his subjects, *at* his accession to the throne, little better than beasts of burden.

> J. MORSE *Universal Geog.* vol. ii, p. 78.

Common solder, which is a mixture of lead and tin, melts *at* a lower temperature than either lead or tin.

> SPENCER *Principles of Biology* vol. i, § 92, p. 276.

2. Of degree, rate, value, etc.: up to; amounting to; to the extent of; corresponding to; according to; *at* a dollar a yard; interest *at* 6 per cent.

[Here are to be included such phrases as *at least, at most, at any rate,* etc.]

Radiant heat moves *at* the rate of 186,000 miles per second.

> P. G. TAIT *Recent Advances* lect. 8, p. 204.

3. Denoting connection in a great variety of ways, mostly metaphorical applications of the meanings that apply to space:

engaged in; occupied with; connected with; dependent on; subject to; in a state or condition of; having reference to; involving responsibility for; with direction of thought or intention toward; toward; with; against; as, *at* college; *at* prayer; the country is *at* war; the stag was *at* bay; he was enraged *at* the insult; we were *at* his mercy; they were set *at* liberty; to laugh *at* a person or thing; to talk *at* a person (who is not directly addressed); the guilt will be *at* your door.

> I found them close together,
> *At* blow and thrust.
>> SHAKESPEARE *Othello* act ii, sc. 8.

> An 'twere to me, I should be mad *at* it.
>> SHAKESPEARE *Merchant of Venice* act v, sc. 1.

> And Lancelot marvell'd *at* the wordless man.
>> TENNYSON *Elaine* st. 9.

> It is better to fight for the good than to rail *at* the ill.
>> TENNYSON *Maud* xxviii, st. 5.

> True religion is, *at* its soul, spiritual sympathy with, spiritual obedience to God.
>> PHILLIPS BROOKS *Light of the World* ser. v, p. 77.

> My ambition will keep my brain *at* work, I warrant thee.
>> SCOTT *Kenilworth* vol. i, ch. 15, p. 242.

> Base Envy withers *at* another's joy,
> And hates that excellence it cannot reach.
>> THOMSON *Seasons, Spring* l. 284.

> His stern, stoical face was like that of a lion *at* bay.
>> MOTLEY *John of Barneveld* vol. ii, ch. 18, p. 246.

> The world's a stately bark, on dang'rous seas,
> With pleasure seen, but boarded *at* our peril.
>> YOUNG *Night Thoughts* vi, l. 83.

> The free waves
> Will not say, No, to please a wayward king,
> Nor will the winds turn traitors *at* his beck.
>> LOWELL *Glance Behind the Curtain* st. 4

The citizens were all *at* liberty to walk and gather fruit in his gardens and grounds near the town.

> KEIGHTLEY *Greece* pt. ii, ch. 1, p. 154.

The King's chagrin *at* the cautious limitations imposed upon the State's special embassy was, so he hoped, to be removed by full conferences in the camp.

> MOTLEY *John of Barneveld* vol. i, ch. 4, p. 217.

An Amazonian woman, indignant *at* the cowardice of the magistrates, attempted to interfere, but was carried away and inclosed in Bridewell.

> ABEL STEVENS *History of Methodism* vol. i, bk. iii, ch. 8, p. 282.

The sporting men gave it away by betting *at* odds that Mr. Lincoln would never reach Washington.

> CHITTENDEN *Recollections of Lincoln* ch. 10, p. 60.

Distinctions

At—in: "He is now living *at* Paris." Correct usage requires us to say rather, "He is now living *in* Paris." Always *in* a country; either *at* or *in* a city, town, or village; *at*, if the place is regarded as a point; *in*, if it is inclusive. "We arrived *at* Paris"; "He lives *in* London"; "There are three churches *in* this village." In England the use of *in* before towns and cities is more restricted than in the United States; the distinctions observed there between *at* and *in* often seem arbitrary.

[*At* is less definite than *in*. *At* the church may mean *in*, or *near* the church. Hence, *at* does not make a reference to the *interior* prominent. It is proper to use *at* before the names of small towns, villages, foreign cities far remote, and houses; as, "He lived *at* Fishkill, lectured *at* Winnebago, died *at* Pekin."

In should be used before the names of the great geographical or political divisions of the globe, countries, and large cities; as, He teaches *in* Paris; she sings *in* New York. *At* should be used before the number of a street, and *in* (not *on*) before the name of the street; as, The officer was found *at* the Court House *in* Clark street.

At or *in* may often be used interchangeably; as, He was crowned *in*, or *at* Paris; Both *at* Belfast and *in* Dublin riots occurred.

At is used after the verb TOUCH; as, The vessel touched *at* Queenstown. *At* or *in* may be used after the verb ARRIVE; as, They arrived *at*, or *in* Liverpool. *At* or *in* may be used after the verb TO BE; as, He has been at Boston.—*in* Baltimore.

FALLOWS *100,000 Synonyms and Antonyms.*]

At last—at length: These two prepositional phrases are quite distinct in meaning and are not, in strict usage, interchangeable. The assumption that *at length* means the same as *at last*, and is therefore superfluous, is an error. Both *at length* and *at last* presuppose long waiting; but *at last* views what comes after the waiting as a *finality; at length* views it as *intermediate* with reference to action or state that continues, or to results that are yet to follow; as, "I have invited him often, and *at length* he is coming"; "I have invited him often, and *at last* he has come"; "*At length·* he began to recover"; "*At last* he died." "*At last* he concluded" is correct, but "*At last* he began" would seem somewhat grotesque.

Scarce thus *at length* failed speech recovered sad.
> MILTON *Paradise Lost* bk. iv, l. 857.

O, then, *at last* relent.
> MILTON *Paradise Lost* bk. iv, l. 79.

At length the freshening western blast
Aside the shroud of battle cast.
> SCOTT *Marmion* can. 6, st. 26.

There *at last* it lay, the bourn of my long and weary pilgrimage.
> R. F. BURTON *El Medinah* ch. 25, p. 899.

All work must be done *at last*, not in a disorderly, scrambling, doggish way, but in an ordered, soldierly, human way.
> RUSKIN *Crown of Wild Olive* lect. i, p. 26.

Every hero becomes a bore *at last*.
> EMERSON *Representative Men, Uses of Great Men* p. 26.

At last as marble rock he standeth still.
> TASSO *Godfrey of Bulloigne* tr. by Fairfax, bk. vi, st. 27.

AT ALL

The phrase *at all* has been objected to by some critics, probably because—like all idioms—it defies analysis. It is certainly not, as some urge, superfluous, except as every word or phrase used merely for emphasis is superfluous. "I see nothing *at all*" is more emphatic than "I see nothing." It is as if the speaker replied to unspoken cross-questioning, saying, "nothing *of any kind*," "nothing *whatever*," "nothing *at all*."

The phrase is sustained by the usage of the very best authorities.

And they shall be no more two nations, neither shall they be divided into two kingdoms any more *at all*.   *Ezek.* xxxvii, 22.

I find in him no fault *at all*.   *John* xviii, 38.

God is light, and in him is no darkness *at all*.   *1 John* i, 5.

Now, this no more dishonors you *at all*
Than to take in a town with gentle words.
SHAKESPEARE *Coriolanus* act iii, sc. 2.

'Tis better to have loved and lost
Than never to have loved *at all*.
TENNYSON *In Memoriam* xxvii, st. 4.

Verbs and Other Antecedents

[*At* has been referred in a continually more extensive measure to the idea of a motion or direction pressing towards or aiming at a person or thing. To the verbal notions *come*, *reach*, *fall*, *hasten*, to which *at* is added only in definite combinations, are attached others, as, *throw*, *aim*, *shoot*, *strike*, *grasp*, *reach*, *bask*, *spit*, *hiss*, and the like, mostly with the expression of a hostile tendency.   MAETZNER *English Grammar* vol. ii, p. 379.]

It may be added that in many of these cases *at* carries a distinct implication of not attaining, as in its use with *strike*, *grasp*, *catch*, *snatch*, *reach*, etc.   A man *strikes* at another if the blow falls short; if it reaches, he is said to *strike* him rather than to *strike at* him. So in the proverb, "Drowning men *catch at* straws." The player *strikes at* or *catches at* the ball that goes

by him.   The same is true of the use of *at* with certain nouns,
as *attempt, endeavor,* etc.   An attempt *at* eloquence is a failure
to be eloquent.

Erroneous Usage

" *Where* was I *at*, Mr. Speaker ? " This celebrated utterance
justly raised a question as to the sobriety of the honorable member.   *Where* is not to be followed by *at* or *to*.   The correct
phrase is not " *where* is it *at* ? " but " *where* is it ? " not " *where*
are you going *to* ? " but simply " *where* are you going ? "   The
sense of *at* is virtually included in *there* and *where*, so that the
repetition of *at* is redundant.   (Compare p. 313, Note.)

ATHWART

Athwart is derived from *thwart*, from the Icelandic *thvert*,
across, from *thverr*, cross, plus the prefix *a-*.

I. Of place or space :

1. In nautical use, from side to side of (a ship, etc.) ; across
the course of ; across ; as, a framework *athwart* the deck ; a fleet
sailing *athwart* our course.

> And so our ship fell *athwart* the Portuguese ship's hawse.
>   DEFOE *Capt. Singleton* ch. 11, p. 187.

> While sheeting home, we saw the Agacucho standing *athwart*
> our bows, sharp upon the wind, cutting through the head seas
> like a knife.   DANA *Two Years before the Mast* ch. 10, p. 47.

> Jones now determined to lay his ship *athwart* the enemy's
> hawse.   A. S. MACKENZIE *Paul Jones* vol. i, ch. 8, p. 182.

2. Of position, direction, or motion in general, from side to
side of ; in the direction of the breadth of ; across the course or
path of, so as to meet or fall in with ; hence, into the notice or
observation of.

> She drew her casement-curtain by,
> And glanced *athwart* the glooming flats.
>   TENNYSON *Mariana* st. 2.

II. Figuratively, so as to cross, thwart, or oppose; in opposition to; contrary to; against; as, *athwart* our plans.

> Whatsoever comes *athwart* his affection.
> SHAKESPEARE *Much Ado about Nothing* act ii, sc. 2.

> Heave him upon your winged thoughts,
> *Athwart* the sea.
> SHAKESPEARE *K. Henry V.* act v, chorus, l. 8.

VI—Prepositions Defined and Illustrated

BARRING, BATING

For the meaning and use of these words, see PARTICIPIAL PREPOSITIONS.

BEFORE

Before is from the Anglo-Saxon *beforan*, which is composed of the prefix *be-*, by, and the adverb *foran*, from *fore*, *for*, before, for.

I. Of place or space:

1. Denoting precedence, ahead of; in advance of; preceding; in front of; as, heralds went *before* the king.

I had rather, forsooth, go *before* you like a man than follow him like a dwarf.

> SHAKESPEARE *Merry Wives of Windsor* act iii, sc. 2.

Sleep, gentle heavens, *before* the prow.

> TENNYSON *In Memoriam* ix, st. 4.

The sparkle and tremor of purple sea
That rises *before* you, a flickering hill,
On and on to the shut of the sky.

> LOWELL *Pictures from Appledore* div. iv, l. 5.

King Solomon, *before* his palace gate
At evening, on the pavement tessellate
Was walking with a stranger from the East.

> LONGFELLOW *Wayside Inn, Azrael* in pt. iii, st. 1.

2. Of position, face to face with; in the presence of; in front of; as, the prisoner stood *before* the court.

O come, let us worship and bow down: let us kneel *before* the Lord our maker. Ps. xcv, 6.

As a being with a will, man cannot avoid putting *before* him certain aims and principles of conduct.

> BOSANQUET *Hist. of Æsthetic* ch. 10, p. 250.

II. Of time:

Prior to; anterior to; earlier than; sooner than; as, blossoms come *before* fruit.

Make me feel the wild pulsation that I felt *before* the strife.
TENNYSON *Locksley Hall* st. 55.

This sad affair had chanced about thirty years *before* the action of our story commences.
HAWTHORNE *House of Seven Gables* ch. 1, p. 27.

The shellbark alone drops its leaves *before* they are tinted in autumn.   W. FLAGG *Year Among the Trees, The Hickory* p. 157.

In the summer [1642] *before* the confederation of the Colonies, the first Commencement of Harvard College was held.
PALFREY *New England* vol. ii, ch. 1, p. 48.

Before selection can take place, the fittest must already be in existence.   JANET *Final Causes* tr. by Affleck, bk. i, ch. 7, p. 307.

The pilot . . . was an old Dutch skipper, and had a habit of spitting on his hands *before* every order he gave, as if the effort was a manual exertion.   MACREADY *Reminis.* ch. 20, p. 287.

III. Of various relations:

1. In advance of, as regards development, condition, or attainment; higher than; superior to; formerly, surpassing in rank or eminence.   (Compare I., 1.)

As Vane was *before* his age in religion . . . so also he was *before* his age in politics.   P. HOOD *Cromwell* ch. 18, p. 206.

2. Within the jurisdiction, cognizance, or power of (compare I., 2); demanding action or attention; as, the motion is *before* the house: sometimes used in solemn invocation, oath, or affirmation; as, *before* God I affirm.   (Compare I., 2.)

3. Driven in front of; moved on by; overcome by; as, the ship sailed *before* the wind; he carried all *before* him.

How many hopes are like the spider's web, woven in the night, bright in the morning dew, perishing *before* the first footfall!
H. W. BEECHER *Norwood* ch. 38, p. 351.

Sooner or later every intellectual canker disappears *before* earnest work.   TYNDALL *Hours of Exercise* ch. 5, p. 62.

Black brumal clouds driven *before* furious blasts.
> R. F. BURTON *Lake Regions Cent. Afr.* ch. 8, p. 65.

4. In preference to; in comparison with; sooner than; rather than; as, they will die *before* yielding.

> Prefer a noble life *before* a long.
>> SHAKESPEARE *Coriolanus* act iii, sc. 1.

> Pay him six thousand and deface the bond:
> Double six thousand, and then treble that,
> *Before* a friend of this description
> Shall lose a hair through Bassanio's fault
>> SHAKESPEARE *Merchant of Venice* act iii, sc. 2.

> As these white robes are soil'd and dark,
>   To yonder shining ground;
> As this pale taper's earthly spark,
>   To yonder argent round;
> So shows my soul *before* the Lamb,
>   My spirit *before* Thee.
>> TENNYSON *Saint Agnes' Eve* st. 2.

BEHIND

Behind is derived from the Anglo Saxon *behindan*, from the adverb *hindan*, behind (connected with *hind, hinder*), plus the prefix *be-*, by, on, etc.

I. Of place or space:

1. At the back of; on the back or farther side of; following after; after; as, stand *behind* me; he is *behind* that tree; *behind* the curtain.

This wild assault was soon checked, by grape from two guns planted *behind* a traverse on the ramparts.   W. F. P. NAPIER *War in the Peninsula* vol. i, bk. v, ch. 2, p. 381.

> *Behind* a cloud the moon doth veil her light.
>> R. H. STODDARD *The Castle in the Air* st. 8.

Behind these came two pursuivants at-arms in tabards.
> HOWARD PYLE *Men of Iron* ch. 24, p. 224.

A . . . screen or net-work, *behind* which the dark forms of the natives were seen glancing to and fro.

PRESCOTT Mexico vol. i, bk. ii, ch. 4, p. 276.

Cuchillo closed *behind* him the wattle of bamboos that served as a door.   MAYNE REID *Wood-Rangers* ch. 9, p. 67.

2. To or toward the rear of; to, toward, or in the space left by; back of; as, look *behind* you.

Look not *behind* thee, neither stay thou in all the plain.

Gen. xix, 17.

Get thee *behind* me, Satan.   *Matt.* xvi, 23.

II. Of time:

In the time previous to; in time left by; remaining after the death or departure of; as, he left a fortune *behind* him.

> Spirits of peace, where are ye? are ye all gone,
> And leave me here in wretchedness *behind* ye?
> <div align="right">SHAKESPEARE <i>K. Henry VIII.</i> act iv, sc. 2.</div>

> But he, whose loss our tears deplore,
> Has left *behind* him more than fame.
> <div align="right">BRYANT <i>In Memory of William Leggett</i> st. 1.</div>

> As in the winters left *behind*,
> Again our ancient games had place.
> <div align="right">TENNYSON <i>In Memoriam</i> lxxviii, st. 8.</div>

III. Of various relations:

1. From the local idea of supporters standing at one's back, in a position to give aid to or make use of; ready to aid or support; sustaining; supporting; as, he has capital *behind* him, the administration is *behind* the movement.

It was not the famous needle-gun . . . which won the late Prussian victories, but the intelligence and discipline of the Prussian soldier, the man *behind* the gun.

MATHEWS Words ch. 1, p. 48.

And every rustler and thief, every road agent and train robber from the Canadian line to Kansas knows that shotgun and the man *behind* it.   *N. Y. World* Oct. 4, 1908.

2. Not so well advanced as; in the rear of, as regards knowledge, development, etc.; inferior to; not equal to; not up to; as, *behind* the times; he is *behind* his class.

The cut of the clothing of even the most buckish young fellows is *behind* the times.
> C. D. WARNER *Saunterings, Amsterdam* p. 84.

Was the Mayflower launched by cowards, steered by men *behind* their time?   LOWELL *Present Crisis* st. 15.

Distinctions

After—behind: See under AFTER.

BELOW

Below is from the adjective *low* plus the prefix *be-*, by, on, etc.

I. Of place:

1. Of position, farther down than; not so high as; lower than; under; beneath; as, *below* the knee; *below* the surface of the water.

I hear one thrumming a guitar *below* stairs.
> THOREAU *Winter, Jan. 13, 1857* p. 172.

> He never counted him a man
> Would strike *below* the knee.
> SCOTT *Lay of the Last Minstrel* can iii, st. 17, l. 8.

2. Of direction, course, etc., lower down than; as, the town *below* this on the river.

> . . . Him I'll desire
> To meet me at the consecrated fount,
> A league *below* the city.
> SHAKESPEARE *Measure for Measure* act iv, sc. 3.

II. Of derived meanings, in figurative use:

1. Lower than in degree, rank, value, dignity, etc.; inferior to; under; as, *below* the captain is the lieutenant; the yield was *below* the average.

A proud and sensitive nature finds it far easier, often, to speak confidingly to one in a station *below* him than to an equal or a superior.   H. W. BEECHER *Norwood* ch. 37, p. 284.

The boy was immediately *below* his grandfather in his class, and   . . 'trapped' or corrected him in his reading.
                    N. MACLEOD *Highland Parish, Peasantry* p. 189.

2. Too low to be worthy of; unworthy of; beneath; as, such action is *below* contempt.

[*Beneath* contempt is more usual and is preferable.]

It is possible to be *below* flattery as well as above it.
                    MACAULAY *England* vol. i, p. 151.

I shall cheerfully bear the reproach of having descended *below* the dignity of history.   MACAULAY *England* vol. i, p. 28.

Distinctions

Below—beneath—down—under—underneath: See DISTINC-
TIONS under BENEATH.

BENEATH

Beneath is derived from the Anglo-Saxon *beneothan*, from the prefix *be-*, by, plus *neothan*, below.

I. Of place or space, in a lower place or position than; lower than; underneath; below; under; as, a hidden rock *beneath* the waves.

[In a local regard, these prepositions (*beneath* and *underneath*) point to the lower position which an object takes or receives with respect to that dependent upon them, whether with perpendicular or non-perpendicular depth, with or without contact with the other, as well with as without covering an object.
                    MAETZNER *English Grammar* vol. ii, p. 459.]

Beneath her stretched the temples and the tombs,
The city sickening of its own thick breath,
And over all the sleepless Pleiades.
                    ALDRICH *Judith* pt. i, st. 2.

From *beneath* the flap of an enormous pocket of a soiled vest, . . projected an instrument.
                    COOPER *Last of the Mohicans* ch. 1, p. 8.

> Seek yonder brake *beneath* the cliff,—
> There lies Red Murdoch, stark and stiff.
>> SCOTT *Lady of the Lake* can. 5, st. 13.

The great elm-trees in the gold-green meadows were fast asleep above, and the cows were fast asleep *beneath* them.
> KINGSLEY *Water-Babies* ch. 1, p. 14.

II. In derived or figurative use:

1. Of influence, power, or control, often denoting subordination, dependence, or protection : influenced or controlled by ; pressed or crushed by; subdued or dominated by; sheltered by; dependent on; under the power, dominion, or protection of ; under; as, the boughs bent *beneath* their load.

One of his [Murillo's] Madonnas was so saintly beautiful in the tranced joy of her divine maternity, that I felt my knees giving way *beneath* me, obedient to the instinct of adoration.
> GRACE GREENWOOD *Haps and Mishaps* ch. 8, p. 56.

> And the waves bound *beneath* me as a steed
> That knows his rider.
>> BYRON *Childe Harold* can. 3, st. 2.

> I think our country sinks *beneath* the yoke;
> It weeps, it bleeds.
>> SHAKESPEARE *Macbeth* act iv, sc. 8, l. 39.

An empirical acquaintance with facts rises to a scientific knowledge of facts as soon as the mind discovers *beneath* the multiplicity of single productions the unity of an organic system.
> MAX MÜLLER *Science of Language* first series, lect. i, p. 25.

2. Of inferiority, inferior to; unsuited to the dignity of; lower in rank than ; unworthy of ; under ; below ; as, he is *beneath* my notice.

It was more dangerous to be above that standard (of female attainments) than *beneath* it.
> MACAULAY *England* vol. i, ch. 8, p. 318.

A most abject and brutified nature, totally *beneath* the human character.   IRVING *Knickerbocker* bk. i, ch. 5, p. 69.

Distinctions

Below — beneath — down — under — underneath:

[*Under* strictly implies that another object is directly upon or over in a vertical line. *Below* signifies that one object is lower than another, so as to be looked down upon from it or hidden from view by it; as, *below* (not *under* nor *beneath*) the horizon.
Standard Dictionary.]

Below, beneath, and *under* are in many cases interchangeable. The distinctions in their use are so subtle as often to seem arbitrary. We may say *below, beneath,* or *under* the stars, but scarcely *below* or *beneath* the sun, though *under* the sun is very common. We may say *below* stairs, though *down*-stairs is more common; as, "I saw that *down*-stairs." *Beneath* or *under* the stairs would indicate that the stairway stretched above the object; as, the incendiary placed the combustibles *under* the stairs The phrase *down-stairs,* or *down the stairs,* has a special meaning of its own implying motion; as, to fall *down-stairs,* where neither *below, beneath,* nor *under* could be used. Similarly we say, "The man has gone *down* the river," meaning along the descending course of the stream; we could not say that the man has gone *below, beneath, under,* or *underneath* the river, unless we referred to the descent of a diver or to passage through a tunnel. So a ship may sail *down,* but not *below, beneath, under,* nor *underneath* the river, unless in the case of a submarine vessel. We may say of a person, "His knees trembled *beneath* him"; it would be impossible to say, "His knees trembled *below* him." Conversely, a student says of another, "He is in the class *below* me," implying simple gradation in rank; "the class *beneath* me" would imply inferiority or contempt, and hence is never used in such connection. *Under* has the special meaning of *subject to,* which is not in either of the associated prepositions. Hence we speak of an object or person as *under* our care or *under* our charge in a worthy sense; as, the jewels or the children *under* our care. *Below* could scarcely be used in such case. We may say contemptuously, "That is *beneath* your care" or "*beneath* your attention," *i e.*, unworthy of it. "*Beneath* one's charge" is not used. *Underneath*, which is practically equivalent to *under* in literal reference to place, has not the derived or metaphorical use. *Below* does not carry the intimation of protection that is often found in *beneath* or *under*. We do not speak of the hen gathering her brood *below* her wings; we might say *beneath* her wings, but more naturally say *under*. The old hymn reads:

> "*Beneath* the shadow of thy throne
> Thy saints have dwelt secure."

For the contrasted prepositions *above — on — over*, see DISTINCTIONS under ABOVE.

BESIDE

Beside is from the Anglo-Saxon *be sidan*, by the side of.

I. Of place or space:

At the side of; in proximity to; near; close to; as, a path *beside* the river.

> *Beside* the bounteous board of home.
> > WHITTIER *For an Autumn Festival* st. 10.

> And I have seen thee blossoming
> *Beside* the snow-bank's edges cold.
> > BRYANT *The Yellow Violet* st. 8.

The faithful Sancho still kept guard *beside* his little master.
> LOUISA M. ALCOTT *Under the Lilacs* ch. 10, p. 98.

Beside him was the croupier, a very boy, whose duty it was to rake in the winnings and pay out the losses, which he did with wonderful dexterity.
> C. B. GILLESPIE in *Century Magazine* June, 1891, p. 262.

> When *beside* me in the dale,   He carrolled lays of love.
> > GOLDSMITH *Hermit* st. 30.

II. Of various relations, more or less based upon the local:

1. In comparison with (as if the objects were placed side by side to be compared); compared with; my merit is little *beside* yours.

Imports there loss, *beside* the present need ?
> MILTON *Comus* l. 287.

Nosegays! leave them for the waking,
   Throw them earthward where they grew.
Dim are such, *beside* the breaking
   Amaranths he looks unto.
Folded eyes see brighter colors than the open ever do.
> E. B. BROWNING *A Child Asleep* st. 2.

2. Outside of:

(*a*) Away or apart from; aside from; as, this discussion is *beside* the matter in hand.

The distinction . . is an altogether false one and *beside* the question.   ROBERTSON *Sermons* third series, ser. xiii, p. 158.

(*b*) Alienated from; deviating from; out of; far from; as, the man is *beside* himself.

> In faith, my lord, you are too wilful-blame,
> And since your coming hither, have done enough
> To put him quite *beside* his patience.
> SHAKESPEARE *1 K. Henry IV.* act iii, sc. 1.

My father . . . was as one *beside* himself, being in ecstasy or rapture of mind. W. BESANT *For Faith and Freedom* ch. 21, p. 150.

'Ecstasy' was madness; it is intense delight; but has in no wise thereby broken with the meaning from which it started, since it is the nature alike of madness and of joy to set men out of and *beside* themselves.
> TRENCH *On the Study of Words* lect. vi, p. 274.

(*c*) In addition to; over and above; other than; except; as, I have no treasure *beside* this.

Beside the sabbaths of the Lord, and *beside* your gifts, and *beside* all your vows, and *beside* all your freewill offerings, which ye give unto the Lord.   *Lev.* xxiii, 38.

[In this sense *besides* is the proper form, and now commonly used.   *Standard Dictionary.*]

Distinctions

Along — beside — by : See under ALONG.

BESIDES

Besides is etymologically the same as *beside*, and was formerly used interchangeably with it, as·

> Alas, Sir, how fell you *besides* your five wits.
> SHAKESPEARE *Twelfth Night* act iv, sc. 2, l. 92.

Now, however, *besides* is quite closely restricted to the sense of *beside*, II., 2 (c), in which sense *beside* is now little used, except in poetry or elevated style, the process of discrimination elsewhere referred to, which is working throughout our language toward the result of one word for one meaning, making its way also here, to distinguish these closely related forms.

1. In addition to; in connection with; other than; over and above; as, *besides* this we have as much more.

> The caloristic doctrine, *besides* its fundamental hypothesis, which we now know to be wrong, had given an absurd and illogical test for quantity of heat in a body.
> WM. THOMSON in *Encyc. Brit.* 9th ed., vol. xi, p. 557.

2. Apart from; beyond; except; bating; save; as, I care for nothing *besides* this.

> The Marquis had not much *besides* his palace.
> N. P. WILLIS *Lady Jane* can. 2, st. 82.

Distinctions

Besides—but—except—save—without: See under BUT.

VII—Prepositions Defined and Illustrated

BETWEEN

Between is derived from the Anglo-Saxon *betweŏnum*, from *be-*, by, plus *tweŏnum*, dative plural of *tweŏn*, double, two

I. Of place:

In or at some point within the space which separates (two places or objects); as, *between* two fires; he stepped *between* the combatants.

[*Between* is strictly applicable only to two things, but this may be understood as including cases where a number of things are discriminated collectively as two wholes or as taken in pairs, or where one thing is set off as against a number of others; *among* is used in cases of distributive discrimination.
Standard Dictionary.]

And he [Abram] went on his journeys from the south even to Beth-el, unto the place where his tent had been at the beginning, *between* Beth-el and Hai. *Gen* xiii, 8.

A break *between* the house tops shows   The moon.
MATTHEW ARNOLD *A Summer Night* st. 1.

Every step of the way lies *between* two precipices, and under toppling crags. TYNDALL *Hours of Exercise* ch. 8, p. 80.

When the distance *between* two bodies is doubled their mutual attraction falls off to one-fourth of what it formerly was.
P. G. TAIT *Recent Advances* lect. xiv, p. 856.

And, for the winter fireside meet,
Between the andirons' straddling feet, .   .
The apples sputtered in a row.
WHITTIER *Snow-Bound* st. 9.

What silence dwells *between*   Those severed lips serene!
JEAN INGELOW *The Snowdrop Monument* st. 4.

II. Of time:

Intermediate in relation to (two times or periods of time); as, *between* morning and noon; *between* 6 and 7 o'clock.

> *Between* the acting of a dreadful thing
> And the first motion, all the interim is
> Like a phantasma, or a hideous dream.
> > SHAKESPEARE *Julius Cæsar* act. ii, sc. 1, l. 63.

> *Between* the dark and the daylight,
> When the night is beginning to lower.
> > LONGFELLOW *The Children's Hour* l. 1.

No true form of figurative art intervened *between* Greek sculpture and Italian painting.
> J. A. SYMONDS *Renaissance in Italy, Fine Arts* p. 8.

III. Of various relations:

1. Intermediate in relation to, as qualities, conditions, characters, etc.:

(*a*) Denoting transition, agreement, or likeness; as, the flavor is *between* sour and sweet; he is something *between* knave and fool.

> Stood on the bound *between*
> Man social and man savage, dark and massive.
> BULWER-LYTTON *Lost Tales of Miletus, The Secret Way* st. 34.

The English cabinet . . . resolved to follow a middle course *between* peace and war.   LINGARD *England* vol. vi, ch. 1, p. 88.

Virtue is nothing but a just temper *between* propensities any one of which, if indulged to excess, becomes vice.
> MACAULAY *England* vol. i, ch. 2, p. 190.

He was now in a chrysalis state—putting off the worm and putting on the dragon-fly—a kind of intermediate grub *between* sycophant and oppressor.   MACAULAY *Essays, Bacon* p. 248.

(*b*) Denoting contrast, difference, or unlikeness; as, the difference *between* violet and red.

The chasm *between* vertebrates and invertebrates is one which it has taxed the ingenuity of transmutationists to bridge.
> WINCHELL *Doctrine of Evolution, Objections* p. 63.

That difference which is always to be seen *between* the stroke of talent and the stroke of genius.

HELEN HUNT JACKSON *Ramona* ch. 1, p. 15.

There is such a difference *between* far-reaching and far-fetching.   LOWELL *Among My Books, Shakespeare Once More* in first series, p. 198.

Between saving a cent and spending a cent there is two cents difference.   C. C. COFFIN *Caleb Krinkle* ch. 12, p. 107.

The difference *between* extreme temperatures at a station is called a range.   A. W. GREELY *American Weather* ch. 10, p. 120.

2. Denoting joint or reciprocal action in agreement or opposition; with relation to both (or all) of; involving both (or all) of; as, a compact or a quarrel *between* friends; *between* ourselves.

And I will put enmity *between* thee and the woman, and *between* thy seed and her seed; it shall bruise thy head, and thou shalt bruise his heel.   *Gen.* iii, 15.

The struggle *between* the two fierce Teutonic breeds [Saxon and Dane] lasted during six generations.

MACAULAY *England* vol. i, ch. 1, p. 8.

The consummation of peace *between* Great Britain and the United States of America was the sublime result of powers which were conspiring together for the renovation of the world.

BANCROFT *United States* vol. v, epoch v, ch. 1, p. 461.

There was a triparite treaty afterwards agreed to *between* England, France, and Austria.

MCCARTHY *Our Own Times* vol. ii, ch. 28, p. 344.

The daily widening schism *between* Lutherans and Calvinists seemed to bode little good to the cause of religious freedom.

MOTLEY *Dutch Republic* vol. iii, pt. iv, ch. 4, p. 6.

They had captured a wolf *between* them, and had brought in his scalp for bounty.   COOPER *Pioneers* ch. 9, p. 142.

3. From one to another of: implying motion or a continuous connection; as, the steamer *between* New York and Hamburg; the railway *between* New York and Boston.

I did go *between* them [the lovers] as I said.

SHAKESPEARE *All's Well* act. v, sc. 3, l. 259.

He may come and go *between* you both.

     SHAKESPEARE *Merry Wives of Windsor* act. ii, sc. 2, l. 180.

The appearance of Joseph in Egypt is the first distinct point of contact *between* Sacred and secular history.

     A. P. STANLEY *Jewish Church* vol. i, pt. i, lect. iv, p. 67.

Distinctions

Between—betwixt: Though no close line can be drawn, it may be said that *betwixt* in modern use seems to incline rather to the sense of separation than of union. We should hardly say, "This will be a bond of union *betwixt* them," but "a bond of union *between* them." So we say, "I mention this in confidence *between* [not *betwixt*] ourselves."

Erroneous Use

The impossible combination of *between* with a singular object is a somewhat common error; as, "There were ten boats with a space of twenty feet *between* each." The number of objects governed by *between* can never be less than two; in other words, *between* can not be used of a single object, as in the following ·

And with a gap of a whole night *between* every one.

     DICKENS *Martin Chuzzlewit* ch. 8, p. 152.

Correct usage requires us to say, "—— *between* each two," "—— *between* every two," or "—— *between* one and another."

BETWIXT

Betwixt is kindred in derivation to and a close synonym of *between.*

You shall see, as I have said, great difference *betwixt* our Bohemia and your Sicilia.

     SHAKESPEARE *Winter's Tale* act i, sc. 1, l. 4

         Nor can the foot
Of disembodied spirit, nor angel wing,
Transgress the deep inexorable gulf
Betwixt the worlds of darkness and of light.

BICKERSTETH *Yesterday, To-day, and For Ever* bk. iii, l. 650.

BEYOND

Beyond is derived from the Anglo-Saxon *begeondan*, from *be-*, by, plus *geond*, yond, yonder.

I. Of place or space:

Farther than; more distant than; on the farther side of; past; over; as, *beyond* the turn of the road; *beyond* the river.

[The transfer of this preposition to other fields is peculiar to modern times; the oldest period of the language employs it for relations of space only. MAETZNER *English Grammar* vol. ii, p. 470.]

> Sweet the memory is to me
> Of a land *beyond* the sea,
> Where the waves and mountains meet.
>
> LONGFELLOW *Amalfi* st. 1.

The first settlers *beyond* the Alleghanies were a heroic race.
E. KIRKE in *Harper's Monthly*, Feb., *1888* p. 420.

He [Philip II.] had long since descried the dark storm that was mustering *beyond* the Alps.
PRESCOTT *Philip II.* vol. i, bk. i, ch. 5, p. 147.

> Time doth not breathe on its fadeless bloom,
> For *beyond* the clouds, and *beyond* the tomb,
> It is there, it is there, my child!
>
> MRS. HEMANS *The Better Land.*

II. Of time:

According to the analogy of spatial relations, extending farther than; later than; past; as, *beyond* the usual hour.

My grief stretches itself *beyond* the hour of death.
SHAKESPEARE *K. Henry IV.* act iv, sc. 4, l. 57.

III. Of various relations:

Surpassing; exceeding; superior to; better than; more than; out of reach of; past; over and above; above; over; as, to live *beyond* one's means; tempted *beyond* endurance; beautiful *beyond* description; it is *beyond* my knowledge.

A mere stroll, which requires no exertion, and does not fatigue, will not be injurious before or after eating, but exercise *beyond* this limit is hurtful at such times. COMBE *Physiology* ch. 5, p. 127.

Latimer went *beyond* everybody else in the miscellaneous assortment of topics he used to bring together.

　　　　　CRAIK *Eng. Lit. and Lang., Latimer* in vol. i, p. 488.

Your bounty is *beyond* my speaking;
But though my mouth be dumb, my heart shall thank you.

　　　　　NICHOLAS ROWE *Jane Shore* act ii, sc. 1.

What's fame? a fancy'd life in others' breath,
A thing *beyond* us, e'en before our death.

　　　　　POPE *Essay on Man* ep. iv, l. 287.

BUT

But is derived from the Anglo-Saxon *būtan*, except, without, being originally an adverb meaning outside, from the prefix *be* by, plus *ūtan*, out.

I. [Obsolete or dialectic.] Of place or space :

Outside of; out; without; as, to gang *but* the house.

This sense, which is now known chiefly as a Scotticism, is worth considering, as showing the fundamental meaning, on which the ordinary and accepted usage is based.

II. Of relations in general:

Leaving out; with exception of; excepting; except; save saving; barring; as, I found all *but* one.

I have known ministers who always unconsciously sifted their audience and preached to nothing *but* the bolted wheat.

　　　　　H. W. BEECHER *Yale Lectures* lect. vii, p. 162.

Nothing ought to be held laudable or becoming, *but* what nature itself should prompt us to think so.

　　　　　STEELE *Spectator* Mar. 7, 1710.

Nothing was audible *but* the hum of the evening insects and the regular muffled beat of the oars over the water.

　　　　　G. W. CURTIS *Trumps* ch. 4, p. 27

Thieves' language, or that dialect for which there is no name, *but* one from its own vocabulary, viz. Slang, is of greater value in philology than in commerce.

　　　　　R. G. LATHAM *English Language* pt. vii, p. 579

Such was old Arthur Gride, in whose face there was not a wrinkle, in whose dress there was not one spare fold or plait, *but* expressed the most covetous and griping penury.

DICKENS *Nicholas Nickleby* vol. ii, p. 288.

There was nothing for it *but* to give way.

FROUDE *Hist. Essays, Erasmus and Luther* lect. i, p. 25.

[This last quotation is an example of what readily occurs in English, though less frequently than in Latin and Greek—the use of an infinitive as the object of a preposition.]

Distinctions

Besides—but—except—save—without: But, except, and *save* (the last-named now chiefly poetical) are all restrictive, denoting something taken out of a general statement, an enumeration, or the like; as, I saw no one *but* (or *except*) him. *Besides* and *without* have a more positive meaning; as, I have much more *besides* this; I have enough *without* that; in neither of which cases could we use *but, except*, or *save*.

BY

By is from the Anglo-Saxon *bt*, big, having the same essential meaning.

I. Of place or space :

1. Next to; near; alongside of; beside; as, he came and sat *by* me; the house stands *by* the river.

Then I was *by* him, as one brought up with him.

Prov. viii, 30.

Jesus took a child and set him *by* him.   *Luke* ix, 47.

> Moors *by* his side under the lea,
> While night invests the sea.

MILTON *Paradise Lost* bk. i, l. 207.

> Should I leave behind
> The inviolate island of the sage and free
> And seek me out a home *by* a remoter sea?

BYRON *Childe Harold* can. 4, st. 8.

And a tree with a moulder'd nest
On its barkless bones, stood stark *by* the dead.
TENNYSON The Dead Prophet st. 5.

I live in a cottage secluded and small,
By a gnarly old apple-tree's shade.
TROWBRIDGE My Brother Ben st. 2.

2. Along the line or course of; alongside of; beside; along; as, to walk *by* the river; the river flows *by* the town.

Siloa's brook that flow'd   Fast *by* the oracle of God.
MILTON Paradise Lost bk. i, l. 12.

By lake and stream, *by* wood and glen,
Our stately drove we follow.
WHITTIER The Drovers st. 4.

Gigantic reeds *by* every oozy stream,
Rank and luxuriant under cloudy skies.
BICKERSTETH Yesterday, To-day, and For Ever bk. iv, l. 674.

3. Near or up to, and beyond; beyond; past; as, the train flashed *by* us; we have gone *by* the station.

And I ran *by* him without speaking
Like a flash of light.
TENNYSON The May Queen st. 5, l. 2.

II. Of time :

1. In the course of; in the time of; within the period or lapse of; during; as, birds that fly *by* night; to travel *by* day.

Not alone *by* day, . . .
But in the weird and unsubstantial sphere
Of slumber did her beauty hold him thrall.
ALDRICH Wyndham Towers st. 7.

And Pan *by* noon and Bacchus *by* night, . .
Follows with dancing and fills with delight
The Mænad and the Bassarid.
SWINBURNE Atalanta in Calydon cho., st. 6.

2. On or before; not later than; as, come *by* seven o'clock.

Let me have Claudio's head sent me *by* five.
SHAKESPEARE Measure for Measure act iv, sc. 2, l. 128.

Moonlight, and the first timid tremblings of the dawn, were *by* this time blending.

> DE QUINCEY *Miscell. Essays, Vision of Sudden Death* p. 170.

By half past eleven the battle became general.

> SOUTHEY *Life of Nelson* ch. 7, p. 248.

3. Taking or regarding as a standard; in accordance with; for the period of; according to; as, to work *by* the day.

All the winterers were hired *by* the year.

> A. MACKENZIE *Voyages from Montreal, Fur Trade* p. 19.

III. Denoting agency, cause, means, or instrument :

1. Through the direct action of (especially of personal, voluntary, and intelligent action); as, this wall was built *by* the Romans.

> The fields between
> Are dewy-fresh, browsed *by* deep-uddered kine.
> > TENNYSON *The Gardener's Daughter* st. 8.

The fact that the water is salter than that of the Atlantic is *by* some supposed to account for the indigo blue of the Gulf Stream.   M. M. BALLOU *Equatorial America* ch. 1, p. 4.

The boomerang must have been discovered . . . *by* some savage throwing a crooked branch, and by his observing its curious and unexpected flight.

> DUKE OF ARGYLE *Primeval Man* pt. iv, p. 152.

She has been made singly responsible for all the evil enacted *by* her parliaments.   AGNES STRICKLAND *Queens of England, Mary* in vol. ii, ch. 6, p. 654.

It is a matter of the simplest demonstration, that no man can be really appreciated but *by* his equal or superior.

> RUSKIN *Modern Painters* vol. i, § 1, pt. i, ch. 1, p. 2.

The Ossianic hero, whose dwelling is in the shadows and the mists, is haunted *by* spectres which are at once his terror, his delight, and his inspiration. STEPHEN *Lectures on France* xviii, p. 507.

Oceanic islands are inhabited *by* bats and seals, but *by* no terrestrial mammals.   DARWIN *Origin of Species* vol. i, ch. 7, p. 281.

The absorption of moisture *by* sponges, sugar, salt, etc., are familiar examples of capillary attraction.

MARY SOMERVILLE *Connection of Phys. Sciences* § 14, p. 110.

2. With the perception, feeling, or experience of; as, the attempt was seen *by* all to be a failure; the sorrow was felt *by* rich and poor alike.

We may call art and science touched *by* emotion religion, if we will.   M. ARNOLD *Lit. and Dogma* ch. 1, p. 46.

> And every moral feeling of his soul
> Strengthened and braced *by* breathing in content.
>   WORDSWORTH *Excursion* bk. i, st. 18.

If he [God] could not be pained *by* anything, . . . had no violable sympathy, he would be anything but a perfect character.
                    BUSHNELL *Sermons for the New Life* ser. xviii, p. 347.

Sentimentalism has been already defined as feeling, partially enlightened *by* the intellect, and yet refusing to be controlled *by* it.   PORTER *Science and Sentiment* ch. 1, p. 84.

For *by* the word spirit we mean only that which thinks, wills and perceives. BERKELEY *Principles of Human Knowledge* ed by Simon, § 138, p. 160.

3. Through the agency or operation of, as an indirect or im personal cause: in some connection with, as of enclosing, sup porting, etc.; having or taking as an indication; using as or being a means of action, information, etc.; through; with; as, the house was struck *by* lightning; *by* this decision all was changed.

Eccentricity is the disturbance of the relations enjoined *by* common sense.   E. P. WHIPPLE *Character* p. 87.

> There stood the chaplain, his uncovered brow
> Unmarked *by* earthly passions.
>   L. H. SIGOURNEY *Sailor's Funeral* l. 87.

Little white villages surrounded *by* trees, nestle in the valleys or roost upon the lofty perpendicular sea-walls.
                    MARK TWAIN *Innocents Abroad* ch. 32, p. 339.

Joshua . . . is always known *by* his spear, or javelin, slung between his shoulders or stretched out in his hand.
                    A. P. STANLEY *Jewish Church* vol. i, lect. x, p. 202.

I saw, *by* his eye, that he had squinted oftener over a gun, than through a needle!   COOPER *Pilot* ch. 25, p. 406.

So bleak these shores, wind-swept and all the year
    Washed *by* the wild Atlantic's restless tide.
              CELIA THAXTER *Rock Weeds* st. 1.

The climate is on the whole so tempered *by* the Gulf Stream
that even this part of Norway is pleasantly habitable.
           SARAH M. H. DAVIS *Norway Nights* ch. 6, p. 148.

The young Edward was declared King *by* acclamation, and
presented in that capacity to the approbation of the populace.
           LINGARD *England* vol. iii, ch. 7, p. 270.

4. Through the instrumentality of: through the use of, as a
means or instrument; making use of; taking hold of; through
the action or influence of; as, they led him *by* the hand; he
mentioned me *by* name.

The flame is fed . . . *by* the wick, which draws or sucks up
the oily liquid exactly as a sponge or towel draws up water.
         YOUMANS *Hand-Book Household Science* ¶ 197, p. 110.

'Tis *by* many reaches that the leeward vessel gains upon the
wind.   COOPER *Water-Witch* ch. 15, p. 70

By an inevitable chain of causes and effects, Providence pun-
ishes national sins *by* national calamities.
          BANCROFT *United States* vol. vi, bk. iii, ch. 8, p. 317.

Take Fate *by* the throat and shake a living out of her.
         LOUISA M. ALCOTT *Journals, Oct., 1858* in ch. 5, p. 101.

He who strives to cast out hatred *by* love, may fight his fight
in joy and confidence.
        J. K. HOSMER *Story of the Jews* pt. ii, ch. 14, p. 227.

Words learn'd *by* rote a parrot may rehearse.
            COWPER *Conversation.* l. 7.

We are bound to the jury trial *by* all the holiest traditions of
our past history.   POMEROY *Municipal Law* § 6, p. 6.

The blow was not a hard one, but the boy was so taken *by*
surprise that he started back.
      T. HUGHES *Tom Brown at Rugby* pt. i, ch. 8, p. 181.

5. In consequence of; as a result of; as victorious *by*
submission.
6

No one need expect to be original simply *by* being absurd.
HUGH MILLER *Testimony of the Rocks* lect. x, p. 396.

This emeute has been rendered memorable *by* the destruction of the Bastille.   G. N. WRIGHT *Louis Philippe* ch. 1, p. 88.

Flagrant evils cure themselves *by* being flagrant.
NEWMAN *Apologia* pt. v, p. 202.

The Essay on Man sins chiefly *by* want of central principle, and *by* want therefore of all coherency amongst the separate thoughts.   DE QUINCEY *Essays on the Poets, Pope* p. 168.

6. Using as a means of conveyance; on; upon; over; via; as, to send freight *by* water; to travel *by* rail.

Couriers and relay horses *by* land, and swift-sailing pilot boats *by* sea, were flying in all directions.
JEFFERSON in Randall's *Thomas Jefferson* vol. i, ch. 15, p. 604.

Marlow is only an hour from London *by* rail, and the river from Kingston to Oxford swarms with cheap trippers.
W. GRAHAM in *Nineteenth Century* Nov., 1898, p. 762.

IV. Of various relations:

1. Of quantity, number, or measurement, to the extent, number, or amount of; as, the insects swarmed *by* thousands; reduce the amount *by* one-half.

The time required for light to reach us from the most distant visible stars is measured *by* thousands of years.
S. NEWCOMB *Popular Astronomy* pt. iv, ch. 2, p. 473.

2. Taking as a standard of measurement; according to; as, two hundred yards *by* actual measurement; 96° in the shade *by* the Fahrenheit thermometer.

[In noting temperature the preposition and adjunct are commonly omitted, and we say 212° Fahrenheit; 100° Centigrade.]

We measure their [men's] calibre *by* their broadest circle of achievement.   E. H. CHAPIN *Lessons of Faith* p. 16.

3. Of possession: in or into possession of; in the hands of; near; with; about; as, he came honestly *by* it; I have not so much money *by* me.   (Compare I., 1.)

Say not unto thy neighbor, Go and come again, and to-morrow I will give, when thou hast it *by* thee.   *Prov.* iii, 28.

> In sooth, I know not why I am so sad.
> It wearies me: you say, it wearies you;
> But how I caught it, found it, or came *by* it,
> What stuff't is made of, whereof it is born,
> I am to learn.
> SHAKESPEARE *The Merchant of Venice* act i, sc. 1, l. 3.

4. Of order, arrangement, etc.:   ·

(*a*) In connection with; arranged with or in; taken or considered according to; alongside of; according to; as, item *by* item.

There are thousands of Christians who have never examined the evidences of the Resurrection piece *by* piece.
     ROBERTSON *Sermons* second series, ser. xx, p. 424.

By the common law of England, no alien whatever can hold land, even as a tenant.   MACAULAY *Essays, Social Capacities of Negroes* in vol. vi, p. 366, app.

Moving *by* the right . . . would have brought him [General Grant] into immediate collision with the enemy on a terrain more suitable for field operations.
     NICOLAY AND HAY *Abraham Lincoln* vol. viii, ch. 14, p. 849.

(*b*) Multiplied into; in connection or measurement with; as, seven feet *by* six.

It [St. Croix] lies 65 miles E. S. E. of Porto Rico and is about 20 miles long from E. to W. *by* about 5 miles broad.
     Lippincott's Gazetteer, 1903 p. 1991.

In nautical use: one point toward: used in "boxing the compass"; as, west *by* north; northwest *by* west.

The *Ranger* was under way . . . as her log says, 'going free, course east *by* south half east. . . .'
     AUGUSTUS C. BUELL *Paul Jones* vol. i, p. 82.

5. Denoting the direction of an action toward its object: with reference to; as regards; as affecting; respecting; concerning; as, to do well *by* one's friends or kindred.

> Then Philip put the boy and girl to school,
> And bought them needful books, and every way,
> Like one who does his duty *by* his own,
> Made himself theirs.
> TENNYSON Enoch Arden l. 880.

6. Denoting adhesion, as an extension of the local meaning in I, 1: adhering to; remaining with; acting in defense of; taking the consequences of; as, I will stand *by* you; I stand *by* the statement; I will abide *by* the decision.

[*Abide* is also used transitively, without a preposition; as, I will *abide* the result.]

I am ready to produce my books, and to abide *by* them, in any court of Justice in the world.
MARIA EDGEWORTH Forester, The Bank-Notes p. 104.

Bitter taunts on those who, having stood *by* the King in the hour of danger, now advised him to deal mercifully and generously *by* his vanquished enemies, were publicly recited on the stage. MACAULAY England vol. i, ch. 8, p. 826.

7. As invoking or calling to witness; in the name, presence, or view of; as, to swear *by* all that is sacred.

Swear not at all; neither *by* heaven, for it is God's throne; nor *by* the earth, for it is his footstool. Matt. v 34.

> Lars Porsena of Clusium,
>   *By* the Nine Gods he swore
> That the great house of Tarquin
>   Should suffer wrong no more.
> *By* the Nine Gods he swore it,
> And named a trysting-day.
> MACAULAY Lays of Ancient Rome, Horatius st. 1.

Distinctions

See DISTINCTIONS under BESIDE; WITH.

Verbs and Other Antecedents

Call (in the phrase *call by name*), *see, perceive, know, understand, judge, measure, seem, take,* are followed by *by* of the determining object; as, I saw *by* his glance that he was a rogue; I judge *by* his dress that he is a man of means; etc. *Surrounded* is commonly followed by *by*; as, *surrounded by* mountains, *by* enemies, etc. *Attended* may take either *by* or *with*; as, he was *attended by* a numerous retinue; the attempt will be attended *with* danger. Compare WITH.

Errors

Very little knowledge of their nature is acquired *by* the spelling-book.   LINDLEY MURRAY *English Grammar* p. 21.

Nouns are often formed *by* participles.
     LINDLEY MURRAY *An English Grammar* vol. ii, p. 290.

By in such connection denotes agency, which is not here intended. It is not the participles that form the nouns, nor the spelling-book that acquires the knowledge. These are rather the sources than the agents, and *from* should be used instead of *by* in both cases.

VIII—Prepositions Defined and Illustrated

CONCERNING, CONSIDERING

For the meaning and use of these words see PARTICIPIAL PREPOSITIONS.

DESPITE

Despite, from the noun *despite*, signifies in despite of; in spite of; in defiance of; notwithstanding.

Despite the discouragement received, . . . he (Commodore Daniel Ammen) ordered one or more of the Thompson machines.
> HAMERSLY *Naval Encycl., Deep Sea.*

DOWN

Down (archaic and poetic *adown*) is derived from the Anglo-Saxon *ádún*, *of-dúne*, from *of*, off, plus *dún*, hill.

I. Of place : in a descending direction along, upon, or in ; from a higher to or toward a lower level, part, or place of or in ; from top to bottom of; along the course or current of; along, in a descending direction, or in a direction thought of as descending; as, *down* a shaft; to fall *down* stairs; to run *down* the hill; to sail *down* the river, or *down* stream; to glance *down* the page.

> And *down* the long beam stole the Holy Grail,
> Rose-red, with beatings in it, as if alive.
> > TENNYSON *The Holy Grail* st. 10.

> And sparkle out among the fern,
> To bicker *down* a valley.
> > TENNYSON *The Brook* st. 2.

> The shadows of the convent-towers
> Slant *down* the snowy sward.
> > TENNYSON *St. Agnes* st. 1

> Hurrah!—hurrah!—the west-wind
> Comes freshening *down* the bay.
> > WHITTIER *The Fishermen* st. 10.

We may see a huge boulder or two poised on the end of the glacier, and, if fortunate, also see the boulder . . . plunging violently *down* the slope.   TYNDALL *Forms of Water* § 18, p. 44.

Their long column might be seen winding *down* the breast of the mountain.   HEADLEY *Miscellanies* vol. ii, ch. 4, p. 88.

> And, hurrying *down* the sphery way,
> Night flies, and sweeps her shadows from the paths of day.
> JEAN INGELOW *Song for Night of Christ's Resurrection* st. 22.

II. Of time: from an earlier to a later period of; onward in duration; as, the story has come *down* the ages.

> *Down* the dark future, through long generations,
> The echoing sounds grow fainter and then cease.
> > LONGFELLOW *Arsenal at Springfield* st. 11.

III. Figuratively, of various relations: along in a direction thought of as descending; as, *down* the wind.

Down the wind, in the same direction the wind is blowing.
> > HAMERSLY *Naval Encycl., Wind.*

[The preposition and its object may be used as an adverb or attributive phrase; as, in *down-river*, *down-stream*, *down-town*, etc.   MURRAY'S *New English Dictionary*.]

DURING

During, originally the present participle of the obsolete verb *dure = endure*, has acquired such independent prepositional force that it is never thought of with reference to its verb. Compare PARTICIPIAL PREPOSITIONS.

Of time, exclusively: in or within the time of; at some period in; throughout the course, action, continuance, or existence of; as, I awoke repeatedly *during* the night; *during* the siege of Troy.

Thus hath he lost sixpence a day *during* his life.
SHAKESPEARE *A Midsummer-Night's Dream* act iv. sc. 2, l. 19.

Thousands of Britons, in times of famine, *during* the first century after the Norman Conquest, sold themselves into thraldom.
C. L. BRACE *Gesta Christi* ch. 21, p. 241.

In America, *during* the Eocene, palms, and figs, and evergreens in Dakota, show a temperature there about that of Florida now.   JOS. LE CONTE *Compend of Geology* pt. iii, ch. 5, p. 848.

It was *during* his [Luther's] enforced seclusion in Wartburg, . . . that Bartholomew Bernhardi, pastor of Kammerich, . . . solved the matter in the most practical way by obtaining the consent of his parish and celebrating his nuptials with all due solemnity.   H. C. LEA *Sacerdotal Celibacy* ch. 25, p. 411.

ERE

Ere is the Anglo-Saxon *ǽr*, before, and is used as a strict synonym of *before*, as regards time or preference, signifying earlier or sooner than; rather than.

> True prayers,
> That shall be up at heaven and enter there
> *Ere* sunrise.
> SHAKESPEARE *Measure for Measure* act. ii, sc. 2, l. 126.

> I'll to my book,
> For yet *ere* supper-time must I perform
> Much business appertaining.
> SHAKESPEARE *Tempest* act. iii, sc. 1, l. 96.

EXCEPT, EXCEPTING

Except is derived from the Latin *exceptus*, the past participle of *excipio*, from *ex*, out, plus *capio*, take.   *Excepting* is strictly the present participle of the verb *except*, and is used interchangeably with the briefer form.   Compare PARTICIPIAL PREPOSITIONS.

With the exception or exclusion of; leaving out; not considering or taking account of; omitting; apart from; aside from; save; saving; but; without.

Except May, there is no month like October for roses.
CHRISTIAN REID *Question of Honor* bk. i, ch. 10, p. 107.

FOR

For is derived from the Anglo-Saxon *for, fore*, before, for.

[The import of a position or movement turned to the front of an object belongs originally to the preposition *for*, similarly to the Latin *pro* allied to *præ*. . . . The idea of stepping before anything yields that of representation, when one object seems to take the place of the other, and may pass as its representative, substitute, or equivalent. The person or thing instead of which another appears, with which it exchanges its activity or quality, the object for which another is exchanged, may be introduced by *for*.   MAETZNER *English Grammar* vol. ii, p. 427.]

I. Of place, denoting extent, measurement, etc. (compare III., 9): to the extent of; for the space of; as, the ground is level *for* several miles.

The chips of the mountain strew the cone *for* eight hundred feet below.   WINCHELL *Walks and Talks* ch. 19, p. 108.

II. Of time:

1. Denoting extent or duration (compare III., 9): to the extent of; throughout the period of; till the end of; throughout; as, it is good *for* the next ten years; it will do *for* the present.

The clergy, *for* a time, made war on schism with so much vigor that they had little leisure to make war on vice.
    MACAULAY *England* vol. i, ch. 2, p. 141.

A cook they haden with them *for* the nones,
To boil the chickens and the marrow bones.
    CHAUCER *C. T., Prologue* l. 382.

A serving man on Saturdays   To cater *for* the week.
    BROWNING *Ring and Book* pt. iv, l. 861.

For several years, whenever a slave brought an action at law for his liberty, Mr. Clay volunteered as his advocate.
    EPES SARGENT *Henry Clay* vol. i, ch. 1, p. 21.

On both sides of the east Temple gate, stalls had *for* generations been permitted for changing foreign money.
    GEIKIE *Life of Christ* vol. i, ch. 30, p. 496

The wonderful elaboration, carried on *for* twenty years, . . . has given to the History of Herodotus its surpassing and never-failing charm.   RAWLINSON *Herodotus* vol. i, ch. 1, p. 17.

2. On the occasion of; with reference to, as an occasion, appointment, or the like; as, be ready *for* to-morrow.

Remember that you are booked *for* the 10th of September.
     MACAULAY in Trevelyan's *T. B. Macaulay* vol. ii, p. 271.

In the first Parliament of James the House of Commons refused *for* the first time to transact business on a Sunday.
     GREEN *English People* vol. iii, bk. vii, ch. 1, p. 15.

III. Of various relations:

1. Of cause, reason, or occasion: because of; by reason of; on account of; as, he was respected *for* his virtues; he cried out *for* fear.

Here he prostrated himself, and cried out, 'Hail, sacred Rome, thrice sacred *for* the blood of the martyrs shed here.'
     W. W. STORY in *Scribner's Magazine* Oct., 1891, p. 417.

It is . . . necessary that every officer remain individually answerable *for* his acts.   F. LIEBER *Civil Liberty* ch. 5, p. 159.

> Likewise to them are Poets much beholden
> *For* secret favors in the midnight glooms.
>   HOOD *Plea of Midsummer Fairies* st. 112.

2. Of the purpose, object, or aim of an action : with a view to; in order to effect, reach, benefit, please, etc. :

(a) As a matter of use or enjoyment: with the design of; appropriate to ; as, a place *for* study; a time *for* worship ; a home *for* the aged.

Every work of art should contain within itself all that is requisite *for* its own comprehension.   POE *Works, Critical Essays, Longfellow's Ballads* in vol. iii, p. 369.

After all, the austere virtues—the virtues of Emerson, Hawthorne. Whittier—are the best soil *for* genius.
     T. W. HIGGINSON *Studies of American Authors, Poe* p. 20.

> Win from our public cares a day *for* joy.
>   SOUTHEY *Joan of Arc* bk. iii, st. 4.

That inexorable law of human souls, that we prepare ourselves *for* sudden deeds by the reiterated choice of good or evil
that gradually determines character.
> George Eliot *Romola* ch. 28, p. 208.

A good quarrel was a sort of moral whetstone, always on
hand *for* the sharpening of their wits.
> Harriet B. Stowe *Poganuc People* ch. 14, p. 152.

Men may choose to forget the ends *for* which their 'talents'
were given them ; . . . they may practically deny that they
were given at all ; yet in this word . . . abides a continual me-
mento that they were so given, . . . and that each man shall
have to render an account of their use.
> Trench *On the Study of Words* lect. iii, p. 98.

(*b*) As something to be reached or attained, or toward which
one's inclinations or desires go out : in order to reach or bring
about ; seeking ; reaching after ; tending toward ; toward ; as,
waiting *for* the mail ; planning *for* the future ; eagerness *for*
praise ; a passion *for* jewelry ; a taste *for* music.

We look in vain in the Old Testament *for* the radiant and
overflowing benignity of the New.
> John Young *Christ of History* bk. ii, pt. v, p. 159.

To account *for* the observed motions of the moon and planets,
Ptolemy adopted and extended the theory of epicycles.
> R. Routledge *Popular Hist. Science* ch. 2, p. 48.

A man bids fairer *for* greatness of soul, who is the descend-
ant of worthy ancestors, and has good blood in his veins.
> Addison in *The Guardian* Aug. 18, 1718.

Our thirst *for* applause, . . . if the last infirmity of noble
minds, is also the first infirmity of weak ones.
> Ruskin *Sesame and Lilies* lect. i, p. 8.

Still within my heart I bear   Love *for* all things good and fair.
> Whittier *Andrew Rykman's Prayer* st. 7.

For who, if the rose bloomed forever, so greatly would care *for*
the rose ?   Owen Meredith *Apple of Life* st. 9.

Locke had no taste *for* fiction.
> Leigh Hunt *Men, Women, and Books* vol. i, ch. 1, p. 7.

He called *for* his gun, which he brandished in a manner of no hopeful auspice for the Howadji.

> G. W. CURTIS *Howadji in Syria* pt. i, ch. 16, p. 111.

(c) As referring to a person whose welfare or enjoyment *is* desired, or to an approved object or a wished-for event: in favor of: opposed to *against*; as, he voted *for* Abraham Lincoln; my voice is *for* war.

> The arbiter of others' fate,   A suppliant *for* his own!
> > BYRON *Ode to Napoleon* st. 5.

A suppliant *for* a father's life, I crave an audience of the King.
> SCOTT *Lady of the Lake* can. 6, st. 9.

They [the Utopians] give their voices secretly, so that it is not known *for* whom every one gives his suffrage.

> T. MORE *Utopia* [trans.] bk. ii, p. 86.

The resolutions *for* the annexation of Texas passed both branches of Congress. H. C. LODGE *Daniel Webster* ch. 8, p. 268.

Thrice had that name been sent to the President with the recommendation of his department commander *for* brevets *for* conspicuous and gallant conduct.

> CHAS. KING *Two Soldiers* ch. 1, p. 11.

That is an argument, not *for* Establishment, but *for* voluntaryism. GEORGE TREVELYAN in *Hansard's Parliamentary Debates, Feb. 20, 1891* p. 1810.

We'll tak a cup o' kindness yet, *For* auld lang syne.

> BURNS *Auld Lang Syne* cho.

3. Of possession or destination: belonging to; to be given or assigned to; to be held or used by; in the province or scope of, to designate; as, this package is *for* you; glory is not *for* cowards, success is *for* the industrious.

There is no true strength *for* any man save in inward rectitude,—in right relations between his own soul and God.

> E. H. CHAPIN *Lessons of Faith* ser. xi, p. 194.

To me, it seems that *for* some people all life is a lie, though they never actually utter a falsehood.

> FRANCES P. COBBE *Duties of Women* lect. ii, p. 71.

Nay, 'tis *for* thee to watch God's house, and ward the images,
And let men deal with peace and war; for they were born for
    these.   MORRIS *Æneids of Virgil* bk. vii, l. 448.

Again *for* him the moonlight shone
On Norman cap and bodiced zone.
          WHITTIER *Snow-Bound* st. 11.

It is well *for* the world that in most of us, by the age of thirty,
the character has set like plaster, and will never soften again.
          W. JAMES *Prin. of Psychol.* vol. i, ch. 4, p. 121.

His habit was very proper *for* a scaramouch, or merry-an
drew, being a dirty calico, with hanging-sleeves, tassels, and
cuts and slashes almost on every side.
          DE FOE *Robinson Crusoe* § 43, p. 576.

4. In place of; instead of; as the equivalent of; as an offset
to; in exchange for; as, to buy (or sell) an article *for* a dollar;
here is the money to pay *for* it; to give blow *for* blow.

I would have paid her kiss *for* kiss   With usury thereto.
          TENNYSON *The Talking Oak* st. 49.

          For surely a woman's affection
Is not a thing to be asked *for*, and had *for* only the asking.
          LONGFELLOW *Miles Standish* pt. iii, st. 6.

[The evil of wealth] springs from that criminal haste which
substitutes adroitness *for* industry and trick *for* toil.
          H. W. BEECHER *Lectures to Young Men* lect. iii, p. 88.

Thy purpose hath atoned *for* thy hasty rashness.
          SCOTT *Ivanhoe* ch. 34, p. 287.

Shady groves and cooling grots are abandoned *for* drawing
rooms at ninety-six, and half-a-score sickly orange-trees tubbed
on the top of a staircase.
          HOOK *Humorous Works, Fashionable Parties* p. 322.

And yet, *for* a word spoken with kindness, I would have re-
signed the peacock's feather in my cap as the merest of baubles.
          DE QUINCEY *Opium-Eater, Suspiria* pt. ii, p. 268.

A thousand men to-day care whether the state is pure, *for*
one who cared in the last century.
          PHILLIPS BROOKS *Candle of the Lord* ser. ix, p. 156

5. In the character of; as being, seeming, or supposed to be; as representing; as, he was left *for* dead on the field; he was mistaken *for* a criminal; I take you *for* an honest man.

Ignorance makes many men mistake mere transcripts *for* originals.   Fuller *Ch. Hist. Britain* vol. i, bk. iii, § 6, p. 374.

With a buffalo spread on the grass, and a blanket *for* our covering, our bed was soon made.
         Thoreau. *Week on the Concord, Sunday* p. 119.

Taking art *for* their guide, instead of nature, and substituting the love of excelling for the love of excellence, they [authors] of course became artificial.
       H. N. Hudson *Lect. on Shakespeare* vol. i, lect. iii, p. 104.

6. With reference or regard to; in relation to; in proportion to; as, *for* this time it does not matter; *for* myself, I do not care; he is small *for* his age.

> And fearful *for* his light caique,
> He shuns the near but doubtful creek.
>   Byron *Giaour* st. 6.

Mr. Howard's estimate [of damage], as given in the entomologist's report for 1887, *for* the nine States infested by the chinch bug in that year, was $60,000,000.   *Insect Life* Oct., 1891, p. 12.

The rules of prudence in general, like the laws of the stone tables, are *for* the most part prohibitive.
       Coleridge *Works, Aids to Reflection* in vol. i, p. 126.

7. In spite of; without regard to; despite; notwithstanding: often in connection with *all*; as, I hold my opinion *for all* that.

> The owl, *for all* his feathers, was a-cold.
>   Keats *The Eve of St. Agnes* st. 1.

> The rank is but the guinea's stamp,
> The man's the gowd *for a'* that.
>   Burns *For A' That and A' That.*

8. In honor of; by the name of; after; as, the child was named *for* his grandfather.   Compare after.

A cup to the dead already,—
Hurrah *for* the next that dies!
       Bartholomew Dowling *Revelry in India.*

9. To the extent or number of; to the amount of; as, he is liable *for* a large amount; he failed *for* half a million.

On Saturday last a judgment was entered against —— —— *for* $9,179.   *The New York Times* Oct. 7, 1908.

Verbs and Other Antecedents

Verbs followed by *for* are too numerous to be fully specified, but include those that imply a reaching or tending toward an object or seeking it as an end, as *ask, beg, hope, labor, long, plan, pray, reach, strive, struggle, toil, wish, work,* etc.; also verbs denoting action that may be in behalf of or for the sake of some person or object; as, to *act, argue, care, plan, speak, stand (stand up), think,* etc. Nouns and adjectives allied to such verbs or to the verbal notions they imply are commonly followed by *for;* as, labor *for* others' good; thoughtful *for* our comfort. In the United States a person is said to subscribe *to* something that he supports, but *for* something that he is to receive or obtain; he subscribes *to* a creed, *for* a magazine. One may send in a subscription either *to* or *for* a periodical. A person corresponds *for* a newspaper, *with* a friend; one thing corresponds *to* or *with* another.

Distinctions

During—for—in—through—throughout—within: As applied to time, *during, for, through,* and *throughout* all contemplate extent of duration; as, he will suffer *during, through,* or *throughout* his whole life; it will last *for* a lifetime; imprisonment *for* life. By change of phrase, we might say "imprisonment *during* life," and this form is sometimes used; but in any often-recurring phrase the tendency is to the shorter word, and *for* is most familiar in such connection. But *for* may also signify on the occasion of; as, be ready *for* to-morrow, that is, to meet the

demands of to-morrow. (Compare DISTINCTIONS under AGAINST.)
This meaning is shared by none of the other words here compared. *In* and *within* may refer only to some included point or
points of a specified duration; as, I have seen him two or three
times *in* (or *within*) the past year. Here *during* might also be
used, but not *for, through,* or *throughout*. But a negative may
make a statement with *in* or *within* universal, covering not only
the specified points, but the whole duration including them, so
that with a negative *for* may be used in place of *in* or *within*;
as, "I have not seen him *in* [or *within*] a year" may be changed
to "I have not seen him *for* a year," and become a stronger state
ment by the change, since *for* is comprehensive as *in* is inclusive

    Against — by — for : See DISTINCTIONS under AGAINST.

FROM

    From represents the Anglo-Saxon *from, fram,* used in the
same sense, denoting primarily removal or separation in space
or time, and then cause, reason, or instrumentality. [How ele·
mentary and fundamental this particle is appears from the exceeding difficulty of framing a definition of it, without using
the word itself in its own definition.]

    I. Of place or space: having as a starting-point of motion,
actual or implied; out of; starting at; leaving behind: opposed
to *into, to,* or *unto;* as, he sailed *from* New York *to* Liverpool;
the student went *from* home *to* college; the town is five miles
from the city; the view *from* the summit is fine; keep away
from the machinery.

> *From* all his deep the bellowing river roars.
> > HOMER *Iliad* tr. by Pope, bk. xxi, l. 258

> At intervals some bird *from* out the brakes
> Starts into voice a moment, then is still.
> > BYRON *Childe Harold* can. 8, st. 87.

> He heard the Angelus *from* convent towers.
> > LONGFELLOW *Wayside Inn, King Robert* st. 14

It was Autumn, and incessant
Piped the quails *from* shocks and sheaves.
    LONGFELLOW *Pegasus in Pound* st. 2.

From Paradise first, if I shall not lie,
Was man out chased for his gluttony.
    CHAUCER *C. T.*, *The Sompnour's Tale* l. 208.

I ate a little chocolate *from* my supply, well knowing the miraculous sustaining powers of the simple little block.
    F. MARION CRAWFORD *Mr. Isaacs* ch. 12, p. 258.

The spectacle of the host of Israel, even though seen only *from* its utmost skirts, is too much for . . . Balaam.
    A. P. STANLEY *The Jewish Church* pt. i, lect. viii, p. 217.

From city to city, *from* province to province, *from* isle to isle. of Hellas, her [Helen's] fame was sung, her beauty was extolled.
    S. G. W. BENJAMIN *Troy* pt. i, ch. 2, p. 18.

II. Of time: having as a starting-point of duration; noting the beginning of a period or of some series regarded as occupying time; beginning with; after: often with *till* or *to* as correlative; as, *from* birth *till* death; *from* morning *to* night; the cathedral dates *from* the fifteenth century.

The king [Alfred] . . . *from* his early years had been animated with the most ardent passion for knowledge.
    LINGARD *England* vol. i, ch. 4, p. 169.

From morn *to* noon he fell, *from* noon *to* dewy eve,
 A summer's day. MILTON *Paradise Lost* bk. i, l. 743.

Far in a wild, unknown to public view,
From youth *to* age a reverend hermit grew.
    PARNELL *The Hermit* l. 1.

And so we lay *from* ebb-tide, *till* the flow
Rose high enough to drive us from the reef.
    JEAN INGELOW *Brothers, and a Sermon* st. 6.

All manner of outcries assailed the speaker, *from* his rising *till* he surceased. A. C. COXE *Impressions of England* ch. 31, p. 276.

In this chair, *from* one year's end *to* another, sat that prodigious book-worm, Cotton Mather, sometimes devouring a great book, and sometimes scribbling one as big.

> HAWTHORNE *Grandfather's Chair* pt. ii, ch. 4, p. 107.

Tradition, it is said, occasionally hands down the practical arts with more precision and fidelity than they can be transmitted by books, *from* generation *to* generation. WEBSTER in *Private Correspondence, Dec. 29, 1850* in vol. ii, p. 408.

III. Of various relations:

1. Having as a starting-point of change, variation, separation, or diversity:

(*a*) In variant or adverse relation to; starting or beginning at or with; as, free *from* fault; the supply is far *from* adequate: often followed by *to ;* as, *from* grave *to* gay.

Withdrawal of custom *from* a tradesman . . . decreases his welfare, and perhaps injures his belongings.

> SPENCER *Data of Ethics* ch. 15, p. 560.

From all the gay and tinsel vanities of the world their [the Quakers'] discipline has preserved them.

> COLERIDGE *Works, Lay Sermon* in vol. vi, p. 197.

Queen Mary saw the minstrel's pain,
And bade *from* bootless grief refrain.

> HOGG *Queen's Wake* pt. iii, 1, 26.

Woolen garments . . . always feel warm and free *from* chill.

> J. J. POPE *Number One* talk v, p. 116.

(*b*) Noting unlikeness, distinction, deviation, or difference; as, the idea of right is quite distinct *from* the idea of expediency.

We cannot disassociate the idea of Causation *from* the idea of Force or Energy. DUKE OF ARGYLL *Unity of Nature* ch. 4, p. 188.

The basis of morals is a distinct question *from* the basis of theories of morals. LECKY *Hist. Eur. Morals* vol. i, ch. 1, p. 21.

But some little deviation *from* the precise line of rectitude might have been winked at in so tortuous and stigmatic a frame. CHARLES AND MARY LAMB *Mrs. Leicester's School Sir Jeffery Dunstan* p. 291.

It is within and quite distinct *from* the corona, and is usually called the 'chromosphere,' being a sort of sphere of colored fire surrounding the sun.   LANGLEY *New Astronomy* p. 61.

Science is as far removed *from* brute force as this sword *from* a crowbar.   BULWER-LYTTON *Leila* bk. ii, ch. 1, p. 88.

[NOTE.—The adjective *different* is correctly followed by *from*. *Different to* has a certain use in England, and is found even in Thackeray, but is regarded as colloquial and avoided by careful writers. The verb *differ* is followed either by *from* or by *with*, *from* being used with reference to qualities, *with* with reference to views, opinions, etc.; an apple differs *from* a pear; a man differs *from* another in stature, complexion, etc.; he differs *with* another in opinion. Compare WITH.]

The mind is a substantive existence, possessing a uniform structure, of a character, however, fundamentally different *from* the bodily structure.

     G. T. CURTIS *Creation or Evolution* ch. 18, p. 470.

Clay had remained essentially different . . . *from* the ordinary pro-slavery man.   CARL SCHURZ *Henry Clay* vol. i, ch. 11, p. 801.

This epoch of ours differs *from* all bygone epochs in having no philosophical nor religious worshippers of the ragged godship of poverty.   RUSKIN *A Joy For Ever* lect. i, p. 2.

Most single topics admit or require a considerable variety of books, each different *from* the other and each supplementing the other.   PORTER *Books and Reading* ch. 4, p. 44.

2. Having as a cause, reason, or origin : noting the source, foundation, or instrument; because of; by reason of; by means of ; by aid of ; as, the river flows *from* the glacier; his skill comes *from* practise ; his precaution sprang *from* distrust ; a quotation *from* Shakespeare ; reasoning *from* analogy ; let me hear *from* you.

Verbs and Other Antecedents

The numerous verbs, adjectives, etc., that take *from* before their objective term are well set forth in the following extract :

[*Have, get, borrow from* make *from* interchange with *of*. . . . With the notions *take away, extort, exact, from* is always preferred.

Demand, desire, enquire, learn, hear from. See OF.

Other employments of *from* rest upon the idea of distance . the notions contemplated are of privative nature.

Intransitive verbs attach themselves in part immediately to verbs of movement, or coincide with them (in figurative meaning).

Deviate, decline, shrink, dissent, etc. Here occur *withdraw, swerve, stray, turn, shrink, quail, flinch, start, deviate, decline, vary, dissent, differ,* used figuratively, and similar ones.

Cease, desist, abstain, rest, and the like.

Transitive verbs of different sorts permit, along with an accusative of the person or of the thing, an adverbial determination with *from.*

Free from—with various shades of the notion of the activity, as *free, rid, save, deliver, extricate, rescue, release, redeem, resuscitate, absolve, excuse,* etc.

Protect, preserve, guard, cover, hide, in various shades of the notions, as *shield, screen, protect, guard, defend, keep, preserve, shelter, hide, conceal, shade, shadow, wrap,* border hard on the series just cited. Here also *privilege, sanctify,* and others are to be referred, which, so far as they are to denote a rendering secure, may be combined with *from.*

Part, disjoin, divide, separate, sever, sift, screw, disturb, discourage, divorce, detract, divert, dissuade, deter, curb, warp, refrain, seduce, alienate, estrange, hinder, inhibit, shut, forbid, prevent, except, exempt, exclude, etc., to which in part, only through the combination with *from,* the privative meaning is allotted.

Distinguish attaches itself to the preceding verbs; but it is to be observed that verbs of knowing and perceiving with *from,* like *know, see,* are [often] substituted for this verbal notion.

Adjectives which attach themselves to the series of notions cited are likewise combined with *from.* They are not numerous, and are chiefly of Romance origin. Many of them take *of* instead of *from.*

Here belong *free, clear, secure, safe, different, exempt, separate, alien, foreign, innocent, entire,* and the like.

The use of *from* with the notions *become, make, transmute,* likewise borders on the idea of distance; on the other hand, the object introduced with *from* appears as the material from which anything is produced.

MAETZNER *English Grammar* vol. ii, pp. 265–268.]

Distinctions

[*Against—from:* These two words are often interchangeable; as, "Shelter *from* the blast or *against* the blast."

Thus we may say, "Defend us *against* or *from*, protect us *against* or *from*, secure us *against* or *from*, our enemies."
FALLOWS *100,000 Synonyms and Antonyms* p. 368.]

But it will be found that there is always a difference in the thought according to the word used. *From* suggests escape or relief; *against* suggests defense or resistance.

From—of: See DISTINCTIONS under OF.

Errors

As a matter of fact, metaphysical philosophy substitutes entities *to* will and Nature *to* the Creator. L. LEVI BRUHL *Philosophy of Auguste Comte* (tr. from French by K. de Beaumont) p. 45, l. 7.

After *substitute* or *substitution* correct usage requires *for* and not *to*

Instead *for* consultation he uses consult.
JOSEPH PRIESTLEY *The Rudiments of English Grammar* p. 143.

Instead is always followed by *of* and not by *for.*

From misunderstanding the directions, we lost our way.
Murray's Key p. 201.

From in such use is perhaps not incorrect, but it is not the best word. *Through* misunderstanding, etc., would be better; or a phrase, as *because of* or *in consequence of* might well be employed.

IX—Prepositions Defined and Illustrated

IN

In is the Anglo-Saxon *in*, and, as stated by Maetzner, "seems to point to a local abiding." *In* may be termed specifically the preposition of inclusion.

I. Of place or space:

1. Denoting the object as surrounding or including in space:

(*a*) Within the bounds of; within the contour, surface, or exterior of; enveloped or restrained by; contained or included within; pertaining to or connected with the interior of; within; inside; as, the stars *in* the sky; the prisoner *in* chains; a story *in* a book; a room *in* the house; she clasped the child *in* her arms.

> Finds tongues *in* trees, books *in* the running brooks,
> Sermons *in* stones, and good *in* everything.
> > SHAKESPEARE *As You Like It* act ii, sc. 1.

> Nor night-bird, chambered *in* the rocks.
> > WORDSWORTH *Peter Bell* pt. ii, st. 18.

> My foreign friends, who dream'd us blanketed
> *In* ever-closing fog, were much amazed.
> > TENNYSON *Queen Mary* act iii, sc. 2.

In every representative body properly constituted the people are practically present.
> > SUMNER *Speeches and Addresses* July 7, 1858, p. 207.

Pretty faces framed *in* pretty bonnets are meant to be seen.
> > HOLMES *Autocrat* ch. 8, p. 225.

(*b*) Within the class or group of; comprised or included within the number of; among; as, *in* the army; one *in* a thousand.

Jonathan Edwards . . . was bred *in* the family of a Connecticut minister. HOLMES *Pages from an Old Volume* essay xi, p. 367.

She is the only genuine 'bucker' *in* the outfit, . . . the only bonâ fide bucking horse that ever threw me.

> BAILLIE-GROHMAN *Camps in the Rockies* ch. 4, p. 100.

She never had a fire; one in a sleeping-room would have been sinful luxury *in* the poor minister's family.

> MARY E. WILKINS *Humble Romance, Moral Exigency* p. 221.

(c) With the compounds of *self*, as *himself, herself, itself,* etc., denoting separation from all else, and nearly equivalent to *by;* as, to know the thing *in* itself.

A man was not made to shut up his mind *in* itself; but to give it voice and to exchange it for other minds.

> CHANNING *Works, Self-Culture* p. 19.

2. Denoting the object or that which it surrounds as a goal or end of motion:

(a) Toward, so as to enter; into, so as to remain within; into; to; as, to sink *in* the mire; to dip the pen *in* ink; to put one *in* a rage; to break *in* pieces.

[NOTE.—Such phrases as "Come *in* the house," "He fell *in* the water," are used, but in such cases *into* is preferred. See INTO.]

> Golden tresses, wreathed *in* one,
> As the braided streamlets run !
> > LONGFELLOW *Maidenhood* st. 2.

Never put yourself *in* the wrong with an audience. It has every advantage of you.

> N. SHEPPARD *Before an Audience* ch. 8, p. 180.

It is singular how much fonder civilians are of urging measures that end *in* blood than those whose profession is arms.

> S. LOVER *Handy Andy* ch. 19, p. 175.

Expecting immediate support from Normandy, the conspirators hastened to put themselves *in* a military posture.

> W. RUSSELL *Modern Europe* vol. i, letter xxiii, p. 144.

This is the first time my honour was ever called *in* question.

> GAY *Beggar's Opera* act ii, sc. 2.

(b) Toward, so as to rely or rest on; as, to hope *in* God; to trust *in* one's innocence.

I believe *in* . . . the holy Catholic Church.   *Apostles' Creed.*

The belief *in* astrology was almost universal in the middle of the 17th century.   SCOTT *Guy Mannering* ch. 4, p. 89.

I believe fully, enthusiastically, without break, pause, or aberration, *in* the divinity of Christ.

H. W. BEECHER *Doctrinal Beliefs, Faith in Christ* p. 17.

Trust *in* the certitude of compensatory justice.

SWINBURNE in *The Athenæum* July 10, 1886, p. 49.

II. Of time:

1. Included within; occupying all or a part of; during; within; as, *in* the forenoon; *in* the evening; *in* the past century.

'Tis vain! *in* such a brassy age   I could not move a thistle.

TENNYSON *Amphion* st. 9.

The bridge was *in* the very act of being thrown and grappled to the ramparts.   W. WARE *Zenobia* vol. ii, letter xiv, p. 188.

It is not once only that the well-planned schemes of swindling turfites have been quietly strangled *in* their birth.

Contemporary Review June, 1878, p. 28.

There are certain intellectual products which are only possible *in* hours or minutes of great cerebral excitement.

HAMERTON *Intell. Life* pt. x, letter v, p. 360.

2. Denoting the final point of a specified or indicated period: at the end of; at the close of; after the lapse or expiration of; after; as, *in* an hour it will fall; *in* a year I shall return; due *in* three months.   The period may be indefinite; as, *in* time he will conquer.

In an hour everything indicated an immediate and bloody conflict.   WEBSTER *Works, Bunker Hill* p. 90.

III. Of various relations:

1. Denoting something as limiting or specifying: with regard to; as regards; with respect to; on the part of; for; to; of; as, round *in* the shoulders; weak *in* faith; you are deceived *in* him; he is unfortunate *in* his friends.

We . . . should be ashamed *in* this same confident boasting.
2 Cor. ix, 4.

The contrivances of nature surpass the contrivances of art *in* the complexity, subtility, and curiosity of the mechanism.
PALEY *Natural Theology* ch. 8, p. 20.

Spanish statesmanship could beat the world *in* the art of delay.   MOTLEY *United Netherlands* vol. iv, ch. 41, p. 166.

Simple honesty of purpose *in* a man goes a long way in life.
SMILES *Character* ch. 1, p. 18.

True as the steel of their tried blades,   Heroes *in* heart and hand.
HALLECK *Marco Bozzaris* st. 2.

In man as *in* lower animals, the thatch of hair indeed forms an effective shelter to the head.
·   E. B. TYLOR *Anthropology* ch. 2, p. 44.

2. Denoting material, means, occupation, instrument, or essence, or the sphere within which anything acts: by means of; with the use of; by; through; as, he spoke *in* a whisper; *in* the king's name; to work *in* gold; to deal *in* hardware; virtue consists *in* doing right.

[We may certainly call this the *instrumental use* of the preposition *in*.   MAETZNER *English Grammar* vol. ii, p. 347.]

The savory pulp they chew, and *in* the rind
Still as they thirsted, scoop the brimming stream.
MILTON *Paradise Lost* bk. iv, l. 336.

In all the sports of children, were it only *in* their wanton breakages and defacements, you shall discern a creative instinct.
CARLYLE *Sartor Resartus* bk. ii, ch. 2, p. 78.

Her rattling shrouds, all sheathed *in* ice,
With the masts went by the board.
LONGFELLOW *Wreck of the Hesperus* st. 19.

Vice is ever conceived *in* darkness and cradled *in* obscurity.
GREELEY *American Conflict* vol. i, ch. 2, p. 24.

Descartes . . . made the essence, the very existence of the soul, to consist *in* actual thought.
HAMILTON *Metaphysics* lect. xvii, p. 218.

[NOTE.—For the phrases *consist in* and *consist of* see DISTINCTIONS under OF.]

That man's mind is apt to become small as a pin point who is employed all his life *in* making a pin point.

MCCOSH Emotions bk. i, ch. 1, p. 20.

Pursuant to the King's orders, I passed the night before last . . . *in* waiting upon the friends of the King.

THACKERAY Henry Esmond bk. iii, ch. 13, p. 442.

3. Denoting a thing or person as the object of an emotion: because of; in the act of; on account of: sometimes nearly equivalent to *at* or *of*; as, to delight *in* strife; to take pleasure *in* doing good; exulting *in* victory.

O, not *in* cruelty, not *in* wrath,   The Reaper came that day.

LONGFELLOW Reaper and the Flowers st. 7.

And now Wentworth exulted *in* the near prospect of Thorough.

MACAULAY England vol. i, ch. 1, p. 71.

The Woodman's heart is *in* his work,   His axe is sharp and good.

HOOD The Elm Tree pt. ii, st. 5.

My mother's son cannot learn to delight *in* thin potations.

SCOTT Quentin Durward int., p. 6.

He lost interest even *in* the dinner parties, with a business squint, that he had been so fond of giving.

EGGLESTON The Faith Doctor ch. 4, p. 42.

Some of Brehm's monkeys took much delight *in* teasing, in various ingenious ways, a certain old dog whom they disliked.

DARWIN Descent of Man vol. i, ch. 2, p. 40.

4. Denoting a cause or occasion present with an action: during the continuance of and because of; because of; on account of; by; through; as, stumbling *in* fear; shouting *in* anger.

In this revival [of religion in Kentucky about 1801] originated our camp-meetings.   P. CARTWRIGHT *Autobiography* p. 45.

The Gothic church plainly originated *in* a rude adaptation of the forest trees with all their boughs to a festal or solemn arcade.

EMERSON Essays, History in first series, p. 24

Mirrors, effaced *in* their own clearness, send
Her only image on through deepening deeps
With endless repercussion of delight.

LOWELL The Cathedral st. 7.

Johnson . . . lives neither *in* his prose nor *in* his verse, but *in* the record of his daily talk at the hand of his friend James Boswell.   E. A. FREEMAN in *The Chautauquan* Aug., 1891, p. 648.

That *in* the creation of the United States the world had reached one of the turning points in its history seems at the time to have entered into the thought of not a single European statesman.   GREEN *Hist. Eng. People* vol. iv, bk. ix, ch. 8, p. 272.

5. Denoting physical, mental, or moral conditions, characteristics, affections, circumstances, or activities: in the midst of; amid; under the influence of; affected by; subject to; with; as, to be *in* health, *in* doubt, *in* error; to depart *in* pursuit; to laugh *in* scorn.

While the king was detained in the north, every cantred in Wales had risen *in* arms.   LINGARD *England* vol. ii, ch. 4, p. 181.

Charles had unhappily long been *in* the habit of perverting his natural acuteness to the mean subterfuges of equivocal language. H. HALLAM *Constitutional Hist. Eng.* vol. ii, ch. 10, pt. i, p. 190.

He came, the gentle satirist [Addison], who hit no unfair blow; the kind judge who castigated only *in* smiling.
THACKERAY *English Humorists* lect. ii, p. 88.

The effect is enhanced if the ride be taken *in* crass darkness.
E. E. HALE *Seven Spanish Cities* ch. 8, p. 98.

Tarry the Lord's leisure.   Wait *in* obedience as a servant, *in* hope as an heir, *in* expectation as a believer.   SPURGEON *Treasury of David, Psalm XXXVII.* in vol. ii, p. 197.

Some capsized *in* an angry breeze.
HOLMES *Old Cruiser* st. 11.

They sounded the bugles an' the trumpets,
And march'd on *in* brave array.
Legendary Ballads ed. by Roberts *Battle of Corrichie* st. 7.

The fibrin of the blood is increased *in* acute rheumatism more than *in* any other disease.
FLINT *Prin. and Prac. of Med.* pt. ii, ch. 2, p. 817.

6. Denoting conformity or appropriateness: conformably to; according to; after; as, *in* my opinion; *in* all reason.

Th' unletter'd Christian, who believes *in* gross,
Plods on to heaven, and ne'er is at a loss.
DRYDEN *Religio Laici* l. 322.

And *in* the visions of romantic youth,
What years of endless bliss are yet to flow !
CAMPBELL *Gertrude of Wyoming* pt. iii, st. 5.

The critic, *in* his conception, was not the narrow lawgiver or the rigid censor that he is often assumed to be.
H. JAMES, JR. in *North American Review* Jan., 1880, p. 56.

The independent continental areas are three *in* number.
DANA *Geology* pt. i, ch. 1, p. 18.

Nature had been left to brighten the spot *in* her own way.
CHRISTINE C. BRUSH *Inside Our Gate* ch. 7, p. 170.

7. Denoting kind, manner, degree, measure, direction, or distribution; as, the hawk flew *in* a circle; ten feet *in* length; *in* fact; *in* truth; false *in* every particular.

I am to lead my reader, perhaps *in* a reluctant path.
DRAPER *Intell. Devel. Europe* vol. i, ch. 1, p. 22.

Nothing so difficult to send, or which is so easily spoilt *in* the carriage, as news.
SMITH in Lady Holland's *Sydney Smith* vol. ii, p. 210.

There is nothing (if you will believe the Opposition) so difficult as to bully a whole people; whereas, *in* fact, there is nothing so easy.   SMITH in Lady Holland's *Sydney Smith* vol. ii, p. 210.

The structure [of Landor's 'Gebir'] is noble *in* the main, though chargeable, like Tennyson's earlier poetry, with vagueness here and there.   E. C. STEDMAN *Victorian Poets* p. 40.

All bodies, whatever their temperatures, constantly radiate heat *in* all directions. GANOT *Physics* tr. by Atkinson, ¶ 415, p. 387.

Verbs and Other Antecedents

From its very extended use, *in* may follow any one of numberless words in some combination of use and meaning. As denoting the quality, aspect, or other relation to which the verb is applied, *in* is especially used after verbs like *equal, match, rival, vie, excel, exceed, surpass,* and the like; also with *abate, advance, fail, fall, grow, improve, increase, rise, sink,* and the like; also with verbs of participation; as, *part, share, engage, interfere, join, meddle* (which also takes *with*), *participate,* and the like.

Distinctions

[*In, at, on:* When these words denote time we may say, "*At* the hour of 12, *on* the 24th of September, *in* the year 1881."

"The old, old story was told again *at* five o'clock *in* the morning."

"*At* nine o'clock *on* the morning of May 4th."

FALLOWS *100,000 Synonyms and Antonyms.*]

[*In, within:* In a few cases these words are interchangeable. *Within,* however, is more emphatic than *in.*

We may say *within* the range of his influence, or *in* the range, etc.; *within* his power, or *in* his power; *within* ten minutes, or *in* ten minutes.

In my Father's house are many mansions.—*John xiv. 2.*

In cases like the following, however, *within* does not mean the same as *in,* and is less emphatic. It was *within* his grasp. It was *in* his grasp. In the first instance it may simply mean it was in the *limits,* or *compass* of his grasp; in the other instance it would mean that it was *actually in* his grasp.

Within means "in the inner or interior part"; "inside of"; "within the limits of"; and is opposite to *without. Within* these doors; *within* this roof; *within* this house; *within* himself; *within* one's income; *within* ten miles. We may say, "Is Mrs. Potter *within,* or *in?*" Id.]

[*In, into:* When entrance or insertion is denoted, *into* should be used and not *in.*

He went *into* the hall. She rode *into* the park. They took a ride with their friends *in* Central Park.

Many innovations were introduced *into* the College.

They looked *into* the book.

He infused life *into* the Review.

When a change is made from one form or state into another, *into* is used.

Water is convertible *into* vapor. He was led by evidence *into* a belief of the truth. The manuscripts were put *into* shape.

In is often used for *into* when the noun is omitted to which it properly belongs; as, These are *in*, those are *out*, *i. e.*, *in* office, or *out* of office. Come *in*, *i. e.*, come *into* the house. The ship has come *in*, *i. e.*, come *into* port.

We may say cut, tear, break *in*, *into*, or *to* pieces. Separated, or divided *into* several parts. He fell deeply *in* love; *into* a melancholy condition; *into* a decline. He was put *in* a hard place, or *into* a sad perplexity. Their conduct came *in* question. They examined *into* his conduct.

Into indicates motion, change, entrance, in a more marked degree than *in*. Id.]

There are cases where either *in* or *into* might be used, but with some difference of meaning.

The most awful idea connected with the catacombs is their interminable extent, and the possibility of going astray *into* this labyrinth of darkness. HAWTHORNE *Marble Faun* ch. 8, p. 89.

Here it would have been correct to say, "going astray *in* this labyrinth of darkness," *i. e.*, within it, so as to be enclosed by it. "Going astray *into* it" suggests the moving on and on *to* and *toward* new, more distant, and more hopeless depths, and is hence the more expressive phrase.

Consist in, consist of: See DISTINCTIONS under OF.

INSIDE

Inside is a modern word compounded of *in* and *side*.

In or into the interior of; within; as, he stepped *inside* the gate; it stands just *inside* the door.

[NOTE.—The common popular usage is of the adverb followed by *of, inside of.*]

The Captain stood well to the westward, to run *inside of* the Bermudas. R. H. DANA *Two Years before the Mast* ch. 88, p. 214.

INTO

Into is derived from the Anglo-Saxon *in*, in, plus *to*, to. *Into* is the preposition of tendency, as *in* is of position or situation.

[In and to; to and in: implying motion: used to express any relation, as of presence, situation, inclusion, etc., that is expressed by *in*, accompanied by the idea of motion or direction inward. *Century Dictionary.*]

I. With reference to place or space, of action tending toward and terminating in: so as to enter or penetrate; to and in; so as to reach or perceive what is within; to or toward the inside of; as, come *into* the house; he thrust the spear *into* the heart of his foe; he looked *into* the room.

[In some phrases of this kind, *in* is also used; as, put it *in* water. Where the idea of remaining or being *in* is more prominent than that of motion *into*, such expressions are allowable, but the present tendency is to discriminate the two words, using *into* where motion or tendency is to be expressed, and *in* to denote the simple fact of being or remaining within; thus, "Come *in* the house" is held to be less elegant as well as less accurate than "Come *into* the house." Compare IN.]

He was more strongly tempted . . . to make excursive bolts *into* the neighboring alleys when he answered the door.
DICKENS *Martin Chuzzlewit* ch. 9, p. 172.

Sforza . . . had first called the barbarians *into* Italy.
PRESCOTT *Ferd. and Isa.* vol. iii, pt. ii, ch. 10, p. 6.

Sunrise threw a golden beam *into* the study, and laid it right across the minister's bedazzled eyes.
HAWTHORNE *Scarlet Letter* ch. 20, p. 255.

I plunged *into* the sea,
And, buffeting the billows to her rescue,
Redeemed her life with half the loss of mine.
OTWAY *Venice Preserved* act i, sc. 1.

His road [lay] open . . . *into* the very bowels of the republic.
MOTLEY *United Netherlands* vol. iv, ch. 44, p. 284.

Our several borrowings were thrust *into* a wallet, which was sometimes in his pocket, and sometimes in mine.
N. P. WILLIS *Prose Writings, Female Ward* p. 108.

We emerge from shade *into* sunshine, and observe the smoke of a distant cataract jetting from the side of the mountain.
TYNDALL *Hours of Exercise* ch. 11, p. 126.

II. Of time: extending within or protracted to; as, this will reach far *into* the twentieth century; the minutes lengthened *into* hours.

How far *into* the morning is it, lords? . . . Upon the stroke of four.   SHAKESPEARE *K. Richard III.* act v, sc. 8, l. 286.

III. Of various relations following the analogy of the relation of place or space.

1. So as to infuse or impart to; so as to become affected by or united with; as, to put meaning *into* the words; to put life *into* the picture; to marry *into* a family.

Whatever passion enters *into* a sentence or decision, so far will there be in it a tincture of injustice.
     ADDISON *The Guardian* July 4, 1718.

One great thought breathed *into* a man may regenerate him.
     CHANNING *Works, Laboring Classes* p. 49.

A moral should be wrought *into* the body and soul, the matter and tendency, of a poem, not tagg'd to the end.
     LAMB *Letters* vol. i, ch. 5, p. 188.

Infuse *into* the purpose with which you follow the various employments and professions of life . . . this sense of beauty, and you are transformed at once from an artisan into an artist.
     E. P. WHIPPLE *Success* essay viii, p. 208.

The man who can't put fire *into* his speeches should put his speeches *into* the fire.   MATHEWS *Oratory and Orators* ch. 4, p. 108.

2. So as to change to; so as to become; as, to convert water *into* steam; to translate Greek *into* English.

One of the Seven Wise Men of Greece boiled his wisdom down *into* [these] words, . . . nothing too much.
     HOLMES *Over the Teacups* ch. 8, p. 181.

The English *into* which Chapman transfuses the meaning of the mighty ancient is often singularly and delicately beautiful.
CRAIK *Eng. Lit. and Lang., Chapman's Homer* in vol. i, p. 574.

.   I cannot shape my tongue
To syllable black deeds *into* smooth names.
     BYRON *Marino Faliero* act iii, sc. 1.

In any great district of caverns, we usually have the underground spaces divided *into* distinct classes of which the uppermost was the earliest to be constructed.
     N. S. SHALER *Aspects of Earth, Caverns* p. 114.

2. In mathematics, so as to unite as a factor with; as, to multiply a *into* x + y.

Verbs and Other Antecedents

[*Into* stands along with *to*, with the notions of becoming or making into something and of transformation into something.

Here also belong the notions of *falling, breaking, bursting,* and *taking to pieces,* and the like, as well as *parting* and *dividing,* where the pieces or parts become, after intransitive and transitive verbs, determinations of the subject or object:

The notion of *uniting* or *blending* is also construed with *into* where the result of the combination is also to be denoted:

Whether with the notion of translating (*into* a language) we should rather join the idea of transmutation or of removal may appear doubtful.   MAETZNER *English Grammar* vol. ii, p. 310.]

Distinctions

In—into: See DISTINCTIONS under IN.

Errors

The following erroneous uses of *in* are given in Goold Brown's *Grammar of English Grammars:*

It will be despatched, *in* most occasions, without resting.
JOHN LOCKE *Small English Grammar.*

Based *in* the great self-evident truths of liberty and equality.
Scholar's Manual.

In the above-quoted sentences correct usage would require one to write "*on* most occasions" and "based *on* the great self-evident truths."

But they have egregiously fallen *in* that inconveniency.
Barclay's Works iii, p. 78.

Here we should say "fallen *into,*" not "fallen *in.*"

If the addition consists *in* two or more words.
LINDLEY MURRAY *English Grammar* p. 176.

Consist in may at times be properly used, but here the correct phrase would be *consist of.* See DISTINCTIONS under OF.

LIKE

See TO, III., 1.

MID, MIDST

See AMID, AMIDST.

MONG, MONGST

See AMONG, AMONGST.

NOTWITHSTANDING

See PARTICIPIAL PREPOSITIONS.

NEAR

See TO, III., 1.

OF

Of is derived from the Anglo-Saxon *of*, from.

[Etymologically and in earliest use the meaning of *of* is that of departure or going away from or out of a particular place or position. (Compare OFF.) But this usage is now the less common one, the genitival relation which *of* also represents having, by transition from the relation of issuance to that of connection, become the customary and usual signification.

Standard Dictionary.]

[A word primarily expressing the idea of literal departure away from or out of a place or position. It passes from this physical application to the figurative meaning of departure or derivation as from a source or cause. Finally it transforms the idea of derivation or origin through several intermediate gradations of meaning into that of possessing or being possessed by, pertaining to, or being connected with, in almost any relation of thought. *Century Dictionary.*]

Such descriptive paragraphs as those above quoted really give a better idea of the meaning of this often-recurring preposition than attempted definitions of its fine shades of meaning, which perpetually merge into each other. In the following arrangement the endeavor has been to abbreviate, condense, and simplify rather than to extend the definitions, which by close analysis may be subdivided almost without limit. As *from* has been called distinctively the preposition of separation, *of* might be termed the preposition of origin or source, though the idea of separation is also included.

Starting with the idea of separation in space, *of* comes to denote any relation as of movement, position, origin, possession, etc., into which the idea of separation from, proceeding from, being derived from, or the like may even remotely enter.

I. Of place or space:

1. Denoting relative position: in distance or direction from; as within a mile *of* the shore; Massachusetts lies north *of* Connecticut.

In the vicinity *of* coral reefs and islands the attrition of the waves imparts a milky complexion to the sea.

WINCHELL *Walks and Talks* ch. 11, p. 66.

They cannot go back *of* the returns. It is their business simply officially to announce the result.

New-York Tribune Nov. 14, 1891, p. 6, col. 8.

Free-will is a fact of consciousness, and we can neither go back *of* the testimony of consciousness nor explain that away.

J. P. THOMPSON *Theology of Christ* ch. 9, p. 115.

Tall gaunt stacks rise out of the waves in front *of* the cliffs of which they once formed a part.

ARCH. GEIKIE *Geol. Sketches* ch. 2, p. 24.

North *of* the town stands the castle of San Carlos—a square fort, with a moat and glacis. R. A. WILSON *Mexico* ch. 7, p. 85.

2. Denoting location in; belonging to or connected with as a locality; as, the tower *of* London; the coast *of* England.

Braw, braw lads *of* Gala Water.

BURNS *Braw Lads of Gala Water* chorus.

The Commons *of* England, the Tiers-Etat *of* France, the bourgeoisie *of* the Continent generally, are the descendants of this class [artisans]. MILL *Polit. Econ.* prelim., p. 12.

3. Noting extent or distance; measuring; covering; amounting to; as, a start *of* twenty yards; a plot *of* two acres.

The buildings [of South Carolina College] disposed about a square *of* ten acres, which is called the Campus.

> R. MILLS *Statistics of South Carolina* [1826] p. 701.

The farm of Cincinnatus consisted *of* about three-and-a-half statute acres.

> C. W. HOSKYNS *Hist. Agriculture, Ancient Period* p. 41.

II. Of time: denoting the occasion, period, age, or the like; pertaining to or connected with; as, the age *of* chivalry; from the moment *of* his birth; I have known him *of* old.

The fate of the Triennial Bill confounded all the calculations of the best-informed politicians *of* that time.

> MACAULAY *England* vol. iv, ch. 20, p. 382.

The outlawed pirate *of* one year was promoted the next to be a governor and his country's representative.

> FROUDE *Eng. in West Indies* ch. 1, p. 10.

III. Of various relations :

1. Denoting separation other than merely local, and often exchangeable with *from.*

(*a*) From by separation, riddance, or removal ; as, free *of* debt; quit *of* blame; cured *of* a bad habit; relieved *of* a burden. See DISTINCTIONS.

Dick at the front door delivered himself *of* the words he had been boggling over for the last two hours.

> KIPLING *Light that Failed* ch. 1, p. 14.

I did consent; And often did beguile her *of* her tears.

> SHAKESPEARE *Othello* act i, sc. 3.

I was like a man bereft *of* life.

> BUNYAN *Works, Grace Abounding* p. 46.

The bereavement of death is never devoid *of* a sense of holy calm, a sort of solemn peace connected with the memory of the lost one.   LEVER *Tom Burke Of 'Ours'* ch. 42, p. 127.

Yes, fortune may bereave me *of* my crown.

> THOMAS KYD *Spanish Tragedy* act i, sc. 1.

The holly, providently planted about the house [of the English peasant], to cheat winter *of* its dreariness.
>> IRVING *Sketch-Book, Rural Life in England* p. 84.

They were born *of* a race of funeral flowers
That garlanded, in long-gone hours,
A templar's knightly tomb.
>> FITZ-GREENE HALLECK *Alnwick Castle* st. 5.

The old Abou Do, being resolved upon work, had divested himself *of* his tope or toga before starting.
>> BAKER *Nile Trib. Abyssinia* ch. 13, p. 388.

[NOTE.—In such connection *out of* is often used.

The besom of reform has swept him *out of* office.
>> HAWTHORNE *Scarlet Letter, Custom House* p. 14.]

(*b*) From as a source, origin, material, or agency; with reference to; as proceeding from; on the part of; as, he is *of* a noble family; born *of* woman; the son *of* David; made *of* gold; it is very good *of* you to say so.

My pride was tamed, and in our grief
I *of* the Parish asked relief.
>> WORDSWORTH *The Last of the Flock* st. 5.

And beauty born *of* murmuring sound
Shall pass into her face.
>> WORDSWORTH *Three Years she Grew* st. 5.

I have made a miserable botch *of* this description.
>> HAWTHORNE *Eng. Note-Books, Furness Abbey* in vol. i, p. 220.

Of small coral about her arms she bare
A pair of beads, gauded all with green.
>> CHAUCER *C. T., Prologue* l. 158.

[NOTE.—In such case, *out of* is often used.

Out of my stony griefs   Bethel I'll raise.
>> SARAH F. ADAMS *Nearer, my God, to Thee* st. 4.]

The light consisted *of* fifteen Argand lamps, placed within smooth concave reflectors twenty-one inches in diameter.
>> THOREAU in *American Prose, Highland Light* p. 358.

[NOTE.—For the phrases *consist of* and *consist in* see DISTINCTIONS under OF.]

Opposite the door hung a target *of* hide, round, and bossed with brass.   MACDONALD *What's Mine's Mine* ch. 7, p. 47.

(c) From as by division or selection (answering to the partitive genitive of Latin and other languages):

(1) As by division, as of a part from a while, or as a portion of something greater; as, a piece *of* bread; a drink *of* water; to partake *of* food; he has none *of* it; does he want all *of* it?

I pray thee, set a deep glass of Rhenish wine on the contrary casket.   SHAKESPEARE *The Merchant of Venice* act i, sc. 2, 1, 95.

All Of It

All of is a popular idiom exactly parallel to the phrase *the whole of*, used in contrast with *a part of* the same substance or collection, "How much of this shall I take?" *All* (*i. e.*, the whole), *of* it": "How many of these men were present?" *All of* them."

All of beauty and of beatitude we conceive and strive for, ourselves are to be sometime.

A. BRONSON ALCOTT *Concord Days, Ideals* p. 272.

Except when such contrast is in mind the *of* is superfluous, and therefore objectionable. Not, "*All of* the members were present," but, "*All* the members———"; "I signed *all* (not *all of*) the letters"; "———with *all* (not *all of*) my heart"; instead of "I know *all of* them," preferably, "I know them *all*."

(2) As by selection, subtraction, or removal from a group, class, number, etc.; from among; among: including the use of *of* after a superlative; as, one *of* the men; some *of* the people; one *of* many; the best *of* books.

[NOTE.—This form can be used even when the enumeration includes the whole number referred to; as, there were twenty *of* us; that is, taking the whole number one by one, there would be twenty. Hence arise such phrases as *all of* this company. Compare preceding note under III., (c) (1).

Here belong such phrases as *of mine, of his, of yours*, etc., *i. e.*, among those that are mine, his yours, or the like—phrases sometimes mistakenly criticized as inaccurate, but which are in general and approved use. These expressions may be used even with reference to a single object; as, "this head *of* mine," that is "*of* or *among* the things belonging to me."]

And he,—the basest *of* the base,   The vilest *of* the vile.
WHITTIER *The New Year* st. 28.

Ecclesiastical tyranny is *of* all kinds the worst; its fruits are cowardice, idleness, ignorance, and poverty.
BANCROFT *United States* vol. i, ch. 10, p. 372.

No more shall grief *of* mine the season wrong.
WORDSWORTH *Intimations of Immortality* st. 8.

Belongings, as an old expression now reinstated in its former rights, is peculiar to the very latest period of our language. The more *of* such vernacularisms we call up from the past, the better.   F. HALL *Modern English* ch. 8, p. 807.

Many *of* them were from the South, and could not bring themselves to the point of accepting the 'Force Bill.'
H. C. LODGE *Daniel Webster* ch. 7, p. 214.

A clearer and larger apprehension *of* God.
STORRS *Divine Origin of Christianity* lect. ii, p. 85.

England, the most calculative, is the least meditative, *of* all civilized countries.
CARLYLE *Essays, Characteristics* in vol. iii, p. 89.

Of all reading, history hath in it a most taking delight.
C. MATHER *Magnalia Christi* vol. ii, bk. iv, pt. ii, ch. 10, p. 158.

2. Denoting association, connection, or possession:

(*a*) Connected with as a component or part, quality or attribute; belonging or pertaining to; made by; possessed by; helping to form or complete; characterizing; as, the handle *of* a knife; the residence *of* the senator; the length *of* his arm; the power *of* the king; a sign *of* grief; on the point *of* yielding.

Thou hast the right arched beauty *of* the brow.
SHAKESPEARE *Merry Wives of Windsor* act. iii, sc. 8.

Catholicism obeys the orders *of* one man, and has therefore a unity, a compactness, a power, which Protestant denominations do not possess.   DRAPER *Conflict between Relig. and Sci.* p. 829.

The building and arrangement *of* a house influence the health, the comfort, the morals, the religion.

    HARRIET B. STOWE *House and Home Papers* No. xi, p. 272.

It has never been questioned that the doctrine *of* the brotherhood *of* mankind and *of* the duty *of* universal benevolence is a main feature of Christianity.

    J. R. SEELEY *Ecce Homo* pt. ii, ch. 15, p. 188.

The dints and furrows *of* time's envious brunt.

    LOWELL *The Oak* st. 2.

The shrill treble *of* the squaws mingles not discordantly with the guttural tones of the bucks.

    H. R. LEMLY in *Harper's Monthly, Mar., 1880* p. 499.

That fulgor and brightness *of* him that made the sun.

    BURTON *Anat. Melancholy* pt. iii, § 4, p. 595.

The self-sacrifice *of* Leonidas, the good faith *of* Regulus, are the glories *of* history.

    J. LUBBOCK *Pleasures of Life* pt. ii, ch. 1, p. 11.

All *of* the Indian tribes . . . are religious—are worshipful.

    CATLIN *N. Am. Indians* vol. i, letter xxii, p. 156.

(*b*) Having as an attribute or quality, feature, function, characteristic, or the like; holding; possessing; marked or characterized by; as, a man *of* power; a heart *of* adamant.

The Elizabethan was a period *of* transition in the history of the English tongue.

    H. E. SHEPHERD *Hist. Eng. Lang.* ch. 20, p. 166.

Drusus . . . was . . . *of* so cruel a temper, that a peculiarly sharp kind of swords were named from him Drusians.

    KEIGHTLEY *Roman Empire* pt. i, ch. 8, p. 54.

The President's patronage is, in the hands of a skilful intriguer, an engine *of* far-spreading potency.

    BRYCE *American Commonwealth* vol. i, pt. i, ch. 6, p. 61.

Full big he was *of* brawn, and eke *of* bones.

    CHAUCER *C. T. Prologue* l. 548.

Great Hector *of* the beamy helm, the son
Of Priam, led the Trojan race.
> HOMER *Iliad* tr. by Bryant, bk. ii, l. 1025

(c) Pertaining to as an object of desire, right, propriety, suitability, need, etc.; as, fond *of* jewelry; desirous *of* gain; worthy *of* praise.

The library, the museum, the aviary, and the botanical garden of Sir Thomas Browne, were thought by Fellows of the Royal Society well worthy *of* a long pilgrimage.
> MACAULAY *England* vol. i, ch. 3, p. 276.

Surely not even the best of men was ever entirely worthy *of* a good woman.   MAARTENS *The Greater Glory* ch. 33, p. 277.

I am not fond *of* rectifying legislative mistakes by executive acts.   WASHINGTON in Sparks's *Writings of Washington* July 6, 1796, vol. xi, p. 137.

Ugly and deformed people have great need *of* unusual virtues.
> GEORGE ELIOT *Mill on the Floss* bk. v, ch. 3, p. 292.

The ruling passion of an Arab is greediness *of* gold, which he will clutch from the unarmed stranger, or filch from an unsuspecting friend.   LYNCH *Dead Sea and Jordan* ch. 22, p. 430.

The Count . . . was a bold and graceful rider. He was fond, too, *of* caracoling his horse.
> IRVING *Crayon, Tour on the Prairies* ch. 7, p. 41.

The boorish driver leaning o'er his team
Vociferous, and impatient *of* delay.
> COWPER *Task* bk. i, l. 296.

We never tire *of* the drama of sunset.
> THOREAU *Winter, Jan. 7, 1852* p. 128.

3. In general reference where the connection may even become a mere indication: in respect to; concerning; because of; about; at; as, wonderful things are told *of* him; to hear *of* an event; to talk *of* business; beware *of* the dog; to make use *of* opportunity; a chance *of* success.

If we speak *of* temples and monuments, the stones of the Incas remain, but the Titans that piled them are gone.
> BUSHNELL *Moral Uses of Dark Things* ch. 4, p. 98.

Franklin warned you a hundred years ago *of* the peril of being divided by little, partial, local interests. FARRAR *Sermons and Addresses in America, Farewell Thoughts* p. 856.

The early literature of Castile could boast *of* the Poem of the Cid, in some respects the most remarkable performance of the middle ages.   PRESCOTT *Ferdinand and Isabella* vol. i, p. 12.

John, like Philip of Macedon, made use *of* gold even more than arms, for the reduction of his enemies.
> PRESCOTT *Ferdinand and Isabella* vol. i, pt. i, ch. 2, p. 58.

Bring eke with you a bowl or else a pan   Full *of* water.
> CHAUCER *C. T., Canon's Yeoman's Tale* l. 496.

IV. In various archaic or obsolete senses, which for the practical purposes of this book need not be particularly considered; as, tempted *of* the devil; come *of* a Sunday; it has been so *of* a long time.

I yet am unprovided   *Of* a pair of bases.
> SHAKESPEARE *Pericles* act ii, sc. 1.

But why *of* two oaths' breach do I excuse thee,
When I break twenty!   SHAKESPEARE *Sonnets* clii.

Let her great Danube rolling fair
Enwind her isles, unmark'd *of* me.
> TENNYSON *In Memoriam* xcvii, st. 8.

That he might joust unknown *of* all, and learn
If his old prowess were in aught decay'd.
> TENNYSON *Elaine* st. 26.

Of an evening, you are kind to the most unattractive of the wall-flowers.   MITCHELL *Reveries of a Bachelor* p. 118.

A hard case that hereupon I should be justly condemned *of* sin.   HOOKER *Ecclesiastical Polity* bk. ii, p. 189.

One is often tempted *of* the Devil to forswear the study of history altogether as the pursuit of the Unknowable. A. BIRRELL *Obiter Dicta, Rogue's Memoirs* in first series, p. 154.

It is only *of* recent years that ensilage, *i. e.*, the preservation of green food for cattle by partial fermentation in silos, has become an important feature in agricultural economy.

Encyc. Brit. 9th ed., vol. **xxii**, p. 67.

Barking dogs sometimes bite, as many a small boy, too trustful *of* the proverb, has found to his cost.

T. W. HIGGINSON *Out-Door Papers, Physical Courage* p. 44.

Columbus had an immediate audience *of* the queen, and the benignity with which she received him atoned for all past neglect.   IRVING *Columbus* vol. i, bk. ii, ch. 7, p. 117.

And unbreached *of* warring waters Athens like a sea-rock stands.

SWINBURNE *Erechtheus* l. 1451.

Verbs and Other Antecedents

Of is used after a vast number of verbs, especially:

(1) Verbs expressing the idea of separation or removal of any kind; as, *acquit, balk, bereave, break* (as *of* a habit), *cheat, cleanse, clear, cure, defraud, deliver, deprive, despair, disappoint, disarm, disburden, discharge, dispossess, divest, drain, ease* (as *of* a load), *fail, heal, lighten, miss* (as *of* a prize), *purge, recover, relieve, rid, rob, shear, spoil, strip, tire, wean, weary,* and many others. Some of these, as *deliver, recover, wean,* may also take *from*.

(2) Verbs conveying some idea of origin or source; as, *be, come, descend, spring,* with some of which *from* may also be used; as, he is *of* a noble family.

(3) Verbs of making and the like, with reference to the material used; as, *build, construct, compose, create, form, frame, make,* etc. In such connection *out of* is frequently used.

(4) Verbs expressing some form of asking or seeking, with reference to the person from whom something is asked or sought; as, *ask* (*of* me, *of* him, etc.), *beg, beseech, crave, demand, desire, entreat, expect, inquire, request, require, seek, want. Deserve* and *merit* take *of* before the word denoting the person from whom reward or the like might come.

(5) Verbs expressing the cause or occasion of an activity, a perception, a result, etc.; as, *accuse, arrest* (now commonly with *for*), *beware, boast, brag, breathe, complain, die* (as *of* a disease), *smell, suspect, taste,* etc.

(6) Verbs of learning or knowing; as, *hear, learn, know,* etc.

(7) Verbs of instructing, convincing, reminding, etc.; as, *acquaint, admonish, advertise, advise, assure, convict, convince, inform, instruct, persuade, remind, warn,* etc.

(8) Verbs of thinking, perceiving, and the like; as, *augur, dream, hold, judge, think,* etc.

(9) Verbs of utterance or expression; as, *murmur* (*of* love or other deep feeling, but *at* or *against* restraint or oppression), *say, sing, speak, talk, tell, treat,* etc.

(10) Many other verbs, especially those of Romance origin; as, *admit, allow, approve, avail* (oneself *of*), *dispose* (as *of* a matter), and the like. Some of these, as *admit, allow, approve,* may take instead a direct object without a preposition.

Of adjectives followed by *of* the following may be specified:

(1) Adjectives connected with the verbs already mentioned; as, *dead, free, sick, tired,* etc.

(2) Adjectives denoting some mental state, as of attention, recollection, etc., or their contraries; as, *afraid, ambitious, ashamed, avaricious, aware, capable, careful, careless, certain, confident, conscious, considerate, desirous, distrustful, eager* (commonly with *for*), *enamored, envious, fearful, fearless, fond, forgetful, glad, greedy, heedful, heedless, hopeless, ignorant, impatient, incapable, indulgent, insensible, insusceptible, jealous, mindful, neglectful, negligent, observant, patient, prolific* (now oftener with *in*), *proud, reckless, regardless, sensible, studious, sure, suspicious, tender, thoughtful, thoughtless, uncertain, unconscious, unmindful, vain, watchful,* and many others.

(8) Adjectives denoting certain moral relations; as, *guiltless*, *guilty*, *innocent*, *worthy*, *unworthy*. But while we say *worthy of*, we say *fit for*. It is noticeable that while we use *glad* with *of*, we say *sorry for*, *considerate*, or *thoughtful of*; but *attentive to* (compare 4) or *indifferent to*; *conscious* or *unconscious of*, but *sensitive to*.

(4) Many adjectives in *-ive* derived from verbal stems; as, *apprehensive*, *descriptive*, *destructive*, *expressive*, *indicative*, *productive*; but *attentive*, *conducive*, *relative*, and others are followed by *to*.

Nouns or pronouns without number may be followed by *of*, since *of* with its object becomes the exact equivalent of the possessive case, "The house *of* John" having the same meaning as "John's house," though in reverse order of statement. The local, descriptive, and partitive uses, as, "A citizen of London," "A man of wealth," "A member of the board," etc., extend the range of such employment of this preposition almost without limit.

Distinctions

About—of—on: See Distinctions under ON.

By—from—of: Of was formerly used indiscriminately for almost any connection of thought, but is now greatly restricted, so that in modern usage we say tempted *by* the devil; come *on* a holiday; it has been so *for* a long time. In each of these cases *of* would formerly have been used. Such phrases as *free of*, *relieved of*, are still in good use, but in many cases *from* is preferred; as, free *from* blame; relieved *from* a burden, *from* care, etc. A process of division and differentiation is going on here as elsewhere, working toward the ideal of having one word and one only to stand for one meaning.

Consist in — consist of: Consist in is used of essence, while *consist of* is used of material; virtue *consists in* right living; granite *consists of* quartz, feldspar, and mica.

OFF

Off is etymologically the same as *of*, but taking especially the meaning *away from.*

Starting with the idea of place, noting deviation, separation, removal, or distance.

1. From; distant from; separated or removed from; as, the the car is *off* the track; as easy as falling *off* a log; the matter is *off* my hands; *off* duty; *off* one's guard.

Off his own beat his opinions were of no value.
EMERSON English Traits ch. 1, p. 27.

2. Extending away from; leading out of; as, Wall Street leads *off* Broadway.

Watling Street, Bow Lane, Old Change, and other thoroughfares *off* Cheapside and Cornhill.
MAYHEW London Labour and London Poor vol. ii, p. 201.

3. In nautical use, opposite and to seaward of at a short distance; as, the ship lies *off* the harbor; there is a reef six miles *off* shore.

Add to this the gale *off* Point Conception.
R. H. DANA Two Years before the Mast ch. 11, p. 58.

On a low island of barren gneiss-rock *off* the west coast of Scotland an Irish refugee, Columba, had raised the famous mission-station of Iona.   GREEN *Hist. Eng. People* vol. i, p. 49.

A steamer flying signals of distress had been sighted *off* that port.   *New-York Tribune* Oct. 15, 1891, p. 1, col. 1.

4. In less approved use, for *of* or *on;* as, to dine *off* or make a meal *off* sandwiches. In this sense, *on* is now preferred. Such expressions as "to get eggs *off* the farmer," etc., are distinctly vulgar or provincial. Compare ON, III., 6.

ON, UPON

On is derived from the Anglo-Saxon *on, an,* related to *in. Upon* is practically identical with *on* both in meaning and use.

[*Upon* now differs little in use from *on,* the former being sometimes used for reasons of euphony or rhythm, and also preferably when motion into position is involved, the latter when merely rest or support is indicated.   When *upon* has its original meaning of *up* and *on*, that is, by means of ascent into a relation of resting or support, it is written as two words, *up* having its adverbial force; as, let us go *up on* the roof.

Standard Dictionary.]

I. Of place or space:

1. In contact with the upper surface of; in or into contact with from above; within the superficial limits of; above and supported by; as, the hair *on* one's head; the people *on* the earth; the stones fell *on* the ground.

Pepin was exalted *on* a buckler by the suffrage of a free people, accustomed to obey his laws and to march under his standard.   GIBBON *Rome* vol. v, ch. 49, p. 29.

He alighted *on* the roof . . . and bubbled out a few notes.
OLIVE T. MILLER *In Nesting Time* ch. 8, p. 48.

The cattle bellowed *on* the plain.
BRET HARTE *John Burns of Gettysburg* st. 2.

Wing-like sails *on* her bosom gliding
Bear down the lily and drown the reed.
JEAN INGELOW *Divided* vii, st. 1.

The ceiling [of the Library at Washington] is iron and glass, and rests *on* foliated iron brackets each weighing a ton.
MARY CLEMMER AMES *Ten Years in Washington* ch. 18, p. 180.

The figure [of an athlete], being in a sitting posture, had been placed *on* a stone capital of the Doric order, as *upon* a stool.
R. LANCIANI in *Century Magazine, Feb., 1887* p. 608.

2. So as to be supported by, as in suspension or the like; as, the fish *on* the hook; the fruit *on* the tree.   [In such cases, the weight rests *on* the point of support, though the object hangs below it.   Compare OVER, I., 8.]

Aloft *on* the stayless verge she hung.
HOGG *Queen's Wake, Abbot M'Kinnon* st. 14.

Loose rock and frozen slide,   Hung *on* the mountain-side.
WHITTIER *To a Friend* st. 4.

The gooseberry produces fruit buds and spurs *on* wood two years old.   P. BARRY *Fruit Garden* pt. iii, ch. 2, p. 262.

So the dew   Globes *on* a grass-blade.
          EDWIN ARNOLD *Light of the World* bk. v, p. 323.

Hundreds of dressed deodar logs had caught *on* a snag of rock, and the river was bringing down more logs every minute to complete the blockade.
          KIPLING *Mine Own People, Namgay Doola* p. 25.

3. In such a position as to cover, overspread, strike, touch, or be attached to the outside of, without reference to elevation; as, nail a strip *on* the under side of the box; he would bet the shoes *on* his feet.

'Bravo!' cried Captain Nutter, rapping *on* the table encouragingly.   ALDRICH *Story of a Bad Boy* ch. 16, p. 180.

Some new English ballet happened to be *on* the boards.
          ALDRICH *Queen of Sheba* ch. 2, p. 28.

As the gentle dip of the swallow's wing
Breaks the bubbles *on* the sea.   HALLECK *Love* st. 1.

The people of the land appeared to slumber; but, like vigilant and wary soldiers, they might be said to sleep *on* their arms.
          COOPER *Lionel Lincoln* ch. 5, p. 91.

Great storms beat *on* this beach, and *on* the cliffs of Nahant.
          A. LEWIS *Hist. Lynn* ch. 1, p. 10.

When, even *on* the mountain's breast,
The chainless winds were all at rest.
          BRYANT *Romero* int., l. 25.

Autographs of famous names were to be seen in faded ink *on* some of the flyleaves.
          HAWTHORNE *Mosses from an Old Manse* p. 28.

4. In such a position as to be supported and borne on by; with the support of; by means of; as, to travel *on* the cars; to go *on* all fours.

All pale extended *on* their shields,   And weltering in his gore.
          PERCY *Reliques, Hermit of Warkworth* fytte ii, st. 69.

The next year Penn himself arrived *on* the ship Welcome with one hundred emigrants, mostly Friends.

> A. GILMAN *American People* ch. 7, p. 89.

Next view in state, proud prancing *on* his roan,
The golden-crested haughty Marmion.

> BYRON *English Bards* st. 12.

People of every age, sex, and condition were borne away *on* the tide of excited feeling that swept over the land.

> J. S. MOSBY *War Reminiscences* ch. 1, p. 5.

While *on* white wings descending Houres throng,
And drink the floods of odour and of song.

> ERASMUS DARWIN *Loves of the Plants* can. 4, l. 324.

'Who comes?' The sentry's warning cry
Rings sharply *on* the evening air.

> BRET HARTE *The Goddess* st. 1.

[NOTE.—Here belong such phrases as *on board of*, sometimes shortened to *on board*, which is used like a preposition before the object. Compare ABOARD.

This was my first day's duty *on board* the ship.

> R. H. DANA *Two Years before the Mast* ch. 28, p. 187.

The stubborn conservative is like a horse *on board* a ferryboat. The horse may back, but the boat moves on, and the animal with it. GREELEY in Parton's *Horace Greeley* ch. 21, p. 280.]

5. In the relation of sequence or approach: following after; in the wake of; after; drawing near to; in direction or movement along; as, pestilence followed *on* the heels of famine; to press *upon* an antagonist; to move *on* (or *upon*) the enemy; he is *on* the way; *on* (or *upon*) the road.

The first of these encroachments *on* the monastic spirit was chivalry, which called into being a proud and jealous military honour that has never since been extinguished.

> LECKY *Hist. Eur. Morals* vol. ii, ch. 4, p. 199.

Close *on* the heels of the straining pack, all a-yell up the hill.

> J. WILSON *Christopher North* fytte i, p. 15.

Every thing dear to nations was wagered *on* both sides.

> MACAULAY *England* vol. ii, ch. 6, p. 107.

> Slight withal may be the things which bring
> Back *on* the heart the weight which it would fling
> Aside for ever.   BYRON *Childe Harold* can 4, st. 23.

> Now fades the glimmering landscape *on* the sight,
> And all the air a solemn stillness holds.
> > GRAY *Elegy* st. 2.

6. Near, or adjacent to, not necessarily multiplying contact or support; at; by; near; along; as, *on* the coast of Africa; *on* the border of the stream.

> My boat is *on* the shore,   And my bark is *on* the sea.
> > BYRON *Lines to Mr. Moore* st. 1.

In city walls, . . . where there is a superabundant abutment *on* either hand to counteract any thrust, the horizontal principle is entirely misplaced. JAMES FERGUSSON *Hist. Ind. and East. Arch.* bk. ii, ch. 2, p. 211.

I advanced forward, and cast anchor *on* the lee side of the island.   SWIFT *Works, Gulliver* pt. i, ch. 8, p. 187.

> *On* the brow o' the sea Stand ranks of people.
> > SHAKESPEARE *Othello* act ii, sc. 1.

Victorious banners were already floating *on* the margin of the Great Desert.   DE QUINCEY *The Cæsars* ch. 6, p. 242.

II. Of time:

1. Within the duration of; during the lapse of; as, *on* that day he arrived.

> If you repay me not *on* such a day,
> *in* such a place, such sum or sums.
> > SHAKESPEARE *Merchant of Venice* act. i, sc. 8.

> May Heaven augment your blisses,
> *On* every new birthday ye see.
> > BURNS *A Dream* st. 1.

On the 18th day of March, 1864, at Nashville, Tennessee, I relieved Lieutenant-General Grant in command of the Military Division of the Mississippi.
> W. T. SHERMAN *Memoirs* vol. ii, ch. 15, p. 5.

In a long ramble . . . *on* a fine autumnal day, Rip had unconsciously scrambled to one of the highest parts of the Kaatskill mountains.   Irving *Sketch-Book, Rip Van Winkle* p. 51.

On this sad day fell the flower of the Aztec nobility.
    Prescott *Mexico* vol. ii, bk. iv, ch. 8, p. 283.

[Note.—With *day*, *time*, and the like, *on* is often omitted; as, come *another day*.

That he came down yesterday was no guarantee that he would do it next time. For [*on*] every day antecedent and consequent varied.   Drummond *Natural Law* int., pt. ii, p. 89.]

2. At the exact point or period of; as, *on* the instant; *on* the stroke of twelve; he arrived *on* time (*i. e.*, at the designated or appointed moment of time).

The sun went down *on* the night of the 14th of February, 1862, leaving the army confronting Fort Donelson.
    U. S. Grant *Personal Memoirs* vol. i, ch. 22, p. 308.

The first natives whom Cortes met *on* landing in Mexico were the Totonacos.
    D. G. Brinton *Am. Race, N. Am. Tribes* ch. 8, p. 189.

3. At the moment of, and in connection with or because of; at; as, *on* the assembling of Congress the controversy began; *on* the signal he arose; *on* my entrance he withdrew.

On the death of their kings they [the Panebes] bury the bodies, first cutting off the head, which they enframe in gold and offer worship to it in a temple.   Lenormant *Beginnings of Hist.* tr. by Lockwood, ch. 5, p. 208, note.

But if *on* a temporary superiority of the one party, the other is to resort to a scission of the Union, no federal government can ever exist.
Jefferson in Randall's *Thomas Jefferson* vol. ii, ch. 9, p. 447.

On a review of this whole transaction, two topics come forth into prominence, the 'name' of Jesus and 'faith' in that name.
    Howson *Meditations on the Miracles* ch. 18, p. 275.

III. Of various relations, more or less closely allied to the idea of position above in space:

1. Having as a foundation, basis, or support; by means of or as if supported or upheld by; sustained or confirmed by; by the authority or assurance of; as, *on* my word; he was appointed *on* your recommendation; to make oath *on* the Bible.

There are some secrets, *on* the keeping of which depends oftentimes the salvation of an army. WASHINGTON in Sparks's *Writings of Washington, Feb. 24, 1777* in vol. iv, p. 380.

Hildebrand . . . determined to lay the corner-stone of his great structure *on* a celibate priesthood.
T. STARR KING *Substance and Show* lect. v, p. 206.

Wrong ever builds *on* quicksands.
LOWELL *Prometheus* st. 2.

I never yet saw a banker who charged *on* paper more than one per cent., and yet through thimble-rigging of piastres, I somehow never get but about nineteen pounds sterling *on* a draft of twenty.
J. P. THOMPSON *Photographic Views of Egypt* ch. 2, p. 17.

Nothing is more injurious in science than assumptions which do not rest *on* a broad basis of fact.
AGASSIZ *Geol. Sketches* sketch vi, p. 154.

The destinies of the human race were staked *on* the same cast with the freedom of the English people.
MACAULAY *Essays, Milton* p. 10.

2. In consequence of; depending upon; having as a reason or ground; by reason of; because of; in accordance with; as, *on* certain conditions; he did it *on* purpose.

After the worship was ended, Haliday made up to the minister, among many others, to congratulate him *on* the splendour of his discourse. HOGG *Tales* in vol. i, p. 319.

The arrest of Shaftesbury *on* a charge of suborning false witnesses to the Plot marked the new strength of the Crown.
GREEN *Short Hist. Eng. People* ch. 9, § 5, p. 640.

The Carlovingian crown may indeed be said to have been worn *on* the tenure of continual conquests.
JAMES STEPHEN *Lect. on France* lect. iii, p. 67.

I think that, if required, *on* pain of death, to name instantly the most perfect thing in the universe, I should risk my fate on a bird's egg.   T. W. HIGGINSON *Out-Door Papers* p. 297.

I . . . was felicitating myself *on* occupying one of the best positions in the House.

HOLMES *Our Hundred Days in Europe* ch. 2, p. 97.

[Hence such prepositional phrases as, *on the part of, on account of.*

This occasioned great excitement, much caucusing and threatening *on the part of* the Southern members, but nothing else.

NICOLAY AND HAY *Abraham Lincoln* vol. i, ch. 16, p. 286.

On account of its indestructibility, gold was regarded by the earlier chemists as the king of metals.

ELIOT AND STORER *Inorganic Chemistry* § 505, p. 282.]

3. In or into a state or condition of; in the act or process of; occupied with; as, *on* guard; *on* duty; *on* fire; *on* record; *on* the contrary; *on* the whole.

On an average a strong gale moves at the rate of 40 miles an hour, a storm at about 56 and hurricanes at 90.

MARY SOMERVILLE *Physical Geog.* ch. 21, p. 287.

> The barbarous pit,
> Fanatical *on* hearsay, stamp and shout
> As if a miracle could be encored.
>
> LOWELL *The Cathedral* st. 10.

In this case the ship would be brought to *on* the starboard tack.   JAMES SMITH *Voyage of St. Paul* ch. 8, p. 107.

Candidates were received *on* trial.

ABEL STEVENS *Hist. Methodism* vol. ii, bk. v, ch. 10, p. 282.

His guest did not bore the viceroy. *On* the contrary, he amused him.   KIPLING *Plain Tales, Germ Destroyer* p. 84.

On the whole, no possible resource seems so little burdensome as this betterment tax.

J. RAE in *Contemporary Review* May, 1890, p. 660.

4. Connected with so as to form part of or be attached or appended to; comprised in; attached to; being a dependent or attendant of; engaged in the making of; as, he was *on* the general's staff; he is *on* the commission; a laborer *on* the public works.

> Tendant *on* each knight,
> Rode many a page and armor-bearer bold.
> Tasso *Jerusalem Delivered* tr. by Wiffen, can. 2, st. 57.

You will find them at the head of their respective classes, in the days when students took rank *on* the catalogue from their parents' condition.   Holmes *Autocrat* ch. 1, p. 24.

If any degree *on* the Centigrade scale, either above or below zero, be multiplied by 1.8, the result will, in either case, be the number of degrees above or below 82°, or the freezing point of Fahrenheit.   *U. S. Dispensatory* p. 1996.

He was . . . side-tackle *on* his college foot-ball team.
> *New-York Tribune* Oct. 20, 1891, p. 5, col. 4.

5. Having as a goal, end, or object: with reference to; attending to; directed toward; toward; against; as, to dote *on* (or *upon*) a child; to make war *on* (or *upon*) an enemy; to go *on* (or *upon*) an errand.

[Note.—In such cases the tendency is to use *upon* in reference to that which is more spiritual, solemn, or formal, and *on* in reference to the ordinary and commonplace. We should ordinarily say, she dotes *upon* that child; I am going *on* an errand; to make war *upon* the pirates. Yet this is not an invariable rule, as the shorter form may be preferred for force and vigor with reference to the greatest matters; as, "*on* God and godlike men we build our trust."]

Like schoolboys of old at a barring out, the Virginians resisted their government, not as ready for independence, but as resolved *on* a holiday.   Bancroft *U. S.* vol. iii, ch. 19, p. 80.

Birth, wealth, genius, and virtue could not have been bestowed in such eminent degree *on* any man without carrying with them the determination to assert their value.
> Motley *Dutch Republic* vol. i, pt. ii, ch. 5, p. 441.

And blushed as she gave it, looking down
On her feet so bare, and her tattered gown.
WHITTIER *Maud Muller* st. 11.

Our duty is to take all reasonable pains before we bestow money or material aid *on* persons unknown.
GLADDEN *Applied Christianity, Social Science* p. 225.

Napoleon's tactics of marching *on* the angle of an army, and always presenting a superiority of numbers, is the orator's secret also.
EMERSON *Society and Solitude* p. 78.

My eye dwelt with delight *on* neat cottages, with their trim shrubberies and green grass plots.
IRVING *Sketch-Book, The Voyage* p. 28.

6. Having or using as a means of sustenance, activity, or the like; as, to live *on* vegetables; to batten *on* garbage. Compare OFF, 4

Were the sums which are still lavished *on* ardent spirits appropriated wisely to the elevation of the people, what a new world we should live in! CHANNING *Works, Labor. Classes* p. 58.

The pitcher-plant is carnivorous, and thrives *on* animal diet.
C. VAN NORDEN *Outermost Rim* ch. 8, p. 86.

A young girl betrays, in a moment, that her eyes have been feeding *on* the face where you find them fixed.
HOLMES *Professor* ch. 7, p. 196.

The young lady who dines heartily *on* lamb has a sentimental horror of the butcher who killed it.
R. HILDRETH *The White Slave* ch. 5, p. 21.

The hero is not fed *on* sweets,   Daily his own heart he eats.
EMERSON *Heroism* l. 7.

We are literary cannibals, and our writers live *on* each other and each other's productions to a fearful extent.
HOLMES *Over the Teacups* ch. 2, p. 28.

7. Noting addition or accumulation: added to; as, thousands *on* thousands.

And every wimpling wavelet of the sea
Rolled a white edge of silver *on* the gloom.
EDWIN ARNOLD *Light of the World* bk. 1, p. 99.

Verbs and Other Antecedents

On (or *upon*) is used after :

(1) Verbs denoting dependence; as, *attend, calculate, count, depend, reckon, rely, repose, rest, wait.* *Believe* and *trust* were formerly used with *on* or *upon,* but are now used with *in.*

(2) Verbs of giving, imparting, inflicting, and the like; as, *bestow, confer, enjoin, entail, expend, inculcate, inflict, lavish, waste,* etc.

(3) Verbs denoting action directed toward some object; as, *call, look, smile,* etc. So a pursuer is said to *gain on* or *upon* a fugitive, or a fencer or boxer to *press on* or *upon* his antagonist, a battalion to *charge* or *move on* or *upon* the enemy. We say to *fight with* or *against,* but to *make war on* or *upon* (also *against*) an enemy. To *fall on* or *upon* is used of attack which tends to demolish its object. *Bet, pledge, venture* also take *on* or *upon* with the underlying idea of direction toward, perhaps also of dependence upon.

(4) Verbs of sustenance; as, *batten, fatten, feed, live, thrive,* etc.

Adjectives derived from or expressing the ideas of the verbs above cited take *on* or *upon; as, attendant, dependent,* etc. Addition, accumulation, crowding, etc., are denoted by *on* or *upon,* whose antecedent may be either verb, adjective, or noun.

Distinctions

About—of—on—upon : A person speaks *of* another if he merely mentions his name, or *of* a topic to which he incidentally refers. That which he speaks *about* he treats more at length. He tells some story *about* a person or expresses some opinion *about* a person or thing. But *about* commonly has a suggestion of discursiveness; the most fragmentary, random, careless, or incomplete talk or writing may be made *about* a matter. Pressing this suggestion to the extreme, Pope writes:

> Explain a thing till all men doubt it,
> And write *about* it, Goddess, and *about* it.
>
> *Dunciad* bk. iv, st. 1, l. 252.

That is, go round and round the subject without ever reaching its heart or essence. But a speech or treatise *on* or *upon* a subject is supposed to be methodical and somewhat complete, perhaps even exhaustive; as, the President sent to Congress a special message *on* reciprocity with Cuba.

OUT, OUT OF

Out as a preposition is colloquial or obsolete; as, to fall *out* the window. The phrase *out of* is now preferably used. The chief uses of this phrase are:

1. Denoting source or origin: proceeding from; from.

> I am a word *out of* the speechless years,
> The tongue of time, that no man sleeps who hears.
> <div align="right">SWINBURNE <i>Tiresias</i> pt. i, st. 22.</div>

His nature had attributes as glorious as the music born *out of* them.   W. R. ALGER *Solitudes, Beethoven* p. 268.

Certificates are, for the most part, like ostrich eggs; the giver never knows what is hatched *out of* them.
HOLMES Elsie Venner ch. 2, p. 82.

Out of too much learning become mad.   BURTON *Anatomy of Melancholy* pt. iii, § 4, memb. 1, subsec. 2, l. 652.

The science of anatomy has grown almost wholly *out of* the exposure of the frame to suffering.
CHANNING Works, Death of Dr. Follen p. 608.

A genuine antique, fished up, . . . *out of* the wreck of the old world. FROUDE *Short Studies, Dissolution of Monasteries* first series, p. 888.

> Dipping the jewels *out of* the sea,
> To sprinkle them over the land in showers.
> <div align="right">ALDRICH <i>Before the Rain</i> st. 2.</div>

2. Denoting material, substance, or the like: of.

It is the office of high art to create music *out of* sound, poetry *out of* words, beauty *out of* colors, and form *out of* matter.
J. PULSFORD Supremacy of Man bk. ii, ch. 8, p. 84.

You cannot make an association *out of* insincere men.
CARLYLE Heroes and Hero-Worship lect. iv, p. 150.

Syllabism, the next stage in the progress of writing, finds its best illustration in the development of the Japanese writing *out of* the Chinese.   ISAAC TAYLOR *The Alphabet* vol. i, ch. 1, p. 88.

3. Denoting separation: away from; from; outside of; beyond.

He spent his last years in his own Land of Beulah, Doubting Castle *out of* sight, and the towers and minarets of Emmanuel Land growing nearer and clearer as the days went on.

FROUDE John Bunyan ch. 6, p. 86.

Specialists who never look beyond their own domain are apt to see things *out of* true proportion.

A. MARSHALL Principles of Economics vol. i, bk. i, ch. 5, p. 72.

Resistance to a Turk is now, and has for generations been, so certain to end in assassination, that thought of resistance has almost died *out of* the Christian mind.

D. S. GREGORY in Princeton Review Jan., 1878, p. 69.

London *out of* season seemed still full of life; Paris *out of* season looked vacuous and torpid.

HOLMES Our Hundred Days ch. 7, p. 271.

So here shall silence guard thy fame;
But somewhere *out of* human view.
Whate'er thy hands are set to do
Is wrought with tumult of acclaim.

TENNYSON In Memoriam lxxiv, st. 5.

Gloster: The state is *out of* tune; distracting fears,
And jealous doubts, jar in our public councils.

ROWE Jane Shore act iii.

My old Friend started, and recovering *out of* his brown study, told Sir Andrew, that once in his life he had been in the right.

BUDGELL Spectator Apr. 22, 1712.

It is not in human nature to wink wholly *out of* sight the rights of a fellow-creature.   CHANNING *Works, Slavery* ch. 2, p. 704.

Take a brute *out of* his instinct, and you find him wholly deprived of understanding.   ADDISON *Spectator* July 18, 1711.

She had twelve intimate and bosom friends *out of* the twenty-four young ladies.   THACKERAY *Vanity Fair* p. 10.

OUTSIDE

Outside is a modern word compounded of *out* and *side*.

On or to the exterior of; beyond the limit of; from; out of; without; as, persons waiting *outside* the gate.

[The adverb with *of*, *outside of*, is in very common use.]

Outside his own domain, and unprotected, he was a very sheep for the shearers. He would have taken his gaiters off his legs, to give away.   DICKENS *David Copperfield* ch. 16, p. 119.

Antiquity, *outside* the Jewish world, had no conception of what we call sin.   GEIKIE *Life of Christ* ch. 1, p. 7.

OVER

Over is derived from the Anglo-Saxon *ofer*, having the general meaning of above. It is often, especially in poetry, abbreviated to *o'er*.

I. Of place or space :

1. Vertically above; higher than; hanging or seeming to hang, rest, or move above, or look down upon; as, the sky is *over* our heads; it is good to have a roof *over* us; the cliff hangs *over* the sea.

> Where the katydid works her chromatic reed
> On the walnut-tree *over* the well.
>   WALT WHITMAN *Leaves of Grass* pt. xxxiii, st. 196.

The golden-rod and the aster hung their plumage *over* the rough, rocky road.   H. B. STOWE *Oldtown Folks* ch. 8, p. 102.

There rose *over* the forecastle bulwarks, not the broad hats of peaceful buscarles, but peaked helmets.
    KINGSLEY *Hereward* ch. 6, p. 84.

The arms of the family, carved in freestone, frowned *over* the gateway.   SCOTT *Guy Mannering* ch. 4, p. 24.

[NOTE.—For the phrase *over one's signature*, etc., contrasted with *under one's signature*, etc., see UNDER, III., 5, note.]

2. Upon the surface or exterior of, without special reference to elevation, so as to cover or protect; as, to put an outer coat *over* one's other garments.

[The same idea controls in such compounds as *overalls, over-shoes*, etc.]

Over his tunic flowed a loose eastern robe, . . . glowing in the richest hues of the Tyrian dye.

BULWER-LYTTON *Last Days of Pompeii* bk. v, ch. 1, p. 835.

Over her breast she wore a stomacher of cloth of gold.

HOWELLS *Venetian Life* ch. 19, p. 309.

3. Upon in such a way as to be supported by or suspended from; as, to sling a musket *over* one's shoulders; to throw a cloak *over* one's arm. (Compare ON, I., 2.)

Shocks of yellow hair, like the silken floss of the maize, hung
Over his shoulders.   LONGFELLOW *Evangeline* pt. iii, l. 3.

4. So as to pass or extend across; in motion above or on the surface of; so as to occupy a position on the farther side of; so as to pass across; across; as, to leap *over* a wall; to sail *over* a lake; to dash water *over* a window-pane.

The shallow fishing-boat glides safely *over* the reefs where the noble bark strands.

ROBERTSON *Sermons* second series, ser. xv, p. 368.

5. Reaching to a higher point than, so as to rise above, cover, or submerge; as, the water is *over* my shoes.

A man may go *over* shoes in the grime of it.

SHAKESPEARE *Comedy of Errors* act iii, sc. 2, l. 104.

6. Here and there upon; traversing the surface of; throughout the extent of; touching, affecting, or noting many points throughout the whole extent of; as, to wander *over* the world; the mud was splashed *over* the garment; to glance *over* a document.

The English language is fast being diffused *over* the whole earth.   HOLLIS READ *Hand of God in Hist.* ch. 9, p. 162.

Not a day passes *over* the earth, but men and women of no note do great deeds, speak great words, and suffer noble sorrows.

CHARLES READE *Cloister and Hearth* ch. 1, p. 5.

Light as an elf,
Or wisp that flits *o'er* a morass.

BYRON *Vision of Judgment* st. 105.

II. Of time: during the continuance of; throughout the duration of; to the end of and beyond; as, to stay *over* night; to keep seed-corn *over* winter.

If any thing be wanting for a smith, let it be done *over* night.
Swift *Directions to Servants, Works* vol. vi.

III. Of various relations, often closely analogous to the meanings respecting place:

1. In higher power, authority, or station than; in command or control of; with authority as to; as, the senior officer takes rank *over* the junior; he placed a colonel *over* the regiment.

And he said unto him that was *over* the vestry, Bring forth vestments for all the worshippers of Baal.   *2 Kings* x, 22.

The less of power given to man *over* man, the better.
Channing *Works, Introductory Remarks* p. 9.

2. In higher estimation, excellence, dignity, or value than; in superiority to; surpassing; as, the advantages of the educated *over* the ignorant.

The advantage which old persons possess *over* young ones is experience.   Lieber *Pol. Eth.* vol. ii, bk. iii, ch. 7, p. 105.

3. With supremacy above, as the result of opposition, contest, or controversy; in spite of; notwithstanding; as, to triumph *over* one's enemies; to exult *over* the vanquished; to be victorious *over* temptation.

> Could'st thou boast, O child of weakness!
>   *O'er* the sons of wrong and strife,
> Were their strong temptations planted
>   In thy path of life?
> Whittier *What the Voice Said* st. 8.

Revenge triumphs *over* death; love slights it; honour aspireth to it.   Bacon *Works, Essays, Of Death* p. 262.

4. With consideration of or concern about; with solicitude for; with reference to; about; concerning; as, to watch *over* one's children; to grieve *over* the past; to talk *over* one's affairs; to fret *over* trifles.

> The king,
> His brother, and yours, abide all three distracted,
> And the remainder mourning *over* them.
>> SHAKESPEARE *The Tempest* act v, sc. 1, l. 18.

> I chatter *over* stony ways,   In little sharps and trebles.
>> TENNYSON *The Brook* st. 6.

5. Reaching above or beyond in quantity or amount; in excess of; more than; as, *over* $1,000.

[In this sense the expression *more than* is generally preferable.   *Standard Dictionary.*]

Madame de Villedeuil became indebted to Madame Eloffe to the extent of *over* two hundred livres for a presentation dress.
>> *Fortnightly Review* vol. xlii, p. 287.

6. Pending the enjoyment or participation of; while engaged in or partaking of; as, the bargain was made *over* a bottle of wine.

> *Capulet:*   Peace, you mumbling fool!
> Utter your gravity *o'er* a gossip's bowl,
> For here we need it not.
>> SHAKESPEARE *Romeo and Juliet* act iii, sc. 5, l. 178.

I am certain that nothing can be truly imputed to me beyond some foolish talk *over* a bottle.
>> MACAULAY *England* vol. ii, p. 898.

X—Prepositions Defined and Illustrated

PARTICIPIAL PREPOSITIONS

Many participles, as *barring, bating, concerning, considering, during, excepting, notwithstanding, past, pending, regarding, respecting, saving, touching*, etc., are used without direct connection with a subject, and with the force of prepositions; as, I spoke with him *concerning* this. Verbal or prepositional phrases may often be substituted for these terms; thus, *as concerns* may be used for *concerning; in consideration of* for *considering; as regards, in* or *with regard to* for *regarding; as respects, in* or *with respect to* for *respecting.*

Concerning may be exactly rendered by *about*, though not coextensive with the latter word. *Considering* is commonly used in a depreciatory sense, implying allowance for or deduction of the things considered; as, he did well *considering* his age, or *considering* the difficulties he had to meet.

See DURING, PAST, PENDING in alphabetical place.

See EXCEPTING under EXCEPT and SAVING under SAVE.

Notwithstanding is used as a preposition by a reversal of the participial construction. Thus, "He arrived, all hindrances *not withstanding*" becomes prepositionally, "He arrived *notwithstanding* all hindrances."

In answer to the question sometimes raised, whether *in regard to* and *in respect to* are correct expressions, or whether *with regard to, with respect to* should not be preferred, it should be said, first, that *in regard to* and *in respect to* are accepted idiomatic expressions used by the best writers and speakers; and, secondly, that *in* in such expressions is not used in the sense of inclusion, but of reference or relation, as in the phrase *in relation to*. *In* in such phrases might almost be rendered by *having; as, having reference, relation*, etc., *to.*

PAST

Past, originally the past participle of the verb *pass*, has acquired such complete independence of its verb that it may well be treated independently as a preposition.

I. Of place or space: beyond in position; farther than; by and beyond; by; as, I walked *past* the house; we have gone *past* the gate.

> *Past* the pebbly beach the boat did flee
> On sidelong wing into a silent cove.
> SHELLEY Revolt of Islam can. 8, st. 84.

Friedrich brushes *past* the Liegnitz Garrison, leaves Liegnitz and it a trifle to the right.
CARLYLE Frederick vol. v, bk. xviii, ch. 9, p. 186.

II. Of time: to or at a later period than; later than; beyond; after; as, it is *past* noon; it is *past* the hour.

> What is the time o' the day?
> *Ari.*: *Past* the mid season.
> SHAKESPEARE The Tempest act. i, sc. 2, l. 239.

I received them handsomely at half-*past* seven, as the modern English now is.   JOHN HOADLEY in Garrick's *Private Correspondence, Letter of Sept. 19, 1773.*

III. In general: beyond the reach, scope, influence, or enjoyment of; as, *past* endurance; *past* hope; *past* remedy.

> The Dog-star rages! nay, 'tis *past* a doubt,
> All Bedlam, or Parnassus, is let out.
> POPE Epistle to Dr. Arbuthnot l. 8.

PENDING

Pending, though strictly the present participle of *pend*, await, is used so independently of its verb as to require special treatment as a preposition.

Of time exclusively:

1. During the continuance of; during; in the period covered by; as, *pending* debate.

However, he locked him up and had him sent to the West Side Court yesterday morning, where he was held *pending* investigation of his statement of forgery.

The New York Times Nov. 16, 1908.

2. During the time intervening before; while expecting or awaiting; as, *pending* decision.

The court met and adjourned *pending* the receipt of orders from the convening authority.

CHARLES KING *Two Soldiers* ch. 17, p. 118.

Pending the rule for the new trial, Mr. Quirk greatly increased the allowance of Titmouse.

CYRUS TOWNSEND BRADY *Tittlebat Titmouse* ch. xv, p. 171.

PER

Per is a Latin preposition signifying *by, by means of, through.* It is correctly used as part of certain Latin phrases; as, *per centum*, by the hundred (abbreviated usually to *per cent.*); *per annum*, by the year; *per contra*, on the contrary; *per diem*, by the day; *per se*, by himself, or itself (most commonly used as meaning *in itself*; considered by itself alone; simply as such; in its own nature without reference to its relations; as, cruelty is a sin *per se*).   Compare VIA.

The use of *per* as an English preposition in such phrases as *per day, per gallon, per yard, per steamer, per invoice*, is condemned on the ground that the joining of a Latin with an English word to form a phrase is a barbarism.   Some of these phrases are, however, so convenient that they are likely to hold their own, at least in commercial life, especially since they may plead as examples the use of the Greek preposition *anti* and the Latin preposition *ex* as English formatives, as in *anti*-expansionist, *ex*-president.

ROUND

See AROUND.

10

SAVE, SAVING

Save, the imperative, and *saving*, the present participle (compare PARTICIPIAL PREPOSITIONS), of the verb *save*, are used with the force of prepositions, exactly equivalent to *except* or *excepting*, i. e., with the exception of.

> There is nothing in Heaven or earth beneath
> *Save* God and man.
>> WHITTIER *My Soul and I* st. 85.

In Virginia none could vote *save* those who possessed such a freehold of fifty acres.   FISKE *Crit. Period Am. Hist.* ch. 8, p. 70.

> In the field of thought, nothing *save* the chaff perishes.
>> W. FRASER *Blending Lights* ch. 1, p. 11.

Saving has the further use, though this has now become rare, of signifying without disrespect to; as, *saving* your highness, *saving* your presence.

> *Gremio:*   *Saving* your tale, Petruchio, I pray,
>   Let us, that are poor petitioners, speak too.
>> SHAKESPEARE *The Taming of the Shrew* act ii, sc. 1, l. 72.

> You, that have so fair parts of woman on you,
> Have too a woman's heart; which ever yet
> Affected eminence, wealth, sovereignty:
> Which, to say sooth, are blessings, and which gifts
> (*Saving* your mincing) the capacity
> Of your soft cheveril conscience would receive,
> If you might please to stretch it.
>> SHAKESPEARE *K. Henry VIII.* act ii, sc. 3, l. 31

SINCE

Since is derived from the Anglo-Saxon *siththan*, from *sith*, after, plus *tham*, dative of *thæt*, that, thus signifying *after that*.

Of time exclusively: during or within the time after; ever after; at a time after; from or after the time, occurrence, or existence of; as, it is ten years *since* we began business; I have been here ever *since* I came.

I escaped upon a butt of sack, which the sailors heaved over-
board, by this bottle! which I made of the bark of a tree, with
mine own hands, *since* I was cast ashore.

> SHAKESPEARE *The Tempest* act ii, sc. 2, l. 124.

But *since* she did neglect her looking-glass, . . .
The air hath starv'd the roses in her cheeks.

> SHAKESPEARE *Two Gentlemen of Verona* act iv, sc. 4, l. 154.

My hunger and the shadows together tell me that the sun
has done much travel *since* I fell asleep.

> GEORGE ELIOT *Romola* ch. 10, p. 107.

One thousand eight hundred years *since* their creation, the
Pagan tales of Ovid . . . are read by all Christendom.

> DE QUINCEY *Essays on the Poets, Pope* p. 157.

Amongst mammals, the urus has become extinct from Europe
since the time of Cæsar.   WINCHELL *Preadamites* ch. 27, p. 488.

Since Jeremy Taylor and Richard Baxter, English Protes-
tantism has had no great casuists. *Good Words* May, 1867, p. 829.

Never, *since* the beginning of opera, had the like charivari
greeted the ears of men.   J. MORLEY *Rousseau* p. 59.

Since is often used after an indication of time in a way that
may be explained as an elliptical use of a preposition, but may
be preferably classed as an adverb, equivalent to *ago*; as, many
years *since*; not long *since*.

King: . . . How long is't, count,
    Since the physician at your father's died?
    He was much fam'd.
Ber.:   Some six months *since*, my lord.

> SHAKESPEARE *All's Well that Ends Well* act i, sc. 2, l. 70.

Married three years *since*: how his Countship sulks!

> BROWNING *Ring and Book* bk. vi, l. 415.

THROUGH

Through is from the Anglo-Saxon *thurh*, used in the same
sense.

I. Of place or space:

1. From limit to limit of, as from end to end or side to side; into on one side and out at the other; as, the road runs *through* the village; the nail went *through* his hand; to see *through* glass, air, or water.

> The sun *through* heaven descending
> Like a red and burning cinder.
> > LONGFELLOW *Hiawatha* pt. v, st. 14.

> As an Æolian harp *through* gusty doors
> Of some old ruin its wild music pours.
> > LONGFELLOW *Wayside Inn, Falcon of Ser Federigo* st. 4, l. 18.

> And suddenly *through* the drifting brume
> The blare of the horns began to ring.
> > LONGFELLOW *Wayside Inn, King Olaf's War-Horns* st. 2.

> Old Andes thrusts yon craggy spear
> *Through* the gray clouds.
> > WORDSWORTH *Peter Bell* prol., st. 12.

Self-love is a cup without any bottom, and you might pour the Great Lakes all *through* it, and never fill it up.
> > HOLMES *Mortal Antipathy* ch. 10, p. 188.

The stream that winds *through* Grasmere vale . . . is of great beauty—clean, bright, full, trouty.
> > BURROUGHS in *Century Magazine* Jan., 1884, p. 419.

> And *through* the dark arch a charger sprang.
> > LOWELL *Vision of Sir Launfal* pt. i, st. 8.

If I undertake to look *through* a drop of water, I may be arrested at first, indeed, by the sports and struggles of animalcular life. HOLLAND *Lessons in Life* lesson xi, p. 151.

Through every rift of discovery some seeming anomaly drops out of the darkness. E. H. CHAPIN *Living Words* p. 80.

> And these articulated veins *through* which
> Our heart drives blood !
> > E. B. BROWNING *Aurora Leigh* bk. v, l. 119

He walked fast, hunted by his fears, chattering to himself, skulking *through* the less frequented thoroughfares.
> > R. L. STEVENSON *Dr. Jekyll and Mr. Hyde* ch. 10, p. 77.

Malcolm . . . clomb the narrow duct of an ancient stone stair that went screwing like a great auger *through* the pile from top to bottom.   MacDonald *Malcolm* ch. 44, p. 80.

This magnet is sustained by a very strong axle of adamant passing *through* its middle, upon which it plays.
Swift *Works, Gulliver* pt. iii, ch. 8, p. 169.

By forced and rapid marches We took the shortest way,
A crow-flight *through* the Jerseys,   And added night to day.
R. H. Stoddard *Ballad of Valley Forge* st. 22.

In every city *through* which he [Lincoln] passed, he was greeted with enthusiasm.
J. S. C. Abbott *Lives of the Presidents* ch. 16, p. 404.

We will blaze the trees, and mark our track *through* the forest for you.   Stanley *In Darkest Africa* vol. i, ch. 6, p. 125.

A hole was stove, *through* which daylight and sea poured in alternately.
Harriet Martineau *Biographical Sketches* pt. iii, ch. 6 p. 209.

Cerberus, cruel monster, fierce and strange,
Through his wide three-fold throat, barks as a dog.
Dante *Vision* tr. by H. F. Cary *Hell* can. 6, l. 12.

2. Over or into all parts or portions of; from point to point or part to part of; in all directions in or over; throughout; as, to look *through* a report; to travel *through* Europe; the shock was felt *through* his system; his fame spread *through* all lands.

Through every fibre of my brain,
Through every nerve, *through* every vein
I feel the electric thrill, the touch
Of life that seems almost too much.
Longfellow *A Day of Sunshine* st. 2.

It is better, in going *through* the world, to have the arms chafed in that narrow passage than the temper.
Dickens *Christmas Stories, Battle of Life* pt. ii, p. 94.

And then we stroll'd
For half the day *thro'* stately theatres
Bench'd crescent-wise.   Tennyson *Princess* ii, st. 10.

He heard the baffled dogs in vain
Rave *through* the hollow pass amain.
> SCOTT *Lady of the Lake* can. 1, st. 8.

Stray warblers in the branches dark
Shot *through* the leafy passes.
> MARY M. DODGE *In the Cañon* st. 2.

For this purpose, he distributed his warriors *through* the adjacent forests; and waylaid every pass.
> IRVING *Columbus* vol. ii, bk. viii, ch. 3, p. 86.

The colors were borne in triumph *through* the streets of London, . . . and were put up as trophies in St. Paul's Cathedral.
> IRVING *Washington* vol. i, ch. 28, p. 246.

The praise thrilled *through* every fibre of his big body. and made it tingle with pleasure.
> THACKERAY *Vanity Fair* vol. i, ch. 8, p. 26.

A low chant Swelled *through* the hollow arches of the roof.
> N. P. WILLIS *The Leper* st. 8.

A shock or vibration passing *through* the brain proves more destructive than a wound penetrating its substance.
> CHARLES BELL *Anatomy of Expression* essay ii, p. 46.

Where *through* the long-drawn aisle and fretted vault
The pealing anthem swells the note of praise.
> GRAY *Elegy* st. 10.

Pure rills *through* vales of verdure warbling go.
> BEATTIE *The Minstrel* bk. i, st. 59.

3. In the midst of; having as the medium of motion or passage; along; among; within; as, the bird flies *through* the air; the ship sped *through* the water; to stroll *through* the woods.

> Love will find its way
Through paths where wolves would fear to prey.
> BYRON *Giaour* st. 82.

And ghastly *thro'* the drizzling rain
On the bald street breaks the blank day.
> TENNYSON *In Memoriam* vii, st. 8

Through Solway sands, *through* Tarras moss,
Blindfold, he knew the paths to cross.
> SCOTT *Lay of the Last Minstrel* can. 1, st. 21.

Sometimes it struggles *through* rugged barrancos, or ravines, worn by winter torrents. IRVING *Alhambra* p. 15.

Regiments of turkeys were gobbling *through* the farmyard.
IRVING *Sketch-Book, Sleepy Hollow* p. 427.

All night the surges of the warm southwest
Boomed intermittent *through* the shuddering elms.
LOWELL *The Cathedral* st. 4.

Who can say what telegraphic communication there may be *through* our atmosphere, and without wires?
W. M. BAKER *His Majesty, Myself* ch. 10, p. 87.

This action of the English Regicides did in effect strike a damp like death *through* the heart of flunkeyism universally in this world. CARLYLE *Cromwell* vol. i, pt. iv, p. 828.

In rhythmic motion *through* the dewy grass The mowers swept.
HOLLAND *Kathrina, Childhood and Youth* st. 15.

Through thistle, bent, and tangled fern The startled Cony flits.
HOOD *The Elm Tree* pt. iii, st. 4.

II. Of time : from the first to the last of; from the beginning to the end of; during the whole period of; as, I shall stay *through* the season; it will affect him *through* life.

The original belief respecting the form of the Earth was wrong; and this wrong belief survived *through* the first civilization. SPENCER *Biology* vol. i, § 110, p. 883.

All God's works of providence, *through* all the ages, meet at last, as so many lines in one center.
EDWARDS *Redemption* period iii, ch. 10, p. 485.

III. Of various relations :

1. Over all the steps of; from entrance into to emergence from; into and out of; from the first to the last of; as, to go *through* college; to go *through* a course of training; to pass *through* a varied experience.

The fortune-teller . . . shuffles *through* her meagre and cheerless years, an object alike of suspicion and of contempt.
J. H. BROWNE *Great Metropolis* ch. 14. p. 146.

The priest gabbled *through* the baptismal formula.
> AMELIA B. EDWARDS *Barbara's History* ch. 50, p. 188.

My thinned ranks told the woeful tale of the fierce struggles, indescribable by words, *through* which my division had passed since 7 o'clock in the morning.
> P. H. SHERIDAN *Personal Memoirs* vol. i, ch. 18, p. 235.

To gallop *through* book after book is to turn intellectual Gilpins.
> GEIKIE *Entering on Life, Reading* p. 243.

He [the business man] opens his newspaper and reads it as he swallows his breakfast. . . . In the train he tears *through* the rest of his newspaper.
> R. DOWLING *Indolent Essays, Holiday Making* p. 12.

To walk with you *through* the Fair, . . . and that we should all come home after the flare, and the noise, and the gayety.
> THACKERAY *Vanity Fair* ch. 19, p. 118.

2. Having as an intermediate term, step, or process; by way of; as, to pass *through* youth to manhood.

Fires gleam warmly *through* some of the windows.
> DICKENS *Bleak House* ch. 12, p. 194.

To a clear eye the smallest fact is a window *through* which the Infinite may be seen.   HUXLEY *Lay Sermons* ch. 6, p. 104.

Pantheism and Monotheism are necessary stages, *through* which human thought passes on its way to Christianity.
> CAIRD *Kant* vol. ii, bk. i, ch. 18, p. 128.

The wine bodega in the south of Spain is not a cellar, but a lofty and capacious store, built on a level with the ground, and entered *through* a preliminary court or garden.
> H. VIZETELLY *Facts about Sherry* ch. 2, p. 22.

Our apartment . . . looked out *through* a great apple-tree.
> HARRIET B. STOWE *Oldtown Folks* ch. 38, p. 428.

> Yet sometimes glimpses on my sight,
> *Through* present wrong, the eternal right.
> WHITTIER *Chapel of the Hermits* st. 11.

3. Having as a means or instrument or aid; by means of; as, he spoke *through* an interpreter; this misfortune came *through* you; the purchase was made *through* a third party.

The old political wire-pullers never go near the man they want to gain, if they can help it; they find out who his intimates and managers are, and work *through* them.
> HOLMES *Elsie Venner* ch. 14, p. 249.

He conquering *through* God, and God by him.
> WORDSWORTH *Poems to Liberty, Siege of Vienna* l. 14.

The interior beauty of a soul *through* habitual kindliness of thought is greater than our words can tell.
> F. W. FABER *Spiritual Conferences, Kindness* ch. 2, p. 49.

Examination *through* a good binocular informed us . . . why so much snow was retained on Ruwenzori.
> STANLEY *In Darkest Africa* vol. ii, ch. 30, p. 325.

4. On account of; by reason of; because of; as, he became helpless *through* fear.

England lost her American Colonies *through* her blind conservatism and *through* the domineering, greedy, and insular egotism of her old Colonial system.
> *Westminster Review* Aug., 1891, p. 116.

He . . . became a commercial traveler, but lost his berth *through* drink.   WM. BOOTH *In Darkest Eng.* pt. ii, p. 185.

THROUGHOUT

Throughout is *through* strengthened by *out*, signifying through in the fullest extent; through and in every part of; from beginning to end of; through and through; all through; as, terror spread *throughout* the city.

I have endeavoured *throughout* the body of this whole discourse that every former part might give strength unto all that follow.   HOOKER *Ecclesiastical Polity* bk. i, p. 59.

Ghiberti's fame now spread *throughout* Italy.
H. GRIMM *Michael Angelo* tr. by F. E. Bunnétt, vol. i, ch. 1, p. 38.

TILL, UNTIL

Till is derived from the Icelandic *til*, to, till. *Until* is from *unto* with the substitution of *til* for *to*. The two words *till* and *until* are used with no perceptible difference of meaning.

Of time exclusively: to the time of; as far as; up to; as, I shall remain *till* September; good *till* used; he watched *until* midnight.

No nation can be perfectly well governed *till* it is competent to govern itself.   MACAULAY *Speeches, July 10, 1833* p. 147.

Men are all conservatives; everything new is impious, *till* we get accustomed to it.   KINGSLEY *Yeast* ch. 2, p. 29.

A Probability stands in place of a Demonstration *till* a greater Probability can be brought to shoulder it out.   JOSEPH MEDE *Works, Passages in the Apocalypse* bk. iii, ch. 3, p. 586.

Goethe used to work *till* eleven without taking anything [to eat], then he drank a cup of chocolate and worked *till* one.   HAMERTON *Intell. Life* pt. i, letter iii, p. 15.

Soft fell the shades, *till* Cynthia's slender bow
Crested the farthest wave, then sunk below.
     MONTGOMERY *West Indies* pt. i, st. 8.

Old furniture was waxed *till* it shone like a mirror.
     MARGARET J. PRESTON *Aunt Dorothy* ch. 6, p. 72.

Self-denial is never a complete virtue *till* it becomes a kind of self-indulgence.   BUSHNELL *Work and Play* lect. i, p. 16.

I don't desire my biography to be written *till* I am dead.
     W. T. SHERMAN *Memoirs* vol. i, ch. 11, p. 269.

Till an ocean interposes its mighty barriers, no citadel of freedom or truth has long been maintained.   EVERETT *Orations and Speeches, First Settlement of New England* p. 45.

Chimneys were unknown in such dwellings [cottages] *till* the early part of Elizabeth's reign.
     HALLAM *Middle Ages* ch. 9, pt. ii, p. 492.

Mail armor continued in general use *till* about the year 1800.
     BULFINCH *Age of Chivalry* pt. i, ch. 1, p. 22.

The spider . . . commits her weight to no thread . . . *till* she has pulled on it with her arms, and proved its strength.
     GUTHRIE *Gospel in Ezekiel* ser. iv, p. 71.

We . . . made the trunk glacier our highway *until* we reached the point of confluence of its branches.
     TYNDALL *Hours of Exercise* ch. 22, p. 260.

Society can never prosper, but must always be bankrupt *until* every man does that which he was created to do.

EMERSON Conduct of Life, Wealth p. 92.

Sir Isaac Newton humbly said that he had one talent, the ability to look steadily at a problem *until* he saw it through.

E. S. PHELPS Struggle for Immortality p. 215

TO, UNTO

To is from the Anglo-Saxon *to*, used in the same sense. *Unto* is used as the exact equivalent of *to* in all senses except as the sign of the infinitive, but is now archaic, and in modern speech practically unused except in poetry or elevated style. *To* and *unto* are used interchangeably in the authorized version of the Bible.

As *to* the Lord and not *unto* men.   *Gal.* iii, 28.

The meanings of *to* must be rather classified than defined.

[*To* is an elementary word not susceptible of formal definition in any of its various uses except by the employment of its derivative *toward*, or in its place a long and awkward periphrasis.   *Standard Dictionary.*]

To may be termed the preposition of tendency, aim, or destination.

I. Of place or space:

1. Denoting motion or action in the direction of and terminating in a place or object: noting tendency and terminus; in the direction of and terminating at or in; toward so as to reach; as, he went *to* London; the fruit fell *to* the ground.

Come *to* me soon at night.

SHAKESPEARE Merry Wives of Windsor act ii, sc. 2, l. 278.

First go with me *to* church, and call me wife,
And then away *to* Venice *to* your friend.

SHAKESPEARE The Merchant of Venice act iii, sc. 2, l. 305.

Ah! that is the ship from over the sea,
That is bringing my lover back *to* me.

LONGFELLOW Maiden and Weathercock st. 3.

> Come *to* us, love us, and make us your own.
>> TENNYSON *A Welcome to Alexandra* l. 28

> And the stately ships go on
> *To* their haven under the hill.
>> TENNYSON *Break, Break, Break* st. 3.

> Count each affliction, whether light or grave,
> God's messenger sent down *to* thee.
>> AUBREY THOMAS DE VERE *Affliction* st. 1.

> Quick *to* the abandoned wheel Arion came
> The ship's tempestuous sallies to reclaim.
>> WILLIAM FALCONER *Wrecked in the Tempest* l. 5.

2. Denoting position: in or tending to close connection or contact with; touching or pressing; by; against; on; upon; as, the child clung *to* his mother; the bird's nest is fastened *to* the limb; pressed *to* one's heart; frozen *to* the surface.

> How they keep their place of vantage,
> Cleaving firmly *to* the rock.
>> AYTOUN *The Island of the Scots* st. 9.

The brushes which are applied *to* the armature are maintained at different potentials when the machine is in action.
> C. F. BRACKETT in *Electricity in Daily Life* ch. 1, p. 4.

In civilized nations the greatest part of mankind are . . . fixtures *to* the soil on which they are born.

JEREMY BENTHAM *Works, International Law* in vol. ii, p. 542.

> Cannon *to* right of them,
> Cannon *to* left of them,
> Cannon in front of them
> Volleyed and thundered.
>> TENNYSON *Charge of the Light Brigade* st. 3.

II. Of time:

As far as; till the end of; for the utmost duration of; till; until; throughout; as, ten minutes *to* twelve; *to* all eternity.

Some venerable specimens of the domestic architecture of the middle ages bear *to* this day the marks of popular violence.
> MACAULAY *England* vol. ii, ch. 10, p. 439.

They go croaking *to* the end of their days, when, reptile-like, they crawl out of life.
> H. W. BEECHER *Pulpit Pungencies* No. cxxi, p. 84.

The hen clucks and broods her chickens, unconscious that *to* the end of the world she is part and parcel of a revelation of God to man.   T. W. Handford *H. W. Beecher, Grand Call to Labor* p. 118.

He wore his hair, *to* the last, powdered and frizzed out.
                    Lamb *Essays of Elia, South-Sea House* p. 4.

The new Latin tongues have pagan roots that retain vitality *to* this day.   D. H. Wheeler *By-Ways of Lit.* ch. 9, p. 181.

To the last the genuine Roman never quitted Rome even for a few months without a wrench to his feelings.
                    Merivale *Gen. Hist. Rome* ch. 22, p. 179.

Thou hast not left me, oft as I left Thee.
On *to* the close, O Lord, abide with me!
                    Henry Francis Lyte *Abide with Me* st. 5.

II. Of various relations:

1. Denoting the object, result, end, or goal of an action, whether it be a person, a thing, an abstract quality, or the like, without reference to locality, and used in a great variety of relations, where many other languages would employ the dative case; as, true *to* his master; devoted *to* his religion; an inclination *to* literary pursuits; driven *to* madness; give it *to* me; the matter is important *to* me; submission *to* the inevitable.

To perform the mercy promised *to* our fathers.   *Luke* i, 72.

They said, What is that *to* us? see thou *to* that. *Matt.* xxvii, 4.

All they that dwelt at Lydda and Saron saw him, and turned *to* the Lord.   *Acts* ix, 85.

That they may have right *to* the tree of life.   *Rev.* xxii, 14.

I will be deaf *to* pleading and excuses.
                    Shakespeare *Romeo and Juliet* act iii, sc. 1, l. 196.

'Zounds! a dog, a rat, a mouse, a cat, to scratch a man *to* death!   Shakespeare *Romeo and Juliet* act iii, sc. 1, l. 104.

If thou dost find him tractable *to* us.
                    Shakespeare *K. Richard III.* act iii, sc. 1, l. 174.

True religion is, at its soul, spiritual sympathy with, spiritual obedience *to* God.
                    Phillips Brooks *Light of the World* ser. v, p. 77.

2. Denoting an end to be accomplished or a result reached or to be reached, a goal attained, destination, design, purpose, aim, or the like: aiming at; resulting in; as, tempted *to* his ruin; roused *to* splendid daring; apprenticed *to* a trade; born *to* trouble; broken *to* saddle; sown *to* wheat.

> I love to give myself up *to* the illusions of poetry.
> IRVING *Sketch-Book, Boar's Head Tavern* p. 145.

3. Denoting that on account of which an obligation is incurred: under obligation respecting; in behalf of; for; toward; as, my duty *to* the church; (in accounting) debtor [Dr.] because of; as, *To* medical attendance $5.

> Free, and *to* none accountable.
> MILTON *Paradise Lost* bk. ii, l. 255.

> *To* twenty poor widows he left two guineas each.
> JAS. PARTON *People's Biography, John Howard* p. 73.

4. In opposition toward; against; opposing, matching, equaling, or confronting; as, face *to* face; the battle was fought hand *to* hand; the betting was ten *to* one.

> What! am I dar'd, and bearded *to* my face?
> SHAKESPEARE *1 K. Henry VI.* act 1, sc. 3.

> Follow us: who knows? we four may build some plan
> Foursquare *to* opposition.   TENNYSON *Princess* v, st. 4.

> Now, man *to* man, and steel *to* steel,
> A chieftain's vengeance thou shalt feel.
> SCOTT *Lady of the Lake* can. 5, st. 12.

The Prince . . . objected *to* the use of the word 'pardon' on the ground that he had never done anything requiring his Majesty's forgiveness.   MOTLEY *Dutch Republic* vol. iii, p. 5.

We are immediately conscious in perception of an ego and a non-ego, known together, and known in contrast *to* each other.
> HAMILTON *Metaphysics* lect. xvi, p. 200.

[Patronage in offices] is utterly abhorrent *to* the ideas on which the . . . government of the United States has been founded.
> H. C. LODGE in *Century Magazine* Oct., 1890, p. 840

To the superstitions that pass under the name of religion, science is antagonistic.   Spencer *Education* ch. 1, p. 90.

The executive government was unequal *to* the elementary work of maintaining peace and order.

    Froude *English in Ireland* vol. iii, bk. viii, ch. 1, p. 5.

5. In correspondence with ; in a manner suitable for ; in accompaniment with ; respecting ; concerning ; as, to dance *to* the music ; to draw *to* scale ; to paint *to* the life ; to speak *to* the resolution ; we will confer as *to* that.

> As *unto* the bow the cord is,
> So *unto* the man is woman.
> Though she bends him, she obeys him,
> Though she draws him. yet she follows.
>   Longfellow *Hiawatha* pt. x, st. 1.

> Till at the last she set herself *to* man,
> Like perfect music *unto* noble words.
>   Tennyson *Princess* vii, st. 21.

> The arched cloister, far and wide,
> Rang *to* the warrior's clanking stride.
>   Scott *Lay of the Last Minstrel* can. 2, st. 8.

A subtile, refined policy was conformable *to* the genius of the Italians. Prescott *Ferdinand and Isabella* vol. ii, pt. ii, ch.1, p. 259.

> And the sounding aisles of the dim woods rang
> *To* the anthem of the free !
>   Felicia D. Hemans *Landing of Pilgrim Fathers* st. 5.

'Bit' is that which has been bit off, and exactly corresponds *to* the word 'morsel,' used in the same sense, and derived from the Latin, *mordere*, to bite.   Mathews *Words* p. 887.

If honors and emoluments could have biassed the independent mind of our countryman, he must have been induced to become a full conformist *to* the English Church.

    T. M'Crie *John Knox* period iii, p. 79.

> Spring has come ! the rills as they glisten
> Sing *to* the pebble and greening grass.
>   W. W. Story *Spring* st. 8.

6. Denoting degree or extent: reaching in amount, degree, or the like; as far as; in comparison with; as, the thermometer rose *to* 90° in the shade; the whole came *to* ten dollars; faithful *to* (or *unto*) death.

> Yet, he prefers thee *to* the gilded domes,
> Or gewgaw grottos of the vainly great.
>
> BYRON *Newstead Abbey* st. 88.

We do not pretend to know *to* what precise extent the canonists of Oxford agree with those of Rome.

> MACAULAY *Essays, Church and State* p. 894.

Philosophy rose *to* its highest level through the Stoics at a time when the Greek mind was declining.

> GLADSTONE *Impregnable Rock* essay iii, p. 102.

The rule of quietness prevails, almost *to* the point of an English dinner-party.   R. H. DANA, JR. *To Cuba* ch. 2, p. 20.

Truth may perhaps come *to* the price of a pearl, that showeth best by day; but it will not rise *to* the price of a diamond or carbuncle, that showeth best in varied lights.

> BACON *Works, Essays, Of Truth* in vol. i, p. 261.

The Congo and its tributaries have been already explored *to* a length of eleven thousand miles.   MRS. H. GRATTAN-GUINNESS *New World of Central Africa* § 1, ch. 1, p. 12.

A general rise or a general fall of prices is merely tantamount *to* an alteration of the value of money.

> .MILL *Political Economy* vol. i, bk. iii, ch. 1, p. 541.

Faculty is properly limited *to* the endowments which are natural to man and universal with the race.   PORTER *Human Intellect* § 96.

7. Denoting addition, superposition, or the like; as an increase or adjunct of; as, add *to* your faith virtue.

The poet Euripides happened to be coupled *to* two noisy Vixens, who so plagued him with their jealousies and quarrels, that he became ever after a professed woman-hater.

> HUME *Essays, Polygamy* p. 106.

> Spurning manhood, and its joys *to* boot,
> To be a lawless, lazy, sensual brute.
>
> SAXE *Spell of Circe* l. 56.

The most valuable additions made *to* legislation have been enactments destructive of preceding legislation.

> BUCKLE *Hist. Civilization* vol. i, ch. 5, p. 200.

> They added ridge *to* valley, brook *to* pond,
> And sighed for all that bounded their domain.
>> EMERSON *Hamatreya* st. 8.

8. Denoting application or attention; as, sit down *to* dinner; to set *to* work; to bend *to* study.

> Now *to* my charms,   And *to* my wily trains.
>> MILTON *Comus* l. 151.

He, therefore, gave much of his time *to* the concerns of vert and venison.   KENNEDY *Horse-Shoe Robinson* ch. 37, p. 402.

I see small girls of ten who might well shame big men of forty as they buckle *to* their lessons.

> R. COLLYER *Life that Now Is* ch. 18, p. 270.

Through the bruteness and toughness of matter, a subtle spirit bends all things *to* its own will.

> EMERSON *Essays, History* in first series, p. 19.

I'm going to bone right down *to* it.

> H. A. BEERS in *Century Magazine* June, 1888, p. 278.

9. Denoting attribution, appurtenance, attendance, possession, or the like: in connection with; appropriate for; as, a cloak with a hood *to* it; the key *to* the barn.

The principle of free governments adheres *to* the American soil.   It is bedded in it, immovable as its mountains.

> WEBSTER *Works, Bunker Hill Monument* in vol. i, p. 77.

Every quality peculiar *to* the Saxons was hateful *to* the Britons; even their fairness of complexion. I. D'ISRAELI *Amenities of Lit., England and the English* in vol. i, p. 26.

He had belonged . . . *to* the armorer's gang on board a British man-of-war.   NORDHOFF *Sailor Life* p. 208.

The application of springs *to* carriages, . . . not only renders them soft-moving vehicles on rough roads, but lessens the pull *to* the horses.   ARNOTT *Elements of Physics* art. 277, p. 154.

11

The roof has a protecting slope *to* it; as one looks at the house, it is like a fluffy, feathery old hen which has settled down in the short grass in the sunshine to cover her chickens.

Atlantic Monthly June, 1882, p. 856.

The emperor [Otho I.] . . . confirmed *to* the Apostolic See the donations made by Pepin and Charlemagne, 'saving in all things,' says he, 'our authority, and that of our son and descendants.'

W. RUSSELL *Modern Europe* vol. i, letter xvi, p. 91.

10. In the relation of; with regard for; for; as, he had this *to* his credit.

> All his frame thrilled with a celestial glory,
> And *to* himself he murmured, 'This is love.'
>
> BULWER-LYTTON *Lost Tales of Miletus, Cydippe* st. 41.

The avenues of public justice everywhere in the United States are equally open *to* all persons.

T. F. BAYARD in *The Forum* May, 1891, p. 240.

> Sceptre and sword were fashion'd *to* his hand!
>
> TASSO *Jerusalem Delivered* tr. by Wiffen, can. 8, st. 59.

'Society is sour grapes *to* those beyond its pale,' said Wemyss, 'but those who can value it press from it the wine of life.'

F. J. STIMSON *First Harvests* ch. 9, p. 92.

Men can be *to* other men as the shadow of a great rock in a weary land.   DRUMMOND *Pax Vobiscum* ch. 2, p. 25.

No Christian man 'liveth *to* himself.'

R. WATSON *Sermons* vol. i, ser. xxvii, p. 316.

They sacrificed their sons and their daughters *unto* devils.

Ps. cvi, 37.

Apply thine heart *unto* instruction.   *Prov.* xxiii, 12.

For I shall sutler be   *Unto* the camp, and profits will accrue.

SHAKESPEARE *K. Henry V.* act ii, sc. 1.

Omission of "to"

To is often omitted after *bring, give, show, tell,* and certain other verbs. That this is a real ellipsis, and not a grammatical fiction, is shown by the fact that if the direct object of the verb intervenes between the verb and the indirect object, *to* is commonly expressed. Thus we say, "*Give* me the book," or "*Give* the book *to* me." Cowper makes John Gilpin say, "Yet *bring* it me," but this is a usage that would not be possible now; we should say, "*bring* it *to* me," and one would scarcely be understood otherwise. We say, "You must *tell* me the truth," or "You must *tell* the truth *to* me." The verb in such use thus has only one real object, called the direct object, as *book, truth,* etc., in the above examples; the so-called indirect object, as *me* in the examples given, being really dependent on the preposition *to,* expressed or understood.

To is commonly also omitted after *hand, pass, offer, telegraph, wire, write,* the indirect object directly following the verb; as, *hand me* that umbrella; please *pass me* the butter; you can not *offer him* so little; *telegraph* (or *wire*) *me* full particulars; *write me* promptly on arrival. In these cases, as with *give* and other like verbs, if the direct object is put first, the indirect must be preceded by *to;* as, *hand* that umbrella *to me;* he *telegraphed* full particulars *to the company.* While *to* is constantly omitted after *tell,* it is now never omitted after *speak;* as, *speak to* me. But formerly *speak* could also be used without *to;* as, you had best *speak him* fair.

Similarly are to be explained the prepositional uses of *like* and *near,* with which the preposition *to* or *unto* was formerly used.

Man is *like to* vanity. Ps. cxliv, 4.

Even such our griefs; . . . *like to* groves, being topp'd, they higher rise. Shakespeare *Pericles* act i, sc. 4.

The children of Israel, a people *near unto* him. Ps. cxlviii, 14.

The *to* is now so uniformly omitted that *like* and *near* have come to have practically the force of prepositions; as, he behaved *like* a child; he stood *near* the door.

Improper Omission of "to"

A prevalent error in some parts of the United States is the omission of *to* after the word *go;* as, "She is always wanting to *go places*"; "I will *go any place.*" In all such cases *to* should be used, its omission being never countenanced by good writers and accurate speakers. The expressions *somewhere, anywhere* may often be used for the meaning which this popular idiom erroneously seeks to express; as, "I want to *go somewhere*"; "I will *go anywhere.*" The omission of *to* before *home* is not a parallel case, but is perfectly correct and justified by the best usage, *home* in such use being an adverb. As an adverb *home* is used with very many verbs; as, *send* him *home*; let him *bring* it *home*. When used as a noun, *home* requires the preposition; as, I am going *to* my *home*.

IV. As the "sign" of the infinitive mode. In this relation the Anglo-Saxon used the preposition *to* followed by a special dative form of the verbal noun, distinguished from the simple infinitive, which was used without *to*. The English, with its constant elimination of inflections, and its tendency to simplicity of form, has dropped the special form of the infinitive and the dative case, but retains the preposition *to* joined with the unmodified form of the verb to express the infinitive.

Endless difficulties have been raised by grammarians in reference to the *to* used as a formative of the infinitive. Says Goold Brown :[*]

"The forms of parsing, and also the rules which are given in the early English grammars, are so very defective that it is often impossible to say positively what their authors did or did not intend to teach. . . . But Murray's twelfth rule of syntax, while it expressly calls *to* before the infinitive a *preposition*, absurdly takes from it this regimen, and leaves us a preposition that *governs nothing* and has apparently nothing to do with the *relation* of the terms between which it occurs.

"Many later grammarians, perceiving the absurdity of calling *to* before the infinitive a preposition without supposing it to govern the verb, have studiously avoided this name; and have either made the 'little word' a supernumerary part of speech, or treated it as no part of speech at all. Among these, if I mistake not, are Allen, Lennie, Bullions, Alger, Guy. Churchill, Hiley, Nutting, Mulligan, Spencer, and Wells. Except Comly, the numerous

---

[*] *Grammar of English Grammars* pp. 616-17.

modifiers of Murray's Grammar are none of them more consistent, on this point, than was Murray himself. Such of them as do not follow him literally, either deny, or forbear to affirm, that *to* before a verb is a preposition; and consequently either tell us not what it is, or tell us falsely; some calling it 'a part of the verb,' while they neither join it to the verb as a prefix, nor include it among the auxiliaries.

"Many are content to call the word *to* a *prefix*, a *particle*, a *little word*, a *sign of the infinitive*, a *part of the infinitive*, a *part of the verb*, and the like, without telling us whence it comes, how it differs from the preposition *to*, or to what part of speech it belongs. It certainly is not what we usually call a prefix, because we never join it to the verb; yet there are three instances in which it becomes such before a noun: viz., *to*-day, *to*-night, *to*-morrow. If it is a 'particle,' so is any other preposition, as well as every small and invariable word. If it is a 'little word,' the whole bigness of a preposition is unquestionably found in it; and no 'word' is so small but that it must belong to some one of the ten classes of speech. If it is a 'sign of the infinitive,' because it is used before no other mood, so is it a 'sign' of the objective case, or of what in Latin is called the dative, because it precedes no other case. If we suppose it to be a 'part of the infinitive,' or a 'part of the verb,' it is certainly no necessary part of either; because there is no verb which may not, in several different ways, be properly used in the infinitive without it. But if it be a part of the infinitive, it must be a *verb*, and ought to be classed with the auxiliaries."

The argument would seem to be sufficiently simple. The *to* was distinctly a preposition in Anglo-Saxon. The inference would be that it is the same in English. This inference must hold unless there is proof to the contrary, and there is no proof to the contrary. No one has ever been able to show why the *to* of the infinitive is not a preposition. The argument supposed to prove this seems to be that a preposition must "govern" an "objective case," and as a verb can have no "case," therefore a preposition can not "govern" it, and consequently the *to* can not be a preposition, but must be something else. What else the word *to* can be in such use no one has been able to show, and many have taken refuge in leaving the word outside of all the parts of speech, landing in the absurdity of a word that is not a part of speech. But, as shown in Chapter I, the "government" of nouns by prepositions is in English a mere grammatical figment. Not one English noun has any different form in the so-called "objective" from what it has in the nominative case. "He fell *to* the ground." How do we know that "ground" is "in the objective case"? Because it is "governed" by the preposition "to." How do we know that "to" is a preposition here? Because it "governs" the "objective case." This is circular reasoning with a very short radius, ending nowhere.

If we drop the fiction of "government," and say simply that a preposition shows some direct *relation* between a preceding and a following term, we solve the whole difficulty; for the *to* of the infinitive does exactly this. In the expression "Tell him *to* go," the "*to*" indicates that the action of the verb "tell" is closely connected with the action of the verb "go," just as in "Tell it *to* John," the "*to*" indicates that the action of the verb "tell" is closely connected with the person called "John." The instances are precisely parallel. So far as grammatical form is concerned, there is as much "objective case" in the word "go" as in the word "John." Neither of them is changed in form in the slightest degree. "Go" remains "go" and "John" remains "John" after the "*to*," however we may construe it. So far as the connection of thought is concerned, "go" is just as much dependent upon "tell" in the one sentence as "John" is upon "tell" in the other, and in either example the "*to*" indicates this dependence, and is, so to speak, the medium of its transfer. All that marks the word as a preposition in the one instance marks it as such in the other. The only answer to this argument is the bald assertion that "a preposition can not govern a verb." But this assertion is disproved by the fact that in the Greek language the preposition does exactly that, so that an infinitive with all its adjuncts will be put in either the genitive, dative, or accusative after a preposition, and often preceded by the definite article in the appropriate case.

What is possible to human thought in one language is possible to human thought in any other language.

If any one pleases to call the "to" simply the "sign" of the infinitive, there can be no special objection, but as a matter of logical analysis the combination of the root-idea of *tendency* expressed by the preposition *to* with the idea expressed in the root-form of any verb gives the most rational and satisfying explanation of the infinitive. The *Standard*, the *Century*, and the *International* dictionary agree in classing *to* in such use as a preposition.

Infinitive Without "to"

That the "to" of the infinitive construction is not "a part of the verb" appears from the fact that the idea of the infinitive can be, and in numerous cases is, expressed without it. This verbal form in infinitive use without "to" Maetzner terms "the pure infinitive."[*] Thus he classes the form of the verb used after auxiliaries as "the pure infinitive," as in the sentences "I may *go*," "he may *come*," and the like. The same explanation of the auxiliary usage is given by the *Standard* and by the *Century* dictionary.

Simple rules are the following:

The infinitive without *to* is used

(1) After auxiliaries, as *do, can, may, must, shall,* and *will.*

(2) After *bid, dare, feel, go, have, hear, help, let, make, need, please,* and *see.*

To be a statesman or reformer requires a courage that *dares* defy dictation from any quarter.

E. P. WHIPPLE *Character* essay iii, p. 91.

(3) After many verbs of perception analogous to *see, hear, feel,* etc.; as, *behold, discern, find, know, mark, observe, perceive, watch,* and some others.

[With many of the verbs specified under (2) and (3) the infinitive with the preposition may also be used.]

(4) After certain elliptical phrases, especially those employing some part of the verb *have* with an adverbial element; as, *had better, had best, had as lief, had rather,* etc.

---

[*] *English Grammar* vol. iii, p. 1.

[The idea that *had* is corrupted from *would* needs no confutation.   MAETZNER *English Grammar* vol. iii, p. 8.]

(5) Somewhat rarely, after the verbs *beg, charge, command, entreat, force, persuade, pray, will,* and some others : after these verbs the prepositional infinitive is now commonly used.

[NOTE.—A usage which is often severely criticized is that of the *split* or *cleft infinitive;* as, *to* suddenly *fall.* Abstractly there seems no more objection to the *split infinitive* than to the *split indicative.* We say, "The value *will* greatly *increase,*" and it seems every way as rational to say "The value is sure *to* greatly *increase.*" The latter is a very popular idiom, and often very forcible, though not commonly found in our best literature. If this usage meets a general popular demand, as now appears probable, it will ultimately win acceptance, but it can not at present be classed as an approved idiom.]

Verbs and Other Antecedents

To is used after numerous verbs, especially of the following classes:

1. Verbs directly denoting motion, to indicate direction or terminus; as, *bear, bring, carry, come, drag, draw, fall, flee, go, hasten, lead, pull, push, rise, send, ship, sink, throw,* and many others.

2. Verbs denoting the direction of some bodily action; as, *bend, bow, kneel, stoop,* etc.

3. Verbs denoting the direction or reference of some act of communication or the like; as, *address, appeal, call, complain, lie, pray, preach, recite, relate, repeat, shout, sing, sue, talk, telegraph, telephone, tell, whisper, write,* etc.

4. Verbs denoting some lasting combination of one object with another, whether literally or figuratively; as, *adhere, ally, append, attach, bind, chain, cleave, cling, fasten, fix, glue, grow, hang, hold, knit, link, marry, nail, pin, rivet, screw, stick, tie, wed.*

5. Verbs denoting sounds, movements of the body, or emotions of the mind which are or seem to be in response to something treated as the object; as, *dance, echo, melt* (to tears, or the like), *quiver, resound, respond, ring, roar, sound, spring, thrill, tremble, vibrate*, and many others.

6. Verbs denoting change take *to* (or often *into*) before the word denoting the resultant effect or condition; as, *alter, burn, change, congeal, contract, diminish, expand, freeze, grow, increase, melt, reduce, transform, transmute, turn*, etc.

7. Verbs denoting appropriateness, agreement, etc.; as, *adapt, agree, conform, consent, fit, suit*, etc.

Adjectives followed by *to* are too numerous to give in full list, but a few classes may be specified:

1. Adjectives of location or situation; as, *adjacent, adjoining, close, contiguous, near* (which by omission of the *to* often seems to be itself a preposition), and many others.

2. Adjectives of comparison, adaptation, or agreement; as, *according, agreeable, congenial, equal, equivalent, like* (which by omission of the *to* seems often to be itself a preposition), *proportionate, similar*, and many others, with their contraries, as *disagreeable, unlike*, etc.

3. Adjectives denoting attraction, approval, and the like; as, *dear, delightful, pleasant, pleasing, precious, sacred, welcome*, with their contraries, as *hateful, indifferent, odious*, etc.

4. Adjectives denoting disposition, treatment, etc.; as, *cruel, false, good, honest, just, kind, mild, obedient, partial, stern, unfair, unjust*, etc.

Numerous nouns take *to* before the object with which the antecedent noun comes into close relation; as, a friend *to* the deserving (where *of* might be used with slight difference of suggestion), a traitor *to* his country, etc.

TOUCHING

Touching is the present participle (see PARTICIPIAL PREPOSITIONS) of the verb *touch*, used with prepositional force in the sense of relating to, concerning, with regard to.

There, with the emperor,
To treat of high affairs *touching* that time.
> SHAKESPEARE *K. John* act i, sc. 1, l. 102.

Any one may have a fancy, and a squirrel has a right to make up his mind *touching* a catamount.   COOPER *Deerslayer* ch. 1, p. 22.

TOWARD, TOWARDS

Toward is derived from the Anglo-Saxon *to*, to, plus -*weard*, -ward, a suffix denoting motion to or from.   It is thus a modified form of *to*, never reaching the full force of the latter word, but always stopping with direction or approach, while *to* indicates attainment or contact.

As in other cases, *towards* is a later form, due to adding the adverbial suffix -es (orig. the mark of a gen. case) to the shorter *toward*.   SKEAT *Etym. Dict.*

[*Towards* is somewhat more common than *toward*, but the two words are interchangeable.   *Standard Dictionary.*]

I. Of place or space: in a course or line leading to; in the direction of; opening, facing, looking, or situated in the direction of; as, he was marching *toward* London; the window opened *toward* the east; there is a tract of fertile land *toward* the north.

The far country, *toward* which we journey, seems nearer to us, and the way less dark; for thou hast gone before.
> LONGFELLOW *Hyperion* bk. iv, ch. 5, p. 342.

The narrow street that clamber'd *toward* the mill.
> TENNYSON *Enoch Arden* st. 3.

Preceded by the beadle, . . . Hester Prynne set forth *toward* the place appointed for her punishment.
> HAWTHORNE *Scarlet Letter* ch. 2, p. 65.

Leslie rises with a grand air from her mother's side . . . and sweeps *toward* him.   HOWELLS *Out of the Question* ch. 8, p. 90.

Two horses have emerged from the ruck, and are sweeping, rushing, storming, *towards* us, almost side by side.
> HOLMES *Our Hundred Days* ch. 1, p. 54.

As the smoke from the calumet moves westward, I behold in it nations of red men, moving . . . *towards* the caverns of the sun.
> F. S. COZZENS *Sparrowgrass Papers* ch. 12, p. 172.

Where strata . . . dip *towards* an axis, forming a trough or basin, it is called a Syncline, or synclinal axis.

> ARCH. GEIKIE *Text-Book Geology* bk. iv, pt. iv, p. 517.

II. Of time: approaching; near to; about; nearly; as, it is now *toward* noon.

It is *toward* evening and the day is far spent.   *Luke* xxiv, 29.

III. In derived or figurative use:

1. Aiming at or contributing to; having as a goal, aim, or end; for the promotion, help, advancement, or furtherance of; in the direction of; being inclined to; for; as, a contribution *toward* an endowment.

The purchase of Louisiana showed the trend of events *toward* nationality to be stronger than the avowed purpose of the party.

> H. C. ADAMS *Public Debts* pt. iii, ch. 2, p. 320.

She [Great Britain] will call on them [the colonies] to contribute *toward* supporting the burdens they have helped to bring on her, and they will answer by striking off all dependence.

> IRVING *Washington* vol. i, ch. 35, p. 329.

There was a certain drift *towards* Dissent among the warmer spirits.   R. W. CHURCH *Oxford Movement* ch. 1, p. 14.

A hopeful, tender, trustful looking *towards* the Cross will keep back the thunder, and God will spare us when he makes inquisition for blood.   J. PARKER *People's Bible, Exodus* ch. 12, p. 78.

A current in people's minds sets *towards* new ideas.

> MATTHEW ARNOLD *Culture and Anarchy* ch. 1, p. 38.

Herodotus was drawn *towards* the most romantic and poetic version of each story, and what he admired most seemed to him the likeliest to be true.

> RAWLINSON *Herodotus* vol. i, bk. i, p. 272, note 9.

2. With respect to; in relation to: in reference to; respecting; regarding; concerning; as, charity *toward* the erring.

She . . . had remained indifferent and fastidiously critical *towards* both fresh sprig and faded bachelor.

> GEORGE ELIOT *Middlemarch* vol. i, ch. 12, p. 180.

The real preparation of the preacher's personality for its trans-
missive work comes by the opening of his life on both sides, *towards* the truth of God and *towards* the needs of man.

> PHILLIPS BROOKS *Lect. on Preaching* lect. i, p. 26.

The feeling of affection of a dog *towards* his master is combined
with a strong sense of submission, which is akin to fear.

> DARWIN *Emotions* ch. 5, p. 120.

UNDER

Under, derived from the Anglo-Saxon *under*, and traced back
to the Gothic *undar* and Old Norse *undir* used in the same sense,
is one of the root-words of our language, and is preserved with
slight variations of form in all Germanic tongues.

I. Of place or space : in a situation lower than ; below ;
beneath.

1. In a place lower than and covered by ; so as to have something directly above ; as, the purse is *under* the table ; the guests
under my roof ; anywhere *under* heaven ; a tunnel *under* Broadway.

> Ere a cable went *under* the hoary Atlantic,
> Or the word Telegram drove grammarians frantic.
>> OWEN MEREDITH *Lucile* pt. ii, can. 4, st. 5, note.

There were bright coals *under* the singing tea-kettle which
hung from the crane by three or four long pothooks.

> SARAH ORNE JEWETT *Strangers and Wayfarers* ch. 7, p. 226.

Each day they camped in a new spot, and while Lita nibbled
the fresh grass at her ease Miss Celia sketched *under* the big umbrella.   LOUISA M. ALCOTT *Under the Lilacs* ch. 12, p. 125.

> On *under* the arch of the star-sown skies.
>> JOAQUIN MILLER *In a Gondola* st. 8.

2. In a place lower than, though not covered by; at the foot or
bottom of ; as, the beach *under* the cliff ; a flower-bed *under* the
window ; the army encamped *under* the walls of the fortress.

Kenelm retraced his steps homeward *under* the shade of his
' old hereditary trees.'

> BULWER-LYTTON *Kenelm Chillingly* bk. i, ch. 15, p. 73.

The sun of Austerlitz showed the Czar madly sliding his splendid army like a weaver's shuttle, from his right hand to his left, *under* the very eyes . . . of Napoleon.   KINGLAKE *Eothen* ch. 8, p. 68.

Alas! for the rarity   Of Christian charity   *Under* the sun!
                              HOOD *Bridge of Sighs* st. 9.

II. Of time: during the period of; in the rule or reign of; pending the administration of; during; as, this system prevailed *under* the Ptolemies; luxury prevailed in France *under* the reign of Louis XIV.

Under no English government, since the Reformation, had there been so little religious persecution.
                              MACAULAY *England* vol. i, ch. 1, p. 128.

III. In derived and figurative use:

1. Denoting inferiority: lower than in quality, character, rank, etc.; less than in number, degree, age, value, or amount; inferior to; below; as, he is *under* twenty; an officer *under* the rank of colonel; he is *under* age.

This conversation was not ended *under* five audiences, each of several hours.   SWIFT *Works*, *Gulliver* pt. ii, ch. 6, p. 155.

2. Denoting dependence, protection, or subordination: subject to the dominion, influence, guidance, instruction, obligation, operation, or employment of; as, *under* British authority; *under* foreign influence; *under* the American flag; *under* oath; *under* compulsion; *under* the circumstances; *under* fire; *under* medical treatment; men *under* arms; (of a vessel) *under* sail, *under* steam, etc.

[NOTE.—It has been questioned whether we should use the common phrase "*under* the circumstances," or whether we should not rather say "*in* the circumstances." It will be seen that *under*, as denoting dependence, is the more expressive word in this connection.]

Both Scotland and Ireland, indeed, had been subjugated by the Plantagenets, but neither country had been patient *under* the yoke.   MACAULAY *England* vol. i, ch. 1, p. 50.

Though I know neither the time nor the manner of the death I am to die, I am not at all solicitous about it; because I am sure that he [God] knows them both, and that he will not fail to comfort and support me *under* them.

ADDISON *Spectator* Mar. 8, 1710–'11.

The only branch of knowledge which the Arabians ever raised to a science was astronomy, which began to be cultivated *under* the caliphs about the middle of the eighth century.

BUCKLE *Hist. Civilization* vol. i, ch. 2, p. 35, note.

Winter snow *under* the action of thawing and freezing temperatures in alternation becomes granular, as we often observe in old snow, especially in early spring.

WINCHELL *Walks and Talks* ch. 8, p. 22.

The American travelling in Europe chafes *under* the restraints of administration. DEPEW *Orations and Speeches, Feb. 22, 1881* p. 47.

It owed its existence to the masterly organizing abilities of McClellan, and ended the war *under* the superb generalship of Grant. DEPEW *Orations and Speeches, Reunion of Army of Potomac, 1887* p. 154.

Their work in the open air, *under* all weathers, is calculated to make them [husbandmen] hardy.

BROUGHAM *British Constitution* ch. 20, p. 380.

It was fortunate for the Constitution that the patriotism of the Peers, acting *under* the sage counsels of the Duke of Wellington, prevented us from having recourse to a measure so full of peril.

BROUGHAM *British Constitution* ch. 17, p. 269.

Under the old Greek and Roman habits of mind, the stranger was mainly looked upon as a barbarian and enemy.

C. L. BRACE *Gesta Christi* pt. ii, ch. 16, p. 190.

I found sleep was out of the question, *under* the incessant attacks of a swarm of peculiarly ravenous mosquitoes.

C. L. BRACE *Hungary in 1851* ch. 15, p. 121.

Over fifteen hundred barrels were packed in 1884, and *under* the new régime, the Kasa-an fishery has distanced its rivals.

ELIZABETH R. SCIDMORE *Alaska* ch. 4, p. 85.

Self-interest is the ruling passion, whether *under* free or despotic governments.

JAMES MONROE *The People the Sovereigns* ch. 2, p. 168.

3. Denoting shelter or protection: covered by; shielded, screened, or defended by; beneath; as, the fleet was moored *under* the guns of the fort; *under* his mother's wing; *under* favor; *under* leave.

> Here, *under* leave of Brutus and the rest, . . .
> Come I to speak in Cæsar's funeral.
> > SHAKESPEARE *Julius Cæsar* act iii, sc. 2, l. 86.

> My lords, then, *under* favour, pardon me,
> If I speak like a captain.
> > SHAKESPEARE *Timon of Athens* act iii, sc. 5, l. 41.

4. Denoting concealment, disguise, or the like: with the assumption of; assuming; as, *under* the mask of friendship; *under* pretense of helping; *under* an assumed name.

> The Jew and the Christian who entered on such themes [atrocities committed by the Government] could only do so *under* the disguise of a cryptograph.   FARRAR *Christianity* ch. 5, p. 46.

> Revelations . . . which he would rather have hidden *under* the ashes of the past.   H. W. MABIE *My Study Fire* ch. 1, p. 5.

> Original vigor was still visible *under* all the rust and batter of seventy years.
> > BAYARD TAYLOR *At Home and Abroad* vol. i, ch. 2, p. 16.

> I here use the word sycophant in its original sense, as a wretch who flatters the prevailing party by informing against his neighbors, *under* pretense that they are exporters of prohibited figs or fancies.   COLERIDGE *Works, Biog. Lit.* in vol. iii, ch. 10, p. 286.

5. Denoting authority, sanction, etc.: by virtue of; in the name of; authorized, substantiated, attested, or warranted by; as, *under* the authority of the United States; *under* my hand and seal; *under* his own signature.

[NOTE.—*Over* is now often used in connection with one's name, signature, or the like; but this is a more recent usage and more local and literal than that of *under*. "*Under* one's signature" denotes not position but authority and attestation, and is thus the more expressive phrase.]

John Paul Jones, with his own hands, raised the first American naval flag, *under* a salute of thirteen guns.

> J. S. C. ABBOTT *Paul Jones* ch. 1, p. 21.

6. In conformity to; in accordance with; as, *under* the terms of the contract; *under* the rules of the game.

The Book of Daniel, and the Apocalypse . . . contain the first germs of the great idea of the succession of ages, of the continuous growth of empires and races *under* a law of Divine Providence.　　A. P. STANLEY *Jewish Church* vol. i, lect. xx, p. 414.

Monarchy, Aristocracy, and Timocracy . . . are, *under* the appropriate circumstances, good forms of government.

> UEBERWEG *Hist. Philos.* tr. by G. S. Morris, vol. i, § 50, p. 170.

7. Denoting classification, arrangement, etc.: with reference to (class, section, division, or the like); as, to treat the subject *under* four heads; these will be considered *under* a later topic; they have been classed *under* the Coleoptera; *under* the name of Cryptogamia.

Blessings may appear *under* the shape of pain, losses, and disappointments.　　ADDISON *The Guardian* July 25, 1718.

Those poems which are classed *under* the appellation of Cyclic, the Hymns, or Proemia, as the ancients termed them.

> R. W. BROWNE *Hist. Class. Lit.* bk. i, ch. 6, p. 93.

In March, 1868, the first woman's club of America was organized *under* the name of Sorosis . . . which, in the pursuit of a name which should not stand in the way of any object desired, Mrs. Croly found in a botanical dictionary.

> *Johnson's Univ. Encyc.* vol. iv, p. 377.

A certain quantum of power must always exist in the community, in some hands, and *under* some appellation.

> BURKE *Revolution in France, French Clergy* in § 1, p. 167.

The Arabs know it well *under* the name Waran (whence the generic name Varanus is derived).

> ALBERT GÜNTHER in *Encyc. Brit.* 9th ed., vol. xiv, p. 784.

UNDERNEATH

Underneath is from the Anglo-Saxon *under* plus *nethe*, lower, as in *nether.*

Of place, almost exclusively: directly below, beneath, or under; as, *underneath* the ground: rarely used in a metaphorical sense, and even then keeping the local and literal meaning prominent; as, to stagger *underneath* a burden.

> Pray God, she prove not masculine ere long;
> If *underneath* the standard of the French
> She carry armour, as she hath begun.
> > SHAKESPEARE *1 K. Henry VI.* act ii, sc. 1, l. 28.

And there, *underneath* the light, lay five or six great salmon, looking up at the flame with their great goggle eyes.
> > KINGSLEY *Water-Babies* ch. 4, p. 147.

UP

Up is from the Anglo-Saxon *up, upp, uppe*, used in the same general sense. *Up* is the preposition of ascent.

[In modern English this preposition is used of motion and direction upwards, but also occurs with continuous movement or direction [even] on level ground, . . . which was originally ruled by the perspective rising of a plain in sight of a person marching.
> > MAETZNER *English Grammar* vol. ii, p. 815.]

Of place exclusively:

1. With reference to motion: from a lower to a higher point or place on or along; toward a higher point of; along the line or ascent of; from the mouth toward the source of (a stream); from the coast toward the interior of (a country) as being higher; as, to climb *up* a tree; to sail *up* a river; I saw him coming *up* the road.

That sprightly Scot of Scots, Douglas, that runs o' horseback *up* a hill perpendicular.
> > SHAKESPEARE *1 K. Henry IV.* act ii, sc. 4, l. 355.

The patient ass, *up* flinty paths,   Plods with his weary load.
> > MACAULAY *Prophecy of Capys* st. 16.

Bogus, in the sense of worthless, is undoubtedly ours, but is, I more than suspect, a corruption of the French 'bagasse' (from low Latin 'bagasea'), which travelled *up* the Mississippi from New Orleans, where it was used for the refuse of the sugar-cane.
> > LOWELL *Biglow Papers* second series, int., p. 242.

He passed *up* the narrow aisle of benches.

> BRET HARTE *Cressy* ch. 1, p. 8.

> Why, there was not a slope
> *Up* which he had not fear'd the antelope.

> KEATS *Endymion* bk. iv, st. 88.

2. With reference to position or situation : at, on, or near a higher place or part of ; on the height or top of ; at, on, or near some point regarded as more advanced ; as, his house is *up* the street ; the next station *up* the line ; a farm *up* the Hudson.

Villas and villages stretched on every side *up* the ascent of Vesuvius, not nearly then so steep or lofty as at present.

> BULWER-LYTTON *Pompeii* bk. ii, p. 96.

VIA

Via is from the Latin, being the ablative of the word *via*, "a way," and signifying "by the way," or as used in English, "by the way of." It is said of the route traveled over, or of any place passed through ; as, ship *via* the Pennsylvania Railroad ; to go to Cincinnati *via* Washington.

This is a usage which is to be condemned on strict rules of grammatical construction, as much as the corresponding use of *anti, ex, per,* etc. But where one word of three letters will say what would otherwise take four words, "by the way of," the short form is sure, in the period of telegraph, telephone, and typewriter, to hold its place when once introduced. It is a tribute to the comprehensive genius, the flexibility, and the vitality of the English language that it can thus adopt a needed or convenient word from any tongue and make it thoroughly at home with the vernacular terms.

WITH

With is from the Anglo-Saxon *with*, which signifies "over against," "opposite"; and, as persons or things may be *over against* or *opposite* each other either in harmony or in conflict, the word *with* came to have the two meanings of *against* and *beside;* to have, *i. e.,* the meaning of opposition and that of association, which has become the controlling sense of the English *with*. The predominance of this latter sense is largely due to the further fact that *with* takes the place of the Anglo-Saxon *mid* (equivalent to the German *mit*), in which the sense of association was the controlling one. The sense of "against" appears in the English *with* in connection with words denoting fighting, war, conflict, and the like.

[It is an interesting fact, however, that the Latin *cum*, strictly denoting association, is used in precisely the same way as the English *with* of hostile relations, *cum hoste confligere* meaning "to fight with [*i. e.*, against] an enemy"; but the Greek prepositions of association σύν and μετά when used of conflict denote cooperation, σύν τινι μάχεσθαι meaning to fight *at* or *on one's side*. The Roman fought *with* his enemy, that is, *against* him. The Greek fought *with* his friend, that is, *on his side, for* him.]

I. Of place or space: *with* is not used distinctively of place, though the local idea inheres in and underlies many of its meanings, as in the sense of companionship, etc. ; as, sit here *with* me.

[The purely local meaning *over against, beside*, was soon lost in English; the decided and sole reference to position in space is at least no longer to be perceived.
     MAETZNER *English Grammar* vol. ii, p. 408.]

II. Of time: denoting simultaneousness; at the time of; in the period, day, hour, moment, or instant of; as, to wake *with* the dawn; his influence ceased *with* his death.

     With every minute you do change a mind.
          SHAKESPEARE *Coriolanus* act. i, sc. 1, l. 182.

Marriage can seldom be celebrated simultaneously *with* betrothment or engagement.
          PARSONS *Contracts* vol. i, pt. i, bk. iii, ch. 10, § 1, p. 543.

The proper era of English newspapers, at least of those containing domestic intelligence, commences *with* the Long Parliament.   CRAIK *Eng. Lit. and Lang., Newspapers* vol. ii, p. 83.

The swallow *with* summer   Will wing o'er the seas.
          HOOD *The Exile* st. 1.

> *With* every anguish of your earthly part
> The spirit's sight grows clearer.
>> LOWELL *On the Death of a Friend's Child* st. 2.

Dream not, *with* the rising sun,   Bugles here shall sound reveillé.
>> SCOTT *Lady of the Lake* can. 1, st. 32.

III. Of various relations:

1. Denoting association, accompaniment, or connection:

(*a*) In a relation of joint activity, cooperation, companionship, mixture, etc.: in the company of; on the side of; so as to have fellowship, union, or harmony concerning; as, to eat, work, read, or visit *with* another; to side *with* one; I wish to consult *with* you.

They enslave their children's children who make compromise *with* sin.
>> LOWELL *Present Crisis* st. 9.

She could not reconcile the anxieties of a spiritual life involving eternal consequences, *with* a keen interest in gimp and artificial protrusions of drapery.
>> GEORGE ELIOT *Middlemarch* vol. i, ch. 1, p. 10.

The digestive organs, unfortunately, are the first to sympathize *with* any mental worry.
>> N. E. YORKE-DAVIES in *Annals of Hygiene* Sept., 1893, p. 534.

The Florentine doctor came down the street . . . *with* a blackamoor who bore a great hamper which contained his medicines.
>> E. E. HALE *In His Name* ch. 2, p. 21.

The loyalty of this gentleman was altogether of a calculating nature, and was intimately connected *with* what he considered his fealty to himself.
>> COOPER *Pilot* ch. 16, p. 188.

> The roar of wintering streams
> That mix their own foam *with* the yellower sea.
>> SWINBURNE *Atalanta in Calydon* st. 99.

We sat down together on the dry, water-worn pebbles, mixed *with* fragments of broken shells and minute pieces of wreck, that strewed the opening of the cave.   HUGH MILLER in Wilson's *Tales of the Borders* in vol. ii, ch. 1, p. 69.

The wide extent of salt marshes and meadows interspersed *with* shallow land-locked washes and lagoons.

H. W. Herbert *Field Sports, Bay Shooting* in vol. ii, p. 7.

[Note.—In the conjoining of unlike or contrasted objects or qualities, *with* has often nearly the meaning of *despite, notwithstanding*.

With all his lucidity of statement, Hamilton was always concise.   H. C. Lodge *Alex. Hamilton* ch. 5, p. 89.]

(b) Denoting guardianship, protection, care, oversight, etc.: (1) In the care of; under the protection of; at the disposal of; as, to leave a child *with* a nurse; to leave one's purse *with* a friend; that matter rests *with* you.

The youngest is this day *with* our father.   *Gen.* xlii, 13.

Lo, I am *with* you alway, even unto the end of the world.
Matt. xxviii, 20.

Factors and Brokers are both and equally agents, but with this difference: the Factor is intrusted *with* the property which is the subject-matter of the agency; the Broker is only employed to make a bargain in relation to it.
PARSONS *Contracts* vol. i, pt. i, bk. i, ch. 4, § 1, p. 78.

(2) Exercising care or protection over; being a guard, guide, or helper to; as, to side *with* the oppressed; God be *with* you.

And the angel of the Lord appeared unto him, and said unto him, The Lord is *with* thee, thou mighty man of valor.
And Gideon said unto him, O my Lord, if the Lord be *with* us, why then is all this befallen us?   *Judges* vi, 12-13.

(3) Under the direction of; in the service of; enrolled in or belonging to; in attendance upon; as, he is *with* a banking-house; he is *with* the army.

[Note.—In business relations, the expression *with* a house, firm, or the like never denotes partnership in, but always employment by, partnership being expressed by *of*.]

Saul arose, and went down to the wilderness of Ziph, having three thousand chosen men of Israel *with* him.   *1 Sam.* xxvi, 2.

(*c*) In the class or group of; numbered among; placed, ranked, or ranged beside; among; as, the amphioxus must be classed *with* the vertebrates; your name was mentioned *with* others; North America *with* South America constitutes the western hemisphere.

The idea underlying all classification is that of similarity. When we group an object *with* certain others, we do so because in some or all of its characters it resembles them.

SPENCER *Psychology* vol. ii, § 310, p. 117.

The tart is national *with* the English, as the pie is national *with* us. HOLMES *Our Hundred Days* ch. 8, p. 807.

(*d*) Denoting some accompanying condition, feeling, act, circumstance, or the like: accompanied by; affected by; having as an attendant circumstance; as, fire and smoke *with* intense heat; the sea surges *with* ceaseless motion.

Contrition is the very sorrow that a man receiveth in his heart for his sins, *with* sad purpose . . . never more to do sin.

CHAUCER *Canterbury Tales, Parson's Tale* div. i.

She was still leaning on the gate *with* one foot on the lower rail and her chin cupped in the hollow of her hand.

BRET HARTE *Cressy* ch. 8, p. 51.

For days, her touching, foolish lines
We mused on *with* conjectural fantasy.

E. B. BROWNING *Aurora Leigh* bk. iv, l. 988.

Overhead was a bower of climbing Waxwork, *with* its yellowish pods scarce disclosing their scarlet berries. T. W. HIGGINSON *Out-Door Papers, Procession of the Flowers* p. 835.

The speaking of a falsehood is not a lie, if it be not spoken *with* an intent to deceive. J. WESLEY *Sermons* vol. ii, ser. lxxxii, p. 450.

A haughty high soul, yet *with* various flaws, or rather *with* one many-branched flaw and crack running through the texture of it.

CARLYLE *Past and Present* bk. ii, ch. 14, p. 92.

2. Denoting an endowment, possession, or characteristic:

(*a*) Having; possessing; conveying; characterized by; as, a man *with* good sense; a cow *with* long horns; Egypt *with* its pyramids; a vase *with* handles.

[NOTE.—*With* in such use often approaches closely the sense of *of*. We may say either a man *of* good sense or a man *with* good sense, *of* denoting the quality more as a possession, and *with* more as an accompaniment.]

The school was in a tall, stately building, *with* a high cupola on the top.

> D. G. MITCHELL *Reveries of a Bachelor, School Days* p. 172.

The Bear has a well-developed paw *with* a flexible wrist.

> AGASSIZ *Methods of Study* ch. 8, p. 114.

And bid creation doff its withered leaves,
To clothe itself *with* spring.

> BONAR *My Old Letters* bk. v, l. 721.

The morning star . . . *with* flaming locks bedight.

> SPENSER *Faerie Queene* bk. i, can. 12, st. 21.

Meantime the other stood
With wide gray eyes still reading the blank air.

> LOWELL *Glance Behind the Curtain* st. 4.

In the centre . . . stood the Indian metropolis, *with* its gorgeous tiara of pyramids and temples.

> PRESCOTT *Conquest of Mexico* vol. iii, bk. vi, ch. 2, p. 81.

(*b*) In a manner expressing, indicating, or pervaded by; as, he worked *with* energy; he gazed on the scene *with* deep dejection.

Brushed *with* extreme flounce   The circle of the sciences.

> E. B. BROWNING *Aurora Leigh* bk. i, l. 404.

The fox-hounds trotting sedately on . . . gave tongue *with* the deep notes of their species.

> ELIZABETH B. CUSTER *Following the Guidon* ch. 22, p. 388.

The play ["As You Like It"] is instinct *with* woodland associations; the spirit of the place is upon its inhabitants.

> H. N. HUDSON *Lect. on Shakespeare* vol. i, lect. vii, p. 278.

Dunning's cross-examination of this villain was carried on *with* an indignant causticity which was long reckoned among his finest efforts.   GEO. CROLY *George IV.* ch. 4, p. 86.

Pitt pressed on every expedition *with* a calculated and sagacious audacity, and his imperious will broke down every obstacle.

> LECKY *Eng. in the Eighteenth Cent.* vol. ii, ch. 8, p. 540.

The Archbishop of New York denies *with* emphasis that there is any such thing as a Culturkampf either existing or imminent in these United States.   *New-York Times* Aug. 5, 1882, p. 4, col. 4.

3. Denoting means, instrument, cause, material, price, accessory, etc.: by; by means of; making use of; by the use or employment of; as, to load a ship *with* coal; to chop wood *with* an ax; to entertain company *with* music; a ring set *with* diamonds.

Feed me *with* food convenient for me.   Prov. xxx, 8.

A population sodden *with* drink, steeped in vice, eaten up by every social and physical malady, these are the denizens of Darkest England.   BOOTH *Darkest England* pt. i, ch. 1, p. 14.

> Earth's crammed *with* heaven,
> And every common bush afire *with* God.
>   E. B. BROWNING *Aurora Leigh* bk. vii, l. 821.

No one can see it [the decay of imperial tombs] without being impressed *with* the reflection that the worship of parents and emperors alike is no longer an active cult in China.
         J. H. WILSON *China* ch. 14, p. 235.

We are at once struck *with* a marked change which takes place . . . in the composition of Parliament.
         GREEN *Short Hist. Eng. People* ch. 5, § 2, p. 247.

Others . . . are overhung, whole months and years, *with* a dreadfully oppressive gloom, . . . never at all to know that this gloom is in their liver.
         BUSHNELL *Moral Uses of Dark Things* ch. 12, p. 257.

One asks one's self *with* astonishment how a doctrine so benign as that of Christ can have incurred misrepresentations so monstrous.   MATTHEW ARNOLD *Essays in Criticism, Marcus Aurelius* in first series, p. 267.

The splendid cathedral spire flamed nightly *with* three hundred burning cressets.   MOTLEY *Dutch Repub.* vol. i, pt. i, p. 207.

With a great sum obtained I this freedom.   *Acts* xxii, 28.

[NOTE.—In its use regarding price, *with* is nearly equivalent to *for*, the latter being the more common.]

4. Denoting result or consequence: because of; through; as, to tremble *with* fear; crushed *with* sorrow; he clapped his hands *with* glee.

I bruised my shin the other day *with* playing at sword and dagger with a master of fence.
SHAKESPEARE *Merry Wives of Windsor* act i, sc. 1.

Witch-elms that counterchange the floor
Of this flat lawn *with* dusk and bright.
TENNYSON *In Memoriam* lxxxviii, st. 1.

Our Savior has brought out very distinctly the fact that the misapplication of small abilities will meet *with* condign punishment.   W. B. STEVENS *Parables Unfolded* p. 88.

I am so worn away *with* fears and sorrows,
So wintered *with* the tempests of affliction.
JOHN FORD *Lover's Melancholy* act iv, sc. 3.

Why blanches Sir Walter *with* fright?
SAXE *Ghost in Armor* pt. ii, st. 8.

They [Chatham's speeches] blaze *with* the authentic fire of imagination.   MATHEWS *Oratory and Orators* p. 283.

5. In respect of; in regard to; in relation to; as regards; as to; as, do not be angry *with* me; that is the way *with* him; what is your business *with* me? to meddle *with* things that do not concern you.

Essex . . . taxed his perfidious friend *with* unkindness and insincerity.   MACAULAY *Essays, Bacon* p. 260.

Thou needst be surelier God to bear *with* us
Than even to have made us!
E. B. BROWNING *Aurora Leigh* bk. vii, l. 1029.

Ay me! what perils do environ
The man that meddles *with* cold iron!
BUTLER *Hudibras* pt. i, can. 3, l. 1.

Vain minds would still be tampering *with* the greatest affairs.
LEIGHTON *Works, Lect. on Rom. xii, 3* in vol. ii, p. 92.

We know that something is wrong *with* our nerves, when they act against our will.   R. C. JEBB *Bentley* ch. 18, p. 210.

Such is ever the case *with* these worthies and *with* nearly all the natives of South Africa.

> GORDON CUMMING *Hunter's Life* vol. i, ch. 10, p. 184.

Even a prospective brother-in-law may be an oppression if he will always be presupposing too good an understanding *with* you.

> GEORGE ELIOT *Middlemarch* vol. i, ch. 8, p. 88.

6. In the region or sphere of; from the standpoint of; in the experience or estimation of; in the sight of; in the case of; among; as, *with* you there is no medium; it is night in the Orient when it is day *with* us.

So great a favourite is the Cairngorum *with* the people of Scotland, that brooches, pins, bracelets, and a variety of ornaments are made with this stone.   URE *Dict.*

People grieve and bemoan themselves, but it is not half so bad *with* them as they say.

> EMERSON *Essays, Experience* in second series, p. 45.

There is something so captivating in personal bravery, that, *with* the common mass of mankind, it takes the lead of most other merits.   IRVING *Knickerbocker* bk. vi, ch. 6, p. 360.

It is thus *with* the vulgar; and all men are as the vulgar in what they do not understand.

> BURKE *Sublime and Beautiful* pt. ii, § 4, p. 43.

Socrates thinks *with* the Christian: Mr. Volney, *with* the deist. Shall we symbolize *with* the Greek or *with* the Frank?

> G. S. FABER *Difficulties of Infidelity* § 1, p. 15.

With a pedant of such magnitude, who would stake a kingdom for the cut of a churchman's cope.

> J. S. BLACKIE *Lay Sermons* ch. 8, p. 247.

7. Denoting analogy, resemblance, or proportion: in the manner of; at the same time or rate as; in proportion to; according to; like; as; as, *with* Berkeley he denied the existence of matter; his influence increases *with* his wealth.

[In mathematics, *with* is used to note a function that is not in exact proportion to its variable, as distinguished from *as;* as, the length varies *with*, but not *as*, the temperature.]

Mars has been an interesting object of telescopic research from the fact that it is the planet which exhibits the greatest analogy *with* our earth.   Newcomb *Popular Astron.* pt. iii, ch. 8, p. 321.

Honorable industry travels the same road *with* duty.

Smiles Self-Help ch. 2, p. 41.

As retorts are expensive in comparison *with* flasks, they are less used than formerly.

Eliot and Storer Inorganic Chemistry app., § 18, p. 28.

You ride quietly along, and the saice follows you, walking or keeping pace *with* your gentle trot, as the case may be.

F. Marion Crawford Mr. Isaacs ch. 4, p. 62.

A comparison of Wickliffe *with* the versions of the sixteenth century would show that in many cases the Early English subjunctive had been replaced by the Elizabethan 'shall.'

E. A. Abbott Shakespearian Grammar ¶ 348, p. 247.

It would be absurd . . . to set down the double marriages of patriarchal times in the same moral rank *with* modern cases of bigamy. Martineau *Studies of Christianity, Ethics of Christendom* p. 318.

8. Denoting opposition, competition, or hostility: in opposition to; opposing; facing; against; as, to fight *with* an enemy; to dispute *with* an opponent; to struggle *with* temptation.

When Christianity comes in collision *with* wrong, evil, and not Christianity, is to compromise.

Joseph Cook Orthodoxy lect. x, p. 300.

Shelley's feud *with* Christianity was a craze derived from some early wrench of his understanding.

De Quincey Essays on the Poets, Shelley p. 46.

You dispute *with* Schelling, and he waves you away as a profane and intuitionless laic. R. A. Vaughan *Hours with the Mystics* vol. i, bk. iii, ch. 3, p. 90.

Frederick II. . . . had his share of brabbling *with* intricate litigant neighbors; quarrels now and then, not to be settled without strokes.   Carlyle *Frederick* vol. i, bk. iii, ch. 8, p. 158.

Feeling that awful pause of blood and breath
Which life endures when it confronts *with* death.

Hood Hero and Leander st. 129.

He conducted himself with a certain stiffness and decorum which contrasted pleasantly enough *with* the exceeding 'bounce' of his earlier career.

         R. F. BURTON *Lake Regions Cent. Africa* ch. 4, p. 108.

In all nature there is not an object so essentially at war *with* the stiffening of frost, as the headlong and desperate life of a cataract.   DE QUINCEY *Essays on the Poets* p. 32.

The manufactures of Flanders perished in the great catastrophe of the religious war of the Low Countries *with* Spain.

         J. R. SEELEY *Expansion of England* course i, lect. v, p. 85.

9. Denoting separation: from; as, to part *with* a keepsake; to dispense *with* a service; to differ *with* a person; to break *with* a friend; to be done *with* a matter.

Fred, when he had parted *with* his new horse for at least eighty pounds, would be at least fifty-five pounds in pocket by the transaction.   GEORGE ELIOT *Middlemarch* ch. 23, p. 220.

And thereupon told them that the Lord has done *with* them. [Cromwell's words at breaking of the Long Parliament.]

         MORLEY *Oliver Cromwell* bk. iv, ch. 6, p. 335.

Verbs and Other Antecedents

Verbs denoting combination or union, or the like, are followed by *with;* as, *accord, agree, ally, combine, concur, confuse, conjoin, connect, consort, fuse, incorporate, interfere, intermeddle, intermingle, intermix, meddle, mingle, mix, reunite, unite,* and many others. Some antonyms of these verbs, as *disagree,* are followed by *with,* though most take *from,* as the preposition of separation; as, to *dissent from, separate from,* etc. *Differ* may take either *from* or *with* (see FROM). *Agree* may take either *about, in, on* (*upon*), *to,* or *with;* as, to agree *about* or *on* a matter; *in* opinion; *to* the terms; *with* a person.

Verbs denoting acquaintance, intercourse, etc., are followed by *with;* as, I am acquainted *with* him; I have met *with* people of that sort. *Meet* may be used absolutely, without a preposition, but in that case denotes less of association than when followed by *with.* *Confer, consult,* and the like are followed by *with.*

Verbs denoting contention, conflict, etc., are commonly fol
lowed by *with*; as, *argue, combat, conflict, contend, debate, discuss, dispute, fight, quarrel, strive, struggle, war, wrangle,* etc.

Adjectives and nouns carrying similar meanings are likewise
followed by *with*; as, *accordant, content, contented, discontented,
displeased, dissatisfied, gratified, pleased, satisfied, united ;* also,
*accord, agreement, concord, gratification, harmony, mixture, sat-
isfaction, union,* etc. We say, however, *hostile to, opposed to,*
or speak of *conflict, contention, war,* etc., *with,* but of *hostility* or
opposition to some person or thing.

Distinctions

By—with: The broad distinction between these two words is
that *by* denotes the agent, and *with* the instrument. The tree
was cut down *by* a man *with* an ax. *By* is, however, often used of
things without life that have the effect of definitely accomplishing
an action; as, the town is surrounded *by* mountains. *With,* as denoting association or cooperation, may be joined with *by* denoting direct agency in the same statement; as, it was done *by* him *with* my
assistance; *by* the President *with* the advice and consent of the Senate.

[*By—with—through :* Whenever a conscious agent is mentioned, and the instrument employed to accomplish his purpose.
by must be used to denote the agent, and *with,* in general, the instrument; as, "He was slain *by* his enemy *with* the sword."

Thus, *by* denotes in general the essential or immediate agent,
and *with,* carrying the idea of companionship, the means or instrument employed by the agent.

He was struck *by* the sun. The sun struck him *with* its rays.
The tree was shaken *by* the wind. The wind shook the tree *with*
its strong hand.

The city was destroyed *by* fire. Here fire is the essential agent.

He destroyed the city *with* fire. Here fire is the auxiliary
means or instrument.

By attention and prompt action he won his case, these being
the essential agents of success.

He won his case *through* attention and prompt action, these
being the important auxiliaries.

SAMUEL FALLOWS, 100,000 Synonyms and Antonyms.]

WITHIN

Within is from the Anglo-Saxon *withinnan*, from *with*, with, plus *innan*, in.

I. Of place or space: in the inner or interior part of; not going beyond; not exceeding; included in; inside of; in; as, *within* the house; *within* the town; it is *within* a mile of this place.

A little way *within* the shop door, lay heaps of old crackled parchment scrolls and discolored and dog's-eared law-papers.
> DICKENS *Bleak House* ch. 5, p. 88.

Within easy range and reach of the great city of London.
> DICKENS *Dombey and Son* ch. 88, p. 549.

And roused the prisoned brutes *within*.
> WHITTIER *Snow-Bound* st. 5.

Within these walls [St. Peter's], the thermometer never varies.
> HAWTHORNE *Marble Faun* vol. ii, ch. 15, p. 171.

The seven hills [of Rome] were first united *within* the cincture of a single wall.
> CHAS. MERIVALE *Rome* ch. 1, p. 88.

During the five winters the [New York trade] schools have been open, no rude or profane word has been heard *within* their walls.
> R. T. AUCHMUTY in *Century Magazine* Nov., 1886, p. 91.

I crept up *within* fifty yards of it [a rhinoceros] unperceived, and sent a zinc bullet close to the ear, which bowled it over dead.
> STANLEY *Through the Dark Continent* vol. i, ch. 17, p. 466.

My brother wears a martial plume,
And serves *within* a distant land.
> T. B. READ *Song of the Alpine Guide* st. 8.

Doubling a creature's activity, quadruples the area that comes *within* the range of its excursions.
> SPENCER *Biology* vol. i, pt. iii, ch. 9, p. 419.

Then said the brave Boanerges, 'Let us for a while lie still *within* our trenches and see what these rebels will do.'
> BUNYAN *Works, Holy War* p. 896.

And now behold *within* the haven rides
Our good ship, swinging in the changing tides.
> MORRIS *Jason* bk. iii, st. 12.

II. Of time: in the limits of a designated time; not beyond or exceeding; included in; inside of; as, he will fail *within* a year; we shall arrive at the house *within* ten minutes.

Within the first week of my passion, I bought four sumptuous waistcoats.   DICKENS *David Copperfield* ch. 26, p. 197.

III. Of general relations: in the limits, range, or scope of; in the reach of; not being, done, or going outside of; as, to live *within* one's means: it is *within* my power; the matter is not *within* our jurisdiction.

> This truth *within* thy mind rehearse,
> That in a boundless universe
> Is boundless better, boundless worse.
>   TENNYSON *Two Voices* st. 9.

> But from *within* proceeds a Nation's health.
>   WORDSWORTH *Sonnet, O'erweening Statesmen* l. 8.

> Truth is *within* ourselves; it takes no rise
> From outward things, whate'er you may believe.
>   BROWNING *Paracelsus* pt. i, l. 728.

Not only is man *within* nature, but his acts and works are *within* nature, and thus human industry itself is *within* nature.
          JANET *Final Causes* tr. by Affleck, bk. i, ch. 8, p. 88.

Educated intelligence keeps radicalism *within* proper limits, and forces it to conserve the highest purposes, by harnessing it to the car of progress.
          DEPEW *Orations and Speeches, May 10, 1882* p. 460.

WITHOUT

Without is from the Anglo-Saxon *withûtan*, from *with*, in the sense of *against*, plus *ûtan*, out.

I. Of place or space: outside of; not in or within; external to; as, *without* the gate; *without* the bounds: in this use less common than formerly.

> The dream's here still: even when I wake, it is
> *Without* me, as within me.
>   SHAKESPEARE *Cymbeline* act iv, sc. 2, l. 307.

II. Of general relations:

1. Out of or beyond the limits of (any society, association, condition, etc.); exceeding the reach of; beyond: closely analogous but not limited to the spatial meaning; as, *without* the pale of civilization.

> Our intent
> Was to be gone from Athens, where we might be
> *Without* the peril of the Athenian law.
> SHAKESPEARE *A Midsummer-Night's Dream* act iv, sc. 1, l. 158.

2. Not having, as the result of loss, privation, negation, or the like; deprived of; destitute of; wanting; lacking; as, *without* money; *without* friends; *without* recourse.

> A tender glow, exceeding fair,
> A dream of day *without* its glare.
> WHITTIER *The River Path* st. 6.

We have seen strong assertions *without* proof, declaration *without* argument, and violent censures *without* dignity or moderation. JUNIUS *Letters* vol. i, letter i, p. 38.

An enterprise undertaken *without* resolution, managed *without* care, prosecuted *without* vigor, will easily be dashed and prove abortive. BARROW *Sermons* vol. iii, ser. xlii.

For no mind ever sailed steadily, *without* moral principle to ballast and right it.
A. J. AND J. C. HARE *Guesses at Truth* second series, p. 508.

For Hugo, man is no longer an isolated spirit *without* antecedent or relation here below. R. L. STEVENSON *Familiar Studies* p. 56.

Plato returned to Athens, and began to teach. Like his master, he taught *without* money and *without* price.
SMILES *Duty* ch. 1, p. 26.

The Cabinets and Chancelleries of Europe were to learn that nothing was to be done any more *without* the authority of England. MCCARTHY *Our Own Times* vol. iv, ch. 64, p. 434.

Let us beware . . . of a Christianity *without* Christ.
J. NEWTON *Letters and Sermons* vol. iv, ser. iii, p. 89.

There is in man a Higher than Love of Happiness; he can do *without* Happiness, and instead thereof find Blessedness!
CARLYLE *Sartor Resartus* bk. ii, ch. 9, p. 148.

PART II

PART II

PART II

Conjunctions Defined and Illustrated

Conjunctions may be regarded as the simplest of connectives, merely conjoining or joining together (Latin *conjunctio*, joining, from *conjungo*, join) words, phrases, or sentences. When words are connected by a preposition those words are in different relations. Thus, when we say, "John went *to* James," *John* is the subject and *James* the object of the action, or, as we commonly say, *James* is "in the objective case." But if we say, "John *and* James went together," there is no difference in the relations of the two nouns. One is as much nominative as the other. Neither is the object of the action, but, as it is the very office of the conjunction to indicate, the two nouns are coordinate.

There are, indeed, some grammarians (as Latham) who will say that conjunctions do not connect words or phrases, but only sentences, and that wherever two words seem to be joined by a conjunction the real union is of two sentences that might be made out of the one. In some cases such division may be made, but in others it becomes ridiculous, as in the sentence last quoted. If we say, "John went together *and* James went together," we utter an absurdity, and do not give the meaning of the original sentence. So if we take the sentence, "The king *and* queen are an amiable pair," and attempt to make two sentences of it, we are landed in the absurdity of saying, "The king are an amiable pair *and* the queen are an amiable pair"; and we do not improve it by putting the verb in the singular and saying, "The king *is* an amiable pair *and* the queen *is* an amiable pair." The fact is that it is exactly and expressly the two nouns which

(195)

the conjunction connects, "The king *and* queen [united] constitute an amiable pair."

The same is true of phrases; as, "to be *or* not to be? that is the question." This could not be resolved into "To be is the question *or* not to be is the question." Neither phrase is "the question" by itself. "The question" is which of the two states that are at once paired and contrasted by *or* shall be preferred.

The English language is much more flexible than the grammarians, and continually bursts out of their petty rules, as a growing tree will burst even an iron band fastened too closely around it.

[A conjunction is a word that conjoins or connects. Conjunctions so often connect sentences, or what may readily be developed into sentences, that it has sometimes been held that they invariably have that office. Mr. Harris, the author of "Hermes," and Dr. Latham are probably the most eminent advocates of that view. The latter says, "there are always two propositions where there is one conjunction"; but the statement, I think, requires limitation. . . . Many words are sometimes pronouns or adverbs, and sometimes conjunctions; and it is not always possible to tell in a given instance which they are. The general test of a conjunction is that it unites two propositions or phrases without being a part of either.

We called (*but*) there was no answer.

The propositions are complete in themselves, and *but* adds nothing to either, but it shows a relation between the two — a relation we may say of disappointment. The conjunction is not necessarily placed between the related propositions.

(*Although*) we called, there was no answer.

When the subject or object is two individuals, acting or acted upon together and united by *and*, the sentence cannot always be decomposed into two propositions without completely recasting it.

"This dog *and* man at first were friends."
If this were developed into:

This dog at first were friends,
and
This man at first were friends,

it would be very like nonsense. The same might be said of —

She mixed wine *and* oil together.

The mother *and* daughter embraced each other.

It is evident then that *and* does not always connect separate propositions.   Ramsey *English Language* ch. 8, pp. 491–94.]

While words and phrases that are connected by conjunctions are commonly coordinate, yet in the connection of sentences the conjunction may have an office very much like that which the preposition has in the connection of nouns or pronouns, showing the dependence of one sentence upon another.

[A conjunction differs from a relative pronoun or adverb, which also connects propositions, in this that the relative belongs to one of the propositions, and the conjunction does not.

This is Mr. A. B. *who* is the secretary of our society.

This is Mr. A. B. (*and*) he is the secretary of our society.
      Ramsey *English Language* ch. 8, p. 494.]

Thus, in the sentence, "I should be very sorry *if* this were the fact," the supposed possibility of the fact is the condition of the sorrow. This subordinate or conditional thought is introduced by *if*, which shows the sentence following to be subordinate or conditional.

The principal conjunctions are the following: *also, although, and, as, because, both, but, either, except, for, however, if, lest, neither, nevertheless, nor, notwithstanding, only, or, provided, save, seeing, since, so, still, than, that, then, therefore, though, unless, what, when, whereas, whereat, whereby, wherefor, wherefore, wherein, whereof, whereupon, wherever (where'er), whether, while, without, yet.*

Correlative conjunctions are: *although—yet, as—as, as—so, both—and, either—or, if—then, neither—nor, not only . . . but also, now—now, now—then, so—as, though—yet, whereas—therefore, whether—or.*

ALSO

Also (Anglo-Saxon *eal swa*, all so, entirely so) is ranked both as an adverb and a conjunction. In the conjunctive use, it may either stand alone or in conjunction with *and, but,* etc., always denoting that what follows is of the same sort as what precedes.

1. In like manner; likewise; wholly so; quite so; as, we must care for the teachers and *also* for the pupils.

There be three things which go well, yea, four are comely in going · a lion, which is strongest among beasts . . .; a greyhound; an he-goat, *also*.   *Prov.* xxx, 29.

Likewise the second *also*, and the third, unto the seventh.   *Matt.* xxii, 26.

> And *also*, I think, thou art not ignorant
> How she opposes her against my will.
> Shakespeare *Two Gentlemen of Verona* act. iii, sc. 2, 1. 25.

2. As something further tending in the same direction, often with increased emphasis or intensity, or as a result or completion : in addition; besides; as well; as, the statesman was *also* a soldier.

And God made two great lights; the greater light to rule the day, and the lesser light to rule the night; he made the stars *also*.   *Gen.* i, 16.

She took of the fruit thereof and did eat, and gave *also* unto her husband with her, and he did eat.   *Gen.* iii, 6.

He hoped *also* that money should have been given him of Paul.   *Acts* xxiv, 26.

There is always a disposition, *also*, to cavil at the conduct of those in command.   Irving *Alhambra, Governor Manco* p. 401.

ALTHOUGH

Although is compounded of *all* and *though*, and is thus a strengthened form of *though*. See THOUGH.

[*Although*—all though—does not differ in meaning from *though*, one of our most primitive conjunctions. It admits the foregoing proposition, but prepares to deny the consequences expected to follow. It is often followed by *still* or *yet* as a correlative.

"*Although* the fig-tree shall not blossom, neither shall fruit be in the vines, . . . *yet* I will rejoice in the Lord."—Hab. iii, 17.   Ramsey *English Language* ch. 8, p. 495.]

Introducing a concessive sentence or clause : admitting or granting that; in spite of the fact that; even though; notwithstanding.

God led them not through the way of the land of the Philistines, *although* that was near.   *Ex.* xiii, 17.

But Peter said unto him, *Although* all shall be offended, yet will not I   *Mark* xiv, 29.

> Good lords, *although* my will to give is living,
> The suit which you demand is gone and dead.
>   SHAKESPEARE *King John* act iv, sc. 2. l. 88

He may not spare, *although* he were his brother.
            CHAUCER *Canterbury Tales* Prologue. l 789.

Oratory is an accomplishment in which Europeans believe that Americans excel, and that this is the opinion of the Americans themselves, *although* they are too modest to express it, may be gathered from the surprise they betray when they find an Englishman fluent before an audience.
            BRYCE *Am. Commonwealth* vol. ii. ch. 8, p. 651.

AND

And is a pure Anglo-Saxon word preserved without change in modern English. *And* may be regarded as the simplest of all connectives, adding one thing to another, or placing one thing beside another, without specification of the kind of connection—a mere plus sign. In usage it has certain derived meanings which are due to the qualities of the things thus brought together, rather than to anything inherent in the meaning of the conjunction.

[*And* joins only things that are grammatically alike and equivalent. It unites nouns, including their substitutes, pronouns, or adjectives, verbs, adverbs, or prepositions, but it does not unite members of these different classes. Moreover it is the only conjunction that unites parts which cannot be construed as separate propositions. RAMSEY *English Language* ch. 8, p. 495.]

I. Copulative or additive :

1. Denoting simple addition : together with ; joined with ; added to ; furthermore ; also : the typical copulative conjunction, as, William *and* Henry ; army *and* navy ; one hundred *and* twenty.

> Dim grows the sky, *and* dusk the air.
>
> R. H. STODDARD *Night Before the Bridal* st. 5.

Little breezes dusk *and* shiver   Thro' the wave that runs forever.

R. H. STODDARD *Night Before the Bridal* st. 5.

TENNYSON *Lady of Shalott* pt. i, st. 2.

We are accustomed to think of a dragon as a winged *and* clawed creature ; but the real Greek dragon . . . was simply a serpent.   RUSKIN *Deucalion* vol. ii, ch. 1, p. 10.

> Where loop the clustered vines ;
> *And* the close-clinging dulcamara twines.
>
> HOLMES *Musa* st. 5.

He does nothing but sit at the table *and* drum with his fingers.   G. W. CURTIS *Trumps* ch. 62, p. 860.

Mirth is short *and* transient, cheerfulness fixed *and* perma nent.   ADDISON *Spectator, May 17, 1712.*

Nobles by the right of an earlier creation, *and* priests by the imposition of a mightier hand.   MACAULAY *Essays, Milton* p. 16.

In choice *and* volition we have the two factors of the will, the constituents of man as a free agent.

HOPKINS *Script. Idea of Man* lect. iii, p. 65.

[NOTE.—In the last quotation above, *and* might be rendered *combined with.* It denotes the close union of the connected nouns, so that both are governed by the same preposition and combine in a single result.

Closely allied to this is the idiomatic expression "*and all,*" which is very emphatic. One or more items are mentioned, which are strictly part of the "all." Then the attempt at enumeration is dropped, and the speaker says "and [in fact] all"— *i. e.*, not only what has been mentioned, but all of which it is a part.

> The total grist unsifted, husks *and all.*
>
> COWPER *Task* bk. vi, l. 108.]

2. Continuing the narrative or following the course of thought: in addition; also; as, they turned *and* ran away

> To such a fame let mere town-wits aspire,
> *And* their gay nonsense their own cits admire.
>> DRYDEN *Prologue III, To the University of Oxford* l. 87.

But when the captains saw how it was, they made a fair retreat *and* entrenched themselves in their winter-quarters.
>> BUNYAN *The Holy War* ch. 5, p. 115.

He managed to continue work till nine o'clock, *and* then marched dumb and dour to his chamber.
>> EMILY BRONTË *Wuthering Heights* ch. 7, p. 49.

> He started back, gazed, nor could aught but gaze,
> *And* cold dread stiffen'd up his hair.
>> LANDOR *Gebir* bk. ii, l. 237.

Cock-fighters trim the hackles and cut off the combs and gills of their cocks; *and* the birds are then said to be dubbed.
>> DARWIN *Descent of Man* pt. ii, ch. 18, p. 408.

Christianity soon eclipsed or destroyed all other sects, *and* became for many centuries the supreme ruler of the moral world.
>> LECKY *Hist. Eur. Morals* vol. i, ch. 2, p. 356.

Honesty goes to bed early, *and* industry rises betimes.
>> CHAS. READE *Cloister and Hearth* ch. 42, p. 198.

> 'Tis distance lends enchantment to the view,
> *And* robes the mountain in its azure hue.
>> CAMPBELL *Pleasures of Hope* pt. i, st. 1.

Suddenly drops the gull *and* breaks the glassy tide.
>> LOWELL *Indian Summer Reverie* st. 24.

> The eve was cradling earth to sleep,
> *And* night upon the mountains hung.
>> GOETHE *Welcome and Departure* tr. by Martin and Aytoun, l. 1.

Thomas Jefferson . . . caught *and* crystallized the spirit of free institutions.
>> DEPEW *Orations and Speeches, April 30, 1889* p. 6.

> 'Twas daybreak, *and* the fingers of the dawn
> Drew the night's curtain.
>> N. P. WILLIS *David's Grief* st. 1.

[NOTE.—Where two or more items are connected in an enumeration, *and* is commonly omitted except before the last of the series; as, he was brave, valiant, *and* noble. (The best present usage retains the comma before the *and* in such an enumeration.)

This ordinary method is, however, subject to several variations:

(*a*) The conjunction may be repeated between every two items of an enumeration; as, fire *and* hail *and* candle-light. This method, which would be tiresome if constantly employed, is very effective in occasional use, seeming at once to emphasize the separate items and to protract the enumeration, thus making it more impressive.

> East *and* west *and* south *and* north
>   The messengers ride fast,
> *And* tower *and* town *and* cottage
>   Have heard the trumpet's blast.
>
> MACAULAY Horatius st. 2.

The chains, *and* the bracelets, *and* the mufflers. *Isa.* iii, 19.

And boy *and* dog, *and* hostler *and* Boots, all slunk back again to their holes.   IRVING *Bracebridge, Stout Gent.* p. 78.

(*b*) The items of the series may be joined in pairs, the two of each pair being connected by *and*; as, king *and* subject, peer *and* peasant, rich *and* poor, man *and* woman are alike interested in the sacred observance of law.

> A fairy realm; where slope *and* stream,
> Champaign *and* upland, town *and* grange, . . .
> Forever blend and interchange.
>
> E. C. STEDMAN Bohemia st. 6.

I might present to you the long catalogue of the noble *and* the good, the wise *and* the brave.

A. McKENZIE Cambridge Sermons ser. xv, p. 290.

(*c*) The conjunction may be omitted altogether, a method forcible by its very abruptness if sparingly used.

Two horses have emerged from the ruck, and are sweeping, rushing, storming towards us, almost side by side.

HOLMES Our Hundred Days ch. 1, p. 54.

Love rules the court, the camp, the grove.
Scott *The Lay of the Last Minstrel* can. 3, st. 2, l. 5.]

3. Denoting emphasis by reduplication:

(*a*) Indicating great but indefinite number, time, extent, etc., by repetition; as, years *and* years; thousands *and* thousands; we walked miles *and* miles; forever *and* ever; greater *and* greater; more *and* more; less *and* less.

Higher still *and* higher,
From the earth thou springest.
Shelley *To a Skylark* st. 2.

The emphasis is sometimes increased by adding something greater after the conjunction in such use; as, it lasted for months *and* years; they came by hundreds *and* thousands.

(*b*) Indicating emphasis by mere repetition of any word, thus causing the mind to dwell upon the thought: one of the simplest and most primitive forms of emphatic statement; as, they talked *and* talked; he raved *and* raved *and* raved; soldiers *and* soldiers *and* soldiers came marching in.

If thou would'st view fair Melrose aright,
Go visit it by the pale moonlight;
*   *   *   *   *   *
When buttress *and* buttress, alternately,
Seem framed of ebon and ivory.
Scott *The Lay of the Last Minstrel* can. 2, st. 1, l. 1.

[Note.—In the case of adjectives other than comparatives, such reduplicative emphasis is usually given without the *and;* as, that tall, tall spire.]

II. Intensive.

1. Denoting advance of thought: also, what is more important; moreover; an intensive use; as, he did the work *and* did it well; I say it *and* [what is more] I mean it.

In this tract the French still had the ascendancy; *and* it was important to dislodge them.
Macaulay's *Essays, Malcolm's Clive* p. 382.

Strictly speaking, all quiescent electricity is static, *and* all electricity in motion, from whatever source, is dynamic.

> B. SILLIMAN, JR. *Physics* ¶ 809, p. 532.

The mark is there, *and* the wound is cicatrized only—no time, tears, caresses, or repentance can obliterate that scar.

> THACKERAY *Henry Esmond* bk. ii, ch. 1, p. 144.

Neither is a dictionary a bad book to read. There is no cant in it, no excess of explanation, *and* it is full of suggestion.

> EMERSON *Society and Solitude, Books* p. 169.

In the eye of the law, all Roman citizens were equal, *and* all subjects of the empire were citizens of Rome.

> GIBBON *Rome* vol. iv, ch. 44, p. 340.

The camp *and* not the soil is the native country of the genuine Tartar.   GIBBON *Rome* vol. iii, ch. 26, p. 7.

> The ruin'd spendthrift, now no longer proud,
> Claim'd kindred there, *and* had his claims allowed.
>
> > GOLDSMITH *Deserted Village* l. 154.

Speak truth *and* the whole truth.   SHELLEY *Cenci* act v, sc. 2.

2. In union of two adjectives, specializing and emphasizing by the latter some quality included in the former; as, these peaches are good *and* ripe; he is nice *and* kind.

This usage is now colloquial and considered inelegant. It has the taint of tautology and consequent feebleness. This criticism does not apply to the union of adjectives where there is a real advance of thought; as, wise *and* good; cheap *and* nasty; strong *and* swift.

III. Adversative or disjunctive:

Denoting the addition of that which is different, contrasted or opposed: a use founded on the fact that nothing brings out a contrast so clearly as the simple placing of the contrasted objects side by side:

    (*a*) On the other hand; yet in addition; yet; but; as, so rich *and* so stingy!

[NOTE.—*And* in such use is nearly equal to *but*. See DISTINCTIONS.]

It is one thing to entertain, *and* another to be entertaining.
    C. D. WARNER *Little Journey in the World* ch. 18, p. 227.

I have brought you here to reason, . . . *and* wrangling is caddish.   E. LYNN LINTON *Patricia Kemball* ch. 20, p. 214.

In schools and colleges, in fleet and army, discipline means success, *and* anarchy means ruin.
        FROUDE *Short Studies. Kerry* in second series, p. 381.

Lord Brougham's wise dictum . . . that it is well to read everything of something *and* something of everything.
        LUBBOCK *Pleasures of Life* pt. i, ch. 3, p. 68.

God made the country *and* man made the town.
        COWPER *The Task* bk. i, l. 749.

(b) Discriminating between things that are united under the same class or name, but are different in character; as, there are apples *and* apples, that is, apples [of one kind] *and* apples [of a very different kind].

(c) Noting the joining of extremes in thought, with consequent inclusion of all that may be between, or noting the matching of opposite or different directions, qualities, etc.; as, alike to rich *and* poor; to travel far *and* wide; he paced to *and* fro; he gazed up *and* down.

        And I would be the necklace,
            And all day long to fall *and* rise
        Upon her balmy bosom,
            With her laughter or her sighs.
        TENNYSON *The Miller's Daughter* l. 182.

IV. Purposive or resultant :

1. Adding a fact or statement which is viewed as the result of what has gone before : consequently; accordingly; hence; as, he found sleep impossible, *and* rose weary and grumbling.

        You bear a gentle mind, *and* heavenly blessings
        Follow such creatures.
        SHAKESPEARE *K. Henry VIII.* act ii, sc. 3.

Were the centrifugal tendency to cease, the centripetal force would be uncontrolled, *and* the body would fall upon the attracting mass.   J. N. LOCKYER *Elements of Astron.* ch. 16. p. 281.

Enlist the interests of stern morality and religious enthusiasm in the cause of political liberty, as in the time of the old Puritans, *and* it will be irresistible.

> COLERIDGE *Table Talk* May 8, 1830.

I was brought up in a New England village, *and* I knew . . . where all those things were that boys enterprise after.

> BEECHER in Abbott's *Henry Ward Beecher* p. 15.

We only know that God is just,   *And* every wrong shall die.

> WHITTIER *At Port Royal* st. 15.

Remember of what blood thou art,   *And* strike the caitiff down!

> AYTOUN *Execution of Montrose* st. 8.

My dragoman had me completely in his power, *and* I resolved to become independent of all interpreters as soon as possible.

> BAKER *Albert Nyanza* ch. 1, p. 8.

The ibis destroyed snakes; *and* Cuvier found the skin of one partly digested in the intestines of one of those mummied birds.

> RAWLINSON *Herodotus* vol. ii, bk. ii, p. 107, note 5.

'Twas summer, *and* the meadow lands
Were brown *and* baked *and* dry.

> ALICE CARY *Fable of Cloud-land* st. 1.

2. In the union of two verbs, especially after *go, come, send,* and *try:* as the result or fulfilment (of an action implied in the preceding verb); as, try *and* find it; go *and* get it.

May's in all the Italian books :
She has old and modern nooks, . . .
And will rise *and* dress your rooms
With a drapery thick with blooms.

> HUNT *May and the Poets* l. 9.

[NOTE.—Many grammarians have been in error in defining *and* in this usage as equivalent to *to*, and hence condemning it as superfluous or incorrect. The usage is sustained by the very highest authority, and, when we come to balance the expressions, is sustained also by the logic of linguistic thought. If we change "try *and* find it" into "try *to* find it," there is an instant loss of force. Why? Because "try *to* find it" refers only to a purpose which is antecedent to the trying, and which may never be fulfilled, while "try *and* find it" contemplates the finding as the sure result of the trying, which may therefore be added to it as an accomplished fact. Instead of being equivalent to an infinite, the *and* with its following verb is more nearly equal to a future tense, "try *and* [you will] find it." Hence this idiom has a conclusiveness to be attained by no other form of expression.

They said unto him, Rabbi, . . . where dwellest thou? He saith unto them, Come *and* see.   *John* i, 38.

He saith unto them, How many loaves have ye? go *and* see.
                                                Mark vi, 38.

Go *and* shew John again those things which ye do hear and see.   *Matt.* xi, 4.

[NOTE—It may be seen that in rapid, emphatic utterance, the *and* of such expressions is often omitted; as, go bring me my hat.]

> Let me not stay a jot for dinner; go get it ready.
>   SHAKESPEARE *King Lear* act i, sc. 4, l. 82.

> Come, gentle dreams, the hour of sleep beguile!
>   LONGFELLOW *The Child Asleep* st. 5.]

V. Certain archaic uses need but be mentioned; as, (*a*) Also; even: often added to *but*, *but and* being equivalent to *but also*. (*b*) If: commonly printed *an* or *an'*, as frequently found in Shakespeare and others of the older writers, and often joined with *if*, which has now completely taken its place.

> No more of that, Hal, *an* thou lovest me.
>   SHAKESPEARE *1 K. Henry IV.* act ii, sc. 4, l. 312.

> God mark thee to his grace!
> Thou wast the prettiest babe that e'er I nursed:
> *An* I might live to see thee married once,
> I have my wish.
>   SHAKESPEARE *Romeo and Juliet* act i, sc. 3, l. 60.

And may stand at the beginning of a sentence, adding what is to come to something previously said, answering the words of some other speaker, or even some unspoken thought or inference supposed to be in his words or acts, joining what the speaker has now to say to some silent thought or reasoning of his own mind, etc.: often passing to sharp adversative use, expressing indignant surprise, reproach, etc.; as, *and* do you mean to tell me you went there? *and* you come to tell me this; *and* [in spite of all] you believe that?

> *And* with one voice the thirty
>   Have their glad answer given:
> 'Go forth, go forth, Lars Porsena;
>   Go forth, beloved of Heaven!'
>
> Macaulay Horatius st. 5.

> *And* still in a voice of dolorous pitch—
> Would that its tone could reach the rich!—
> She sang this 'Song of the Shirt.'
>
> Hood Song of the Shirt st. 11.

And in any case, it is useless to dogmatize about things which God has not revealed.   Farrar *Eternal Hope* p. 94.

Distinctions

And — but: And and *but* are for the most part sharply opposed, *and* being the typical copulative or conjoining, and *but* the typical disjunctive or disjoining particle. *And* expresses proximity, likeness, or union; *but* expresses contrast, unlikeness, or opposition. Yet, in certain uses, these two conjunctions almost coincide. *And,* as in the examples under III., 1 (*a*) is often almost or quite equivalent to *but,* having only this difference that the contrast with *and* is left to inference, while with *but* it is expressly stated. The presentation by *and* is with a lighter touch, and hence sometimes more impressive, as assuming that the contrast is self-evident, and need not be expressly stated by *but,* but only pointed to by *and.*

And — or: See OR.

AS

As is derived from the Anglo-Saxon *eal swā,* all so, entirely so: the particle of comparison, likeness, or illustration.

I. Denoting equality, comparison, equivalence, or proportion:

1. As to extent or character: to the extent of; to the degree in which; in proportion to which; no less than; like: often with one of the correlatives *same, such, so, as;* as, this is the same *as* that; such a one *as* he can not fail.

> Cheerily, then, my little man,
> Live and laugh, *as* boyhood can!
> WHITTIER *Barefoot Boy* st. 5.

> He bade the twelve in all things be *as* brothers,
> And die to self, to live and work for others.
> J. B. O'REILLY *Macarius the Monk* st. 1.

Never . . . can the sight of the gigantic Coliseum full and running over with the lustiest life, have moved one heart, *as* it must move all who look upon it now, a ruin.
DICKENS *Pictures from Italy, Rome* p. 121.

> Her eyes *as* stars of twilight fair,
> Like twilight's, too, her dusky hair;
> But all things else about her drawn
> From May-time and the cheerful dawn.
> WORDSWORTH *She Was a Phantom of Delight* st. 1.

Never was dominion wielded by such unfit hands *as* those of the Spartans. THOMAS ARNOLD *Rome* vol. i, ch. 22, p. 498.

In the early part of life we collect the materials; *as* we grow older we learn to use them.
WAYLAND *Intellectual Philosophy* ch. 5, p. 285.

As the Greeks and Romans became acquainted with other nations they imported their habits of worship.
BULFINCH *Age of Fable* int., ch. 1, p. 6.

We all know the wag's definition of a philanthropist—a man whose charity increases directly *as* the square of the distance.
GEORGE ELIOT *Middlemarch* vol. i, ch. 88, p. 420.

2. In time, denoting simultaneousness: at or during the time when; in or during the act of; while; when; as, the company rose *as* he entered; the king bowed right and left *as* he rode on.

As thus used has often a suggestion of occasion or cause; as, *as* he looked up I saw his meaning.

As daylight failed, Slow, overhead, the dusky night-birds
sailed.   WHITTIER *Pennsylvania Pilgrim* st. 9.

Then shrilled his fierce cry, *as* the riders drew nigh.
         TROWBRIDGE *The Jaguar Hunt* st. 9.

His heart bounded *as* he sometimes could distinctly hear the
trip of a light female step glide to or from the door of the hut.
         SCOTT *Waverley* vol. ii, ch. 87, p. 62.

I was extremely pleased, *as* we rode along, to observe the
general benevolence of all the neighbourhood toward my friend.
         ADDISON *Spectator* July 18, 1711.

As I rounded an elbow in the stream, a black eagle sprang
from the top of a dead tree.   BURROUGHS *Pepacton* ch. 1, p. 16.

I, looking then, beheld the ancient Three, . . .
Still crooning, *as* they weave their endless brede.
         LOWELL *Washers of the Shroud* st. 4.

Fast *as* the fatal symbol flies, In arms the huts and hamlets
rise.   SCOTT *Lady of the Lake* can. 8, st. 14.

Just *as* the sun's slow orb forsook the fulgent west.
         TASSO *Jerusalem Delivered* tr. by Wiffen, can. 4, st. 55.

The pilot grumbled *as* he cast his groggy eyes aloft.
         W. CLARK RUSSELL *John Holdsworth* ch. 8, p. 7.

A most tremendous 'buck' he was, *as* he sat there, serene,
in state, driving his greys.   THACKERAY *Vanity Fair* ch. 6, p. 81.

II. Denoting illustration or representation:

1. Introducing an illustration, example, or citation· for example; for instance; as, an animal that matures slowly, *as* the
elephant, lives long; a poem may be perfect in meter without
rime, *as* Longfellow's *Evangeline.*

Bran-new. . . . The brand is the fire, and brand-new, equivalent to fire-new (Shak.), is that which is fresh and bright, *as*
being newly come from the forge and fire.   SKEAT *Etym. Dict.*

2. Denoting representation: in the character of; presenting
the appearance of; after the manner of; under the name of; as,
I look upon him *as* our foremost author; he was chosen *as*
moderator; Booth appeared *as* Hamlet.

Speech has been bitterly defined *as* the art of hiding thought.
ROBERTSON *Sermons* first series, ser. iii, p. 54.

In the eyes of the West and of the Church in the West
Charlemagne and his successors, who were crowned by the Pope,
were regarded *as* the true emperors of the Christian world, the
true successors of Augustus and Antoninus, *as* the true temporal
heads of the Holy Roman Empire.
BARING-GOULD *Story of Germany* ch. 10, p. 65.

If we mean to keep the blacks *as* British subjects, we are
bound to govern them, and to govern them well.
FROUDE *Eng. in the West Indies* ch. 8, p. 91.

Children are apt to take all stories of fairy, giant, and so on
as gospel.   SULLY *Psychol.* ch. 11, p. 188.

With silence only *as* their benediction, God's angels come.
WHITTIER *To My Friend* st. 6.

I present myself *as* the advocate of my enslaved countrymen,
at a time when their claims cannot be shuffled out of sight.
W. L. GARRISON *Writings and Speeches, Fourth of July Oration* p. 188.

It would therefore pay to melt it up because it was worth
more *as* bullion than *as* coin.
A. L. PERRY *Elements of Polit. Econ.* ch. 10, p. 819.

Peace is now recognized among Christian states *as* their
normal condition, war *as* the exceptional and sad interruption.
STORRS *Divine Origin Christianity* lect. vi, p. 208.

Those books, and those only, were regarded by the primitive
Christians *as* of canonical authority, which were written by apostles, or by the companions of the apostles under apostolic super-
intendence.   C. E. STOWE *Books of Bible* p. 148.

The canter is usually regarded *as* a slow gallop, probably
from the facility with which a change from one gait to the other
can be effected; an important difference will, however, be observed.   EADWEARD MUYBRIDGE *On the Science of Animal Loco-
motion* p. 10.

III. Denoting cause or reason: for the reason that; it being
the case that; considering that; because; since; as, *as* we had
a fair wind, we sailed straight across the open sea; *as* he is poor,
the debt may be remitted; *as* you are here, we will discuss it now.

It was easy enough to buy, *as* nothing was ever given in payment but a promissory note.

> NICOLAY AND HAY *Abraham Lincoln* vol. i, ch. 6, p. 110.

It was an uncomfortable time for us, *as* we momentarily expected it [ice] to 'nip' her sides.

> KANE *U. S. Grinnell Expedition* ch. 16, p. 128.

As the launch drew little water, we had no occasion to follow the circuitous channel.

> FROUDE *Eng. in the West Indies* ch. 14, p. 222.

IV. Denoting concession: however; though; as, bad *as* it is, it might be worse; scarce *as* money is, I do not despair.

Buried *as* she seemed in foreign negotiations, . . . Elizabeth was above all an English sovereign.

> GREEN *Short Hist. Eng. People* ch. 7, § 5, p. 396.

Distinctions

As—like: As denotes closer equivalence, a nearer approach to identity than *like.* "They lived *as* brothers" means somewhat more than "They lived *like* brothers."

BECAUSE

Because is from the prefix *be-* (Anglo-Saxon *be-*), equal to *by*, plus the noun *cause*, and is literally *by cause.* The word is five centuries old, and in the older writings is often spelled *bycause;* it was also often anciently preceded by *for*, as a matter of emphatic reduplication; as, and *for because* the world is populous (SHAKESPEARE *Richard II.* act v, sc. 4, l. 8).

Having as a cause that; for the reason that; as; since; as, this box is light *because* it is empty.

My strength is as the strength of ten,   *Because* my heart is pure.
> TENNYSON *Sir Galahad* st. 1.

But they [the English] have been great and happy *because* their history has been the history of a succession of timely reforms.   MACAULAY *Speeches, July 5, 1831* in vol. i, p. 30.

What's female beauty, but an air divine,
Through which the mind's all-gentle graces shine ?
They, like the Sun, irradiate all between:
The body charms, *because* the soul is seen.
YOUNG *Love of Fame* satire vi, l. 151.

They [the stars and the sun] shine or give out light, *because* they are white hot.   J. N. LOCKYER *Elements of Astron.* int., p. 12.

They pile up reluctant quarto upon solid folio, as if their labours, *because* they are gigantic, could contend with truth and heaven.   JUNIUS *Letters* vol. i, letter xx, p. 129.

It [memory] fails first in names, *because* they are arbitrary and have not numerous correlations to call them up.
McCOSH *Psychology, Cognitive Powers* bk. ii, p. 159.

A lie is contemptible, chiefly *because* it is cowardly.
CHRISTIAN REID *Question of Honor* bk. iii, ch. 6, p. 284.

Never settle upon anything as true, *because* it is safer to hold it than not.   BUSHNELL *Sermons on Living Subjects* ser. ix, p. 180.

We may not be concerned in buttressing any theology *because* it is old.   DRUMMOND *Natural Law, Biogenesis* p. 98.

[NOTE.—*Because* is often joined with *of*, forming the prepositional phrase *because of*, which may be used causatively with nouns, as the conjunction is with clauses or sentences.

And if Christ be in you, the body is dead *because of* sin ; but the Spirit is life *because of* righteousness.   *Rom.* viii, 10.

It is not *because of* its antiquity, or of the character of the times in which it was first believed, that the doctrine of special creations can be shown to be irrational or improbable.
G. T. CURTIS *Creation or Evolution* ch. 4, p. 184.

The beautiful seems right
By force of beauty, and the feeble wrong
Because of weakness.
E. B. BROWNING *Aurora Leigh* bk. i, l. 754.

All things are beautiful
Because of something lovelier than themselves,
Which breathes within them, and will never die.
LUCY LARCOM *Prelude to Poems* st. 1.]

Distinctions

As—because—for—since: See SINCE.

Because—for: See FOR.

BOTH

Both is from the Icelandic *bāthir* or *bādhir*, having as its equivalent in Anglo-Saxon *bā*, used in the same sense.

Strictly as uniting two words, phrases, or sentences, and followed by *and* as its correlative: equally; alike; as well as; as, this remark applies *both* to science *and* to philosophy. See COR-RELATIVE CONJUNCTIONS. *Both* is, however, often used of enumerations including more than two items.

BUT

For the etymology of this word see BUT under PREPOSITIONS.

But may be termed by preeminence the adversative or disjunctive conjunction, though adversative meanings are also expressed by *although, except, neither, nor, notwithstanding, save, than, though, unless, yet,* etc. The adversative meaning of *but* shades off, however, so as to be in some uses scarcely discernible.

[*But* has many and varied uses, so that it is often difficult or impossible to decide whether the word is a conjunction, a preposition, an adverb, or a particle having various offices. As the typical word used in the adversative coordination of sentences, *but* expresses fundamentally opposition, exception, or exclusion, but its meaning is often restricted to slight transition or simple continuance.   *Standard Dictionary.*]

I. Denoting opposition:

1. Of opposition with contrast or contrariety: on the contrary; on the other hand; still; yet; nevertheless; however; notwithstanding; as, he is strong *but* slow; a mind acute *but* narrow; I go, *but* I return.

They prevented me in the day of my calamity: *but* the Lord was my stay.   *Ps. xviii. 18.*

The prudent man may direct a state; *but* it is the enthusiast who regenerates it,—or ruins.

> BULWER-LYTTON *Rienzi* bk. i, ch. 8, p. 111.

Our general principle of unlimited charters has enriched enormously a few individuals, *but* the country as a whole is correspondingly poorer.   ELY *Intro. to Polit. Econ.* p. 99.

Disarmed *but* not dishonored.

> HALLECK *Field of the Grounded Arms* st. 18.

The other pictures were dim and faded, *but* this one protruded from a plain background in the strongest relief, and with wonderful truth of coloring.   IRVING *Traveller, Mysterious Picture* p. 72

It is not to enjoy, *but* to be, that we long for.

> ROBERTSON *Sermons* first series, ser. xix, p. 212.

Beauties in vain their pretty eyes may roll;
Charms strike the sight, *but* merit wins the soul.

> POPE *Rape of the Lock* can. 5, l. 33.

No useless coffin enclosed his breast,
   Not in sheet nor in shroud we wound him;
But he lay, like a warrior taking his rest,
   With his martial cloak around him.

> CHAS. WOLFE *Burial of Sir John Moore* st. 8.

The cross their standard, *but* their faith the sword.

> MONTGOMERY *The West Indies* pt. i, st. 11.

Beauty is Nature's coin, must not be hoarded,
But must be current, and the good thereof
Consists in mutual and partaken bliss.

> MILTON *Comus* l. 789.

'Tis not a lip, or eye, we beauty call,
But the joint force and full result of all.

> POPE *Essay, On Criticism* pt. ii, l. 45.

2. Of opposition with difference: otherwise than; more than; in every direction except: often followed by *that*; as, I can not believe *but* [that] he means well; I can not *but* hope that he will come.

[NOTE.—In place of "can not *but*" in such construction the shortened form "can *but*" is often used with similar (but not identical) meaning. "I *can not but* hope that he will come" means "I can not help hoping," etc., while "I *can but* hope that he will come" means "I *can only* hope," etc., implying a much less confident expectation. *Can but* is thus ordinarily a weaker phrase than *can not but*, though both are in good usage.]

> No one is so accursed by fate,
> No one so utterly desolate,
> *But* some heart, though unknown,
> Responds unto his own.
> LONGFELLOW *Endymion* st. 8.

If one . . . has a teachable disposition, he cannot *but* improve.
H. T. TUCKERMAN *The Optimist, Travel* p. 44.

No human scheme can be so accurately projected *but* some little circumstance intervening may spoil it. *Spectator* Nov. 8, 1714.

As for the birds, I do not believe there is one of them *but* does more good than harm.
LOWELL *My Study Windows, Garden Acquaint.* p. 28.

We cannot *but* believe that there is an inward and essential truth in art.   CARLYLE *Essays, Goethe* vol. i, p. 287.

I could *but* stare upon her; for though I now see very well what she was driving at, . . . I was never swift at the uptake in such flimsy talk.   R. L. STEVENSON *David Balfour* ch. 19, p. 250.

3. Of opposition with concession: though; even if; however; as, that is the rule, *but* there are many exceptions; I think so, *but* am not sure.

The King reigns, *but* his ministers govern.
E. A. FREEMAN *Impressions of the U. S.* ch. 9, p. 122.

His mind, in consequence of his . . . wife's . . . death, had become slightly unhinged, *but* only in one direction.
W. A. HAMMOND *Strong-minded Woman* ch. 1, p. 9.

Compulsion may secure conformity, *but* never obedience.
HOLLAND *Lessons in Life* lesson ix, p. 125.

Paris is not indeed the gentleman, *but* he is the fine gentleman, and the pattern voluptuary, of the heroic ages.
GLADSTONE *Juventus Mundi* ch. 14, p. 516.

> *But* the old three-cornered hat,
> And the breeches, and all that,
>   Are so queer!   HOLMES *Last Leaf* st. 7.

She [Reason] should be my counsellor,   *But* not my tyrant.
                    BRYANT *Jupiter and Venus* st. 1.

We can disprove a particular dogma, *but* in doing so our attitude cannot be purely negative, any more than when we prove it.   CAIRD *Kant* vol. i, int., ch. 1, p. 21.

Major Lefebvre he rallied a little for losing heart, for bungling his business; *but* was not angry with him.
            CARLYLE *Frederick* vol. vi, bk. xx, ch. 12, p. 288.

Borrowing from a sinking fund is always rather a shabby dodge; *but* it is a trick familiar to all statesmen in difficulties.
            McCARTHY *Four Georges* vol. i, ch. 20, p. 309.

Longinus seems to have had great sensibility *but* little discrimination.   MACAULAY *Essays, Athenian Orators* p. 484.

II. Of addition, continuance, or resumption, with slight opposition or contrast, often nearly equal to *and:* further; now· however; *as, but* who comes here?

But in this sense is common in argumentative use; *as,* the whole is greater than any of its parts; *but* the segment is part of the circle; therefore, etc.

Reasons are the pillars of the fabric of a sermon, *but* similitudes are the windows which give the best lights.
        FULLER *Holy and Profane States, Faithful Minister* p. 84.

> *But* where is she, the bridal flower?
>   TENNYSON *In Memoriam* con., st. 7.

The training of children should be so carried on, as not only to fit them mentally for the struggle before them, *but* also to make them physically fit to bear its excessive wear and tear.
                SPENCER *Education* ch. 4, p. 223.

> Unwounded from the dreadful close,
> *But* breathless all, Fitz-James arose.
>   SCOTT *Lady of the Lake* can. 5, st. 16.

Climbing a ladder develops physical strength, [*but*] climbing a mountain feeds nervous energy.

       MUNGER *On the Threshold* ch. 6, p. 187.

Not only in its details should education proceed from the simple to the complex, *but* in its ensemble also.

       SPENCER *Education* ch. 2, p. 121.

III. Of omission, exception, or exclusion: omitting or excluding the fact that; with the exception that; except; unless; as, *but* for human selfishness, all might prosper; there was not a man *but* was ready to go.

> Had we no other quarrel else to Rome, *but* that
> Thou art thence banish'd, we would muster all
> From twelve to seventy; and pouring war
> Into the bowels of ungrateful Rome,
> Like a bold flood o'erbear.
>   SHAKESPEARE *Coriolanus* act iv, sc. 5, l. 188.

> The world is still deceiv'd with ornament.
> In law, what plea so tainted and corrupt,
> *But*, being season'd with a gracious voice,
> Obscures the show of evil? In religion,
> What damned error, *but* some sober brow
> Will bless it and approve it with a text,
> Hiding the grossness with fair ornament?
>   SHAKESPEARE *Merchant of Venice* act iii, sc. 2, l. 74.

With nothing else on earth to do, *But* all day long to bill and coo.

      THACKERAY *Piscator and Piscatrix* st. 7.

> There's not a wind that blows, *but* bears with it
> Some rainbow promise.   KIRKE WHITE *Time* st. 5.

Nothing so prosperous and pleasant, *but* it hath some bitterness in it.   BURTON *Anat. Melancholy* pt. i, § 1, p. 94.

> There is not a nation in Europe *but* labors
> To toady itself and to humbug its neighbors.
> BARHAM *Ingoldsby Legends, The Auto-da-fé* can. 2, st. 1.

And perhaps his greatest glory, both as a poet and as a man, is, that he was no respecter of sects, or parties or persons, *but* simply a teller of the truth.

   H. N. HUDSON *Lectures on Shakespeare* vol. i, lect. ii, p. 70.

IV. Of explanation, furnishing the ground of something preceding: that it is a fact that; that: *but* in such use often takes an added *that*, forming the phrase *but that*; as, I can not deny *but* [that] you have a strong case.

[NOTE.—After *deny, doubt*, and similar words, the simple *that* is now preferred; as, I deny *that* I was present; I do not doubt *that* he said it.]

It must not be denied *but* I am a plain-dealing villain.
SHAKESPEARE *Much Ado About Nothing* act i, sc. 8.

[After negative sentences the dependent sentence introduced by *but that* or *but* is very commonly employed instead of a substantive sentence.
MAETZNER *Eng. Gram.* tr. by Grece, vol. iii, p. 416.]

V. Of comparison, especially of nearness in time : than ; when; before; as, no sooner blown *but* blasted.

The waves do not rise *but* when the winds blow.
BANCROFT *United States* vol. ii, ch. 16, p. 527.

Scarce had I left my father, *but* I met him
Borne on the shields of his surviving soldiers.
ADDISON *Cato* act iv, sc. 4.

This use is still recognized, but is now infrequent. With comparatives *than* is now considered the only elegant construction; as, I had no sooner turned *than* I fell.

EITHER

Either is from the Anglo-Saxon *ǽgther*, allied to *whether*.

As a disjunctive correlative, introducing a first alternative, a second or other alternative being introduced by *or*: in one of two or more cases indeterminately and indifferently ; as, one must *either* go *or* stay.   See CORRELATIVE CONJUNCTIONS.

[NOTE.—There is a colloquial use of *either* standing alone after a negative, in the sense of *at all, in any case, anyway*, which is not approved; as, I did not do it, nor he *either* [often *neither*]; I won't tell you, *either*.]

ERE

Ere is from the Anglo-Saxon *ǽr*, a contraction of *ǽror*, the comparative of *ǽr*, before.

Earlier or sooner than; rather than; before; as, he will die *ere* he will yield.

O thou sword of the Lord, how long will it be *ere* thou be quiet?   *Jer.* xlvii, 6.

> *Ere* the bat hath flown
> His cloister'd flight.
>   SHAKESPEARE *Macbeth* act iii, sc. 2, l. 40.

> And *ere* the early bedtime came
> The white drift piled the window-frame.
>   WHITTIER *Snow-Bound* st. 8.

[The Indians] must be civilized, *ere* they could be Christianized.   COTTON MATHER *Magnalia Christi* vol. i, bk. iii, p. 560.

> After a lingering,—*ere* she was aware,— . . !
> The little innocent soul flitted away.
>   TENNYSON *Enoch Arden* l. 267.

Distinctions

Before—e'er—ere: *Ere* is to be carefully distinguished from *e'er*, the contracted form of *ever*.

This is as strange a thing as *e'er* [ever] I looked on.

It was gone *ere* [before] I could well view it.

Both *e'er* and *ere* are for the most part confined to poetry or to the poetic style, by which fact *ere* is distinguished from *before*.

EXCEPT

For the etymology of this word, see EXCEPT, under PREPOSITIONS.

Noting restriction or limitation: if it were not (or be not) that; if not; unless.

Except these abide in the ship ye cannot be saved.
           Acts xxvii, 31.

Except ye utter by the tongue words easy to be understood, how shall it be known what is spoken?   *1 Cor.* xiv, 9.

> Not resolute, *except* so much were done.
> SHAKESPEARE *King Henry VI.* pt. ii, act iii, sc. 1, l. 267.

[NOTE.—This use of *except* with the subjunctive is archaic, though sometimes adopted by recent writers in imitation of the old style. In the examples given above, we should now use *if—not* or *unless*. *Except* is now used as a conjunction only where it may be viewed as equivalent to a preposition governing an objective clause or phrase, especially when followed by *that*, *for*, or the like.]

[Like all or most prepositions adopted as conjunctions, *except* was originally and properly followed by *that*. It was formerly much used as a conjunction

> "Slack not thy riding *except* I bid thee." *2 Kings* iv., 24.

It is so used sixty-six times in the Bible, and *unless* only eight times. At present the prevailing, and I think better, practice is to use *unless* exclusively as a conjunction and *except* as a preposition.   RAMSEY *English Language* ch. 8, p. 496.]

In ancient Greece, torture was never employed *except* in cases of treason.   LECKY *Rationalism in Eur.* vol. i, ch. 8, p. 332.

Diocletian is supposed never to have seen Rome *except* on the single occasion when he entered it for the ceremonial purpose of a triumph.   DE QUINCEY *The Cæsars* ch. 6, p. 247.

> Parted without the least regret
> *Except that* they had ever met.
> COWPER *Pairing Time Anticipated* l. 59.

Excepting is used as a conjunction in the same way as *except*.

A voice that was by no means bad, *excepting that* it ran occasionally into a falsetto, like the notes of a split reed.
> IRVING *Sketch-Book, Christmas Eve* p. 250.

FOR

The etymology of this word is given in its place under PREPOSITIONS.

[*For* as a conjunction is used only of relations involving cause or reason. It was formerly much used with *that*, in the combination *for that*.]

1. Denoting the reason why the writer or speaker believes in his statement, or that which he wishes to present as a reason to another person, *i. e.* of reason as distinguished from cause: in view of the reason that; seeing that; since; as, it is morning, *for* I hear the birds.

[*For* is the same word as the preposition *for*. It is an abbreviation of [Anglo-Saxon] *"for tham the,"* meaning for the reason that. The *that* continued long to be used:

"And so death passed upon all men *for that* all have sinned."
Rom. v., 12.

"Famed Beauclerc called, *for that* he loved
The minstrel, and his lay approved."
RAMSEY *English Language* ch. 8, p. 497.]

Blessed are the pure in heart: *for* they shall see God.
Matt. v, 8.

The post-boy drove with fierce career,
For threatening clouds the morn had drowned.
WORDSWORTH *Alice Fell* st. 1.

She had evidently made a journey of some length, *for* she was encumbered with travelling wraps.
FRANCES H. BURNETT *That Lass o' Lowrie's* ch. 3, p. 21.

We speak of owls and bats as nocturnal. In reality they are crepuscular, *for* they do not keep on the wing all night, unless it is moonlight.   C. C. ABBOTT *Upland and Meadow* p. 865.

He [man] must not count on distant ages, *for* he is an ephemeron.   H. ROGERS *Origin of the Bible* lect. ix, p. 875.

If you would know the value of money go and try to borrow some, *for*, He that goes a borrowing goes a sorrowing.
B. FRANKLIN *Poor Richard's Almanac* p. 9.

For he always ascribed to his wit that laughter which was lavished at his simplicity.
GOLDSMITH *Vicar of Wakefield* ch. 5, p. 80, note.

For Nature with cheap means still works her wonders rare.
LOWELL *Indian-Summer Reverie* st. 15.

For the people of the village
Saw the flock of brant with wonder.
LONGFELLOW *Hiawatha* pt. xvii, st. 82.

Melancthon himself wrote no hymns, *for* the one or two often attributed to him are really passages from his writings versified by friends.   CATHERINE WINKWORTH *Christian Singers of Germany* ch. 5, p. 115.

2. Denoting the cause of a fact, action, or event, *i. e.* cause as distinguished from reason: owing to the fact that; because; as, the parrot can not fly far, *for* his wings are clipped.

The people were astonished at his doctrine: *For* he taught them as one having authority.   *Matt.* vii, 28, 29.

> My falcon now is sharp, and passing empty;
> And till she stoop, she must not be full-gorg'd,
> *For* then she never looks upon her lure.
> SHAKESPEARE *Taming of the Shrew* act iv, sc. 1, l. 198.

It was late, *for* I had been playing in the last piece; and as it was a benefit night, the performance had been protracted to an unusual length.   DICKENS *Pickwick Papers* ch. 8, p. 48.

The great scope of his work [Don Quixote] was didactic, *for* it was a satire against the false taste of the age.
PRESCOTT *Biograph. Miscell., Cervantes* p. 168.

I never proffer advice, *for* I know nothing is more unwelcome.   H. T. KING *The Egotist* essay lxiii, p. 97.

It was no use to argue the point; *for* she had a very small head.   JULIANA H. EWING *Jackanapes* ch. 1, p. 8.

True science is modest; *for* her keen, sagacious eye discerns that there are deep, undeveloped mysteries, where the vain sciolist sees all plain.
EVERETT *Orations, Scientific Knowledge* in vol. i, p. 276.

We are beginning to hear of a science of charity; and it is sorely needed, *for* old-fashioned alms-giving is a curse.
R. T. ELY *Intro. to Polit. Economy* pt. iv, ch. 7, p. 261.

Distinctions

As—because—for—since: There is a growing tendency to restrict *because* to the cause and *for* to the reason of a fact or action as stated. *For* may enter the realm of *because* and denote cause properly so called, but *because* can not enter the realm of *for* and denote a mere reason which is not a cause. We can not say, "It is going to rain *because* the barometer is falling," the falling of the mercury in the barometer being not a *cause*, since it has nothing to do with producing the rain; but we may use *for* in such case, the observed change in the barometer being the *reason* for the belief that the rain will come. In conversation one will sometimes hear such a remark as, "The sun must have set, *because* it is growing dark." But darkness is not the cause of sunset, but sunset the cause of darkness. It would be more correct to say, "It is dark *because* the sun has set." But this latter sentence would not express the speaker's meaning, which is that the darkness is the *reason* of his belief that the sun has set. This would be exactly and accurately expressed by *for*, thus: "The sun must have set, *for* it is growing dark."

For has also a greater independence than *because*, so that it may stand at the beginning of a sentence, stating the reason of something preceding, the basis of an argument, or the like. But *because* can not stand at the beginning of a sentence, except in the answer to a question where it follows an implied affirmation; as, "Why did you go there?" "[I went] *Because* my business obliged me to go." It would be a violation of good usage to write, "All bodies tend to fall to the earth. *Because* they are drawn downward by gravitation." The sentence must be one: "All bodies tend to fall to the earth, *because*," etc. That is, the sentence introduced by *because* is always subordinate or dependent. But *for* may introduce a coordinate or independent sentence, and we may properly write, "All bodies tend to fall to the earth. *For* they are drawn downward by gravitation." It will be observed that in this latter case the falling is made more emphatic standing as the principal thought in a closed sentence, while in the construction with *because* the mind is led on from the falling to its cause, which becomes the controlling thought, so that we might transpose the sentence to read, "The cause which makes bodies tend to fall to the earth is the attraction of gravitation."

Another distinction between *because* and *for* is that *because* is somewhat more formal, lacking the easy naturalness with which *for* may often come. Thus in the well-known apostrophe to the ocean:

> 'Twas a pleasing fear,
> *For* I was as it were a child of thee.
> > BYRON *Childe Harold* can. 4, st. 184.

Here we could not substitute *because* without giving the artless statement something of the formality of a demonstration. But *as* or *since* would dwarf the reason, which is really important, by seeming to bring it in incidentally and as a subordinate matter.

Of the conjunctions that introduce a cause or reason, *as* unites most completely, and therefore in the most incidental way, assigning the reason as a matter of course. "*As* that was not my name, [of course] I did not answer." "*Since* that was not my name" would imply a more distinct interval of consideration and reasoning. "*Because* that was not my name" would be still more elaborate and argumentative, and is the style one might use if arraigned for silence, and required to give a reason. To the question, "Why did you not answer when I called?" the reply might be, "*Because* that [name which you called] was not my name."

For is intermediate between the incidentality and dependence of *as* or *since* and the argumentative formality of *because*.

FORASMUCH

Forasmuch is an old compound now little used except in legal or other formal or technical style.

Denoting a cause or reason: seeing or considering that; in view of the fact that; seeing that; since; because · followed by *as*.

Forasmuch as God hath showed thee all this, there is none so discreet and wise as thou art.   *Gen.* xli, 39.

Forasmuch as the disease in many of its forms is unattended with organic morbid changes.
> MAUDSLEY *Responsibility in Mental Disease* ch. 9, p. 271.

15

HOWEVER

However, compounded of *how* and *ever*, is used both as an adverb (see ADVERBS) and as a conjunction, in the latter case as follows:

As a word of limitation or abatement interjected into a statement to modify it—a concessive particle: still; yet; though; nevertheless; as, I think it will rain, not, *however*, before we reach home.

> *However*, yet there's no great breach.
> SHAKESPEARE *K. Henry VIII.* act iv, sc. 1, l. 106.

The great value of a federate union of the colonies had, *however*, sunk deep into the minds of men.
> KENT *Commentaries* vol. i, pt. ii, lect. x, p. 198.

This curiosity of theirs, *however*, was attended with very serious effects.   GOLDSMITH *Vicar of Wakefield* ch. x, l. 45.

Distinctions

See NOTWITHSTANDING.

IF

If is from the Anglo-Saxon *gif*, used in the same sense.

[Horne Tooke's plausible conjecture that this word—formerly sometimes written *gif*—is the imperative of *give*, proves to be ill founded, as the Gothic, Old High German, Old Saxon, and Icelandic are without *g*, and the primary meaning of the word is not to give but to doubt,—Icel. *if*, uncertainty, *efa*, to doubt. Moreover the *g* can be accounted for. The Gothic equivalent was *iba* or *ibai*, but to this was sometimes prefixed *yah*, and, making *yabai*, and if; not that it was written with *y* but rather with *j*. Passing into Old Frisian and Anglo-Saxon the word took the form *jef* or *gef*, *g* alternating between the sounds of our *g* and *y*. *If* introduces a proposition as more or less doubtful, connected with another in such wise that if the first holds good, so does the second; if the first fail, the second will fail with it.
MATTHEWS *English Language* ch. 8, p. 497.]

· **1.** Of condition, denoting that in case one statement is true another must be, that in case one event happens another will follow, supposing that one thing is true another must be, or the like: in case that; granting or supposing that; on condition that; as, *if* he falls it will kill him; *if* I said that, I regret it; *if* the sky falls, we shall catch larks; *if* x equals a and y equals a, then x and y must be equal to each other.

If any man be in Christ, he is a new creature.   *2 Cor.* v, 17.

> There's nothing ill can dwell in such a temple:
> *If* the ill spirit have so fair a house,
> Good things will strive to dwell with't.
> SHAKESPEARE Tempest act i, sc. 2, l. 458.

> Or, *if* Sion's hill
> Delight thee more, and Siloa's brook that flow'd
> Fast by the oracle of God.
> MILTON Paradise Lost bk. i, l. 10.

Periander is said to have vowed a golden statue to Jupiter *if* he won the Olympic chariot-race.
RAWLINSON Herodotus vol. iii, bk. v, p. 247, note 8.

Let no guilty man escape, *if* it can be avoided. No personal consideration should stand in the way of performing a public duty. ULYSSES S. GRANT *Indorsement of a Letter Relating to the Whiskey Ring* July 29, 1875.

> And when religious sects ran mad,
> He held, in spite of all his learning,
> That *if* a man's belief is bad,
> It will not be improved by burning.
> PRAED Poems of Life and Manners pt. ii The Vicar st. 9.

2. Of concession: assuming, allowing, or admitting that; even on the supposition that; although; though; as, *if* he was there, I did not know it; *if* he is ignorant, he has good sense; I will go, *if* I die for it.

> The noble Brutus
> Hath told you Cæsar was ambitious:
> *If* it were so, it was a grievous fault;
> And grievously hath Cæsar answered it.
> SHAKESPEARE Julius Cæsar act iii, sc. 2, l. 75

> There is no creature loves me;
> And *if* I die, no soul shall pity me.
> . SHAKESPEARE Richard III. act v, sc. 3, l. 200.

> Thrones, dominations, princedoms, virtues, powers;
> *If* these magnific titles yet remain
> Not merely titular.   MILTON *Paradise Lost* bk. v, l. 774.

> The old mayor climbed the belfry tower,
> The ringers ran by two, by three;
> "Pull, *if* ye never pulled before;
> Good ringers, pull your best," quoth he.
> JEAN INGELOW *High Tide on the Coast of Lincolnshire* l. 1, *sq.*

There is . . . but little *if* any evidence of diminished activity in crustal movement during recent geologic time.
       R. S. WOODWARD in *Am. Geologist* Nov., 1889, p. 280.

Every Sanskrit scholar knows that Nirvâna means originally the blowing out . . . . The human soul, when it arrives at its perfection, is blown out, *if* we use the phraseology of the Buddhists, like a lamp.   MAX MÜLLER *Chips* vol. i, ch. 11, p. 279.

A true gentleman is different from anybody else, even *if* he is sea-sick, and if there is a greater test than that, I do not know what it is!
       H. W. BEECHER in Eleanor Kirk's *Beecher as a Humorist* p. 76.

If he [Browning] had a message, it was a message of belief.
       A. LANG in *Contemporary Review* July, 1891, p. 80.

I'll give you a bit of my mind *if* I never speak again.
       E. E. HALE *Ups and Downs* ch. 14, p. 146.

3. Of doubt, uncertainty, or question: whether; as, I doubt *if* it is wise; I don't know *if* he will stay or go; I am not sure *if* he is at home; tell me *if* you will do it.

Where our expectations have been highly wrought, it is no small gain *if* we are not disappointed.
       W. ALLSTON *Monaldi* ch. 8, p. 94.

As if—as though: See AS.

Distinctions

An—and—if: For *an*, *an'*, or *and* used in the sense of *if* see under AND.

[NOTE.—*If* is often omitted from a conditional clause, and the hypothetical character of the clause indicated by inversion; as the statement "We should have finished *if* we had not been interrupted " may be transformed into " We should have finished *had* we not been interrupted."

> For woman is not undevelopt man
> But diverse.   *Could* we make her as the man
> Sweet love were slain; his dearest bond is this,
> Not like to like but like in difference.
>> TENNYSON *The Princess* vii, l. 260.

Many a man . . . struts abroad a hero, whose claims we would . . . laugh at, *could* we but . . . see his numskull bare.
>> THACKERAY *Critical Reviews* ch. 1, p. 362.

Had they [the Evangelists] been all uniform in their narration, we should have had good cause to suspect fraud and collusion.   HORNE *Intro. to the Bible* vol. i, ch. 3, § 1, p. 185.

Many a member of trades-unions in Scotland would not have been willing to commit outrages upon the person of his neighbors, or even murder, *had* it not been called slating, or by some other technical term.
> F. LIEBER *Manual of Political Ethics* vol. i, § 56, p. 204.]

[NOTE.—*If* with a negative, as *if not*, has nearly or quite the force of *unless*.

There seems to be a constant decay of all our ideas; even of those which are struck deepest, and in minds the most retentive, so that *if* they be *not* sometimes renewed by repeated exercises of the senses, or reflection on those kinds of objects which at first occasioned them, the print wears out, and at last there remains nothing to be seen.   LOCKE *Human Understanding* bk. ii, ch. 10.

He had sat down to two hearty meals that might have been mistaken for dinners *if* he had *not* declared them to be 'snaps.'
> GEORGE ELIOT *Janet's Repentance* ch. 1, p. 3.

If the power to lead is in you, other men will follow; *if* it is *not* in you, nothing will make them follow.
> E. E. HALE *What Career?* ch. 1, p. 27.

A national debt, *if* it is *not* excessive, will be to us a national blessing.   ALEX. HAMILTON *Letter to Robert Morris* April 30, 1781.

We do love beauty at first sight; and we do cease to love it, *if* it is *not* accompanied by amiable qualities.
> LYDIA MARIA CHILD *Beauty*

Be she fairer than the day,
Or the flowery meads in May,
If she be *not* so to me,
What care I how fair she be?
GEORGE WITHER *The Shepherd's Resolution*]

As if or *as though :* Either of these phrases may be used with a verb understood (*as* it would be *if*, or the like), the same or in the same manner that it would be if.

It was *as if* the herald at a tournament had dropped his truncheon, and the fray must end.

T. W. HIGGINSON *Oldport Days* ch. 1, p. 26.

It seem'd *as if* their mother Earth
Had swallow'd up her warlike birth.

SCOTT *Lady of the Lake* can. 5, st. 10.

LEST

Lest is the contraction of the Anglo-Saxon phrase *thȳ lǣs the*, the less that.

Of negative purpose, expectation, or apprehension: in order that . . . not; for fear that; that . . . not; as, watch *lest* the enemy surprise you; he feared *lest* darkness should overtake him.

I saw the sun sinking gradually, and I got quite alarmed *lest* we should be benighted.

VICTORIA *Life in the Highlands,* Sept. 21, '44 p. 46.

Distinctions

Lest — that : Lest includes the meaning of *that* with the addition of a negative, so that it is equivalent to *that not.* "Beware *lest* you fail by neglect" means "Beware *that* you do *not* fail by neglect." When *lest* is used of purpose, the addition of *not* makes the double negative, which is equivalent to an affirmative; "Take care *lest* you do *not* fall asleep" means "Take care *that* you do fall asleep." *Not* should never be used after *lest*, unless the intention is to reverse the apparent meaning. Singular mistakes are often made by failure to observe this distinction, as in the following:

When a young man enters the world, he must take heed *lest* he be *not* ensnared by his companions into vicious practices.

CRABB *Synonyms* under *Heed* p. 506.

The author should have written either "take heed *lest* he be ensnared" or "take heed *that* he be *not* ensnared." The two forms can not be combined. The combination spoils the caution.

NEITHER

Neither is the negative of *either*, commonly used with a following *nor*. See CORRELATIVE CONJUNCTIONS.

Denying the first of two (or more) alternative clauses: not either; as, there was *neither* food nor fire.

If any would not work, *neither* should he eat. *2 Thes.* iii, 10.

The dialects of ancient Greece were *neither* so variant, nor so bad as those of the different districts, and even related countries, of the British isles. COX *Interviews, With Chalmers* p. 69.

NEVERTHELESS

A compound of three English words, *never, the, less.* The meaning can be shown by using the words separately; as, "I should *never* do it *the less* for your threats," equal in meaning to "In spite of your threats I should do it *nevertheless.*"

Denoting adversative coordination: none the less; not the less; notwithstanding; yet.

A man after death is not a natural but a spiritual man; *nevertheless* he still appears in all respects like himself.

SWEDENBORG *Conjugal Love* pt. xxxi.

[With *nevertheless* we may well compare the expression of the same idea in separate words in the phrases *none the less, not the less.*

But *not the less* the blare of the tumultuous organ wrought its own separate creations. DE QUINCEY *Opium-Eater, Suspiria, Affliction of Childhood* pt. i, p. 186.]

Distinctions

See DISTINCTIONS under NOTWITHSTANDING.

NOR

Nor is a contraction of the Middle English *nother*, a variant of *neither*.

As a negative correlative (see CORRELATIVE CONJUNCTIONS) and not; likewise not; also not.

1. As correlative of a preceding negative, usually *neither* or *not*; as, he took *neither* food *nor* drink; he did *not* eat *nor* did he drink.

He shall not fail *nor* be discouraged.   *Isa.* xlii, 4.

> For I have neither wit, *nor* words, *nor* worth,
> Action, *nor* utterance, *nor* the power of speech,
> To stir men's blood.
>   SHAKESPEARE *Julius Cæsar* act iii, sc. 2, l. 222.

> Not spoke in word, *nor* blazed in scroll,
> But borne and branded on my soul.
>   SCOTT *Lady of the Lake* can. 4, st. 6.

> Let not our variance mar the social hour,
> *Nor* wrong the hospitality of Randolph.
>   JOHN HOME *Douglas* act iv, sc. 1.

The appellations in common use to designate these processes, or the capacities for their exercise, as fancy, imagination, invention, reverie, are not applied with technical exactness, *nor* do they answer the ends of a philosophical explanation.
   PORTER *Human Intellect* pt. ii, ch. 6, p. 351.

Spirit is not matter, *nor* matter spirit; . . . the realistic dualism which lies at the bottom of all human convictions, underlies also all the revelations of the Bible.
   C. HODGE *Systematic Theology* vol. i, pt. i, ch. 5, p. 379.

> No Spring, *nor* Summer's beauty, hath such grace,
> As I have seen in one autumnal face.
>   JOHN DONNE *The Autumnal* l. 1.

In this intense eagerness to press forward, he [Pestalozzi] never stopped to examine results, *nor* to co-ordinate means with ends.   JOS. PAYNE *Science of Education* lect. iii, p. 84.

2. As correlative of a negative understood or implied: and not; as, they sat still, *nor* moved a muscle.

[Here the negation of motion is implied in the sitting still. The clause with *nor* expands the idea and carries it to the extreme of immobility.]

> Two dogs of black Saint Hubert's breed
> Unmatched for courage, breath, and speed,
> Fast on his flying traces came,
> And all but won that desperate game;
> *Nor* nearer might the dogs attain,
> *Nor* farther might the quarry strain.
> > SCOTT *Lady of the Lake* can. 1, st. 7.

> Silent, *nor* wanting due respect, the crowd
> Stood humbly round and gratulation bowed.
> > CRABBE *Parish Register* pt. ii, st. 14.

> Go put your creed into your deed,
> *Nor* speak with double tongue.
> > EMERSON *Ode, Concord* July 4, 1857.

> > There his spirit shaped
> Her prospects, *nor* did he believe,—he saw.
> > WORDSWORTH *The Excursion* bk. i, st. 12.

> *Nor* would I change my buried love
> For any heart of living mould.
> > CAMPBELL *O'Connor's Child* st. 16.

3. As an introductory negative in place of neither; used by older writers and in poetic style; as, *nor* praise *nor* blame could move him.

> *Nor* discontents it me to leave the world.
> > THOS. KYD *Spanish Tragedy* act iii, sc. 1.

Distinctions

See DISTINCTIONS under OR.

NOTWITHSTANDING

See explanation of this compound form under PARTICIPIAL PREPOSITIONS.

As denoting adversative coordination: in spite of the fact that; although; though; as, *notwithstanding* that he knew his danger, he took no precautions.

John Hunter, *notwithstanding* he had a bee in his bonnet, was really a great man. De Quincey *Narrative and Miscel. Papers, Coleridge and Opium Eating* p. 141.

Distinctions

Although — but — howbeit — however — nevertheless — notwithstanding — still — though — yet: These terms are very clearly discriminated in the following extract:

[*However* simply waives discussion, and (like the archaic *howbeit*) says, "be that as it may, this is true"; *nevertheless* concedes the truth of what precedes, but claims that what follows is none the less true; *notwithstanding* marshals the two statements face to face, admits the one and its seeming contradiction to the other, while insisting that it can not, after all, withstand the other; as, *notwithstanding* the force of the enemy is superior, we shall conquer. *Yet* and *still* are weaker than *notwithstanding*, while stronger than *but*. *Though* and *although* make as little as possible of the concession, dropping it, as it were, incidentally; as, "*though* we are guilty, thou art good"; to say "we are guilty, *but* thou art good," would make the concession of guilt more emphatic. . . . *Standard Dictionary*.]

OR

Or is a contraction of *other* from the Anglo-Saxon *âwther*, from *â-*, ever, + *hwæther*, whether. See also Correlative Conjunctions

Or is a disjunctive conjunction, without the adversative meaning found in *but*, denoting one of two or more alternatives.

1. Denoting an object the acceptance of which excludes the associated object or objects: either; else; otherwise; as, sink *or* swim: often as correlative of *either* or *whether*; as, *either* go *or* stay; I am considering *whether* I shall ride *or* walk. See Correlative Conjunctions.

> But oars alone can ne'er prevail
>   To reach the distant coast ;
> The breath of Heaven must swell the sail,
>   *Or* all the toil is lost.
>
> Cowper *Human Frailty* st. 6.

By the all-powerful dispensations of Providence, I have been protected beyond all human probability *or* expectation.   WASHINGTON in Sparks's *Writings of Washington* vol. ii, pt. i, p. 89.

In England, in the time of James, a law . . . passed compelling everybody to attend church, *or* pay a fine.
C. C. COFFIN *Building the Nation* ch. 6, p. 79.

Or could *or* should a rational and politically viable people immediately proceed to the solution of such a problem? H. VON HOLST *Constitutional Hist. U. S., 1828–'46* tr. by Lalor, ch. 2, p. 106.

Words that wise Bacon *or* brave Raleigh spake.
POPE *Imitation of Horace* bk. ii, ep. ii, l. 168.

I must soon treat them as the pigeons treat their squabs—push them off the limb, and make them put out their wings *or* fall.   JOHN ADAMS in Seward's *J. Q. Adams* ch. 2, p. 58.

Whenever a column saw him at their head, they knew that it was to be victory *or* annihilation. J. T. HEADLEY *Napoleon and his Marshals, Ney* in vol. ii, p. 818.

2. Denoting equivalence or interchangeableness, as by introducing another name, title, or term, or giving a definition: otherwise called; in other phrase; in other words; that is to say; alias; as, carbonic acid *or* [as otherwise known] carbon dioxid; the solid matter precipitates *or* [to use another word] settles from the solution; the czar *or* emperor; this adventurer Brooks *or* Johnson.

The master *or* commander of any ship, bark, pink, or catch. LONGFELLOW *New England Tragedies, John Endicott* act ii, sc. 2.

The inferior *or* trousered half of the creation.
T. HUGHES *Tom Brown at Oxford* vol. i, ch. 19, p. 809.

The spot selected was a rocky bay, *or* embouchure of a small stream. N. MACLEOD *Highland Parish, Boys of the Manse* p. 45.

[NOTE.—In poetry *or* is often used for *either* as the first of two correlatives; as, *or* in the clouds *or* waves.

> Our acts, our angels are, *or* good *or* ill,
> Our fatal shadows that walk by us still.
> JOHN FLETCHER *Upon an Honest Man's Fortune* l. 37.]

The phrase *or ever* (*or e'er*) is also common in archaic or poetic use, meaning before ever; before the earliest period of; as, in the beginning *or ever* the earth was.

The lions had the mastery of them, and brake all their bones in pieces *or ever* they came at the bottom of the den.   *Dan.* vi, 24.

PROVIDED

Provided is the past participle of the verb *provide*, used independently with the force of a conjunction.

A conditional particle denoting limitation, restriction, or exception: it being stipulated or understood (that); on condition (that); as, *provided* the funds shall be sufficient. Thus, every mortgage is a full conveyance of the mortgaged property to the mortgagee, *provided* that if the loan shall be paid at maturity, the conveyance shall then become null and void.

A man may be a knave or a fool or both (as it may happen), and yet be a most respectable man, in the common and authorized sense of the term, *provided* he saves appearances.

Hazlitt *Table Talk* second series, vol. ii, essay xxxv, p. 194.

SAVE

Save is explained in its place under Prepositions. Its conjunctive force would be at once made evident by supposing the sentence or clause that follows it to be the collective object of the preposition *save;* as, all is still *save* (that the crickets chirp incessantly).

A particle of limitation or exception: except; unless

> The glen was fair as some Arcadian dell,
>   All shadow, coolness, and the rush of streams,
> *Save* where the sprinkled blaze of noonday fell.
>   Bayard Taylor *The Sleeper* st. 1.

SEEING

Seeing is the present participle of the verb *see*, treated by some grammarians as a conjunction, though capable of being treated as a participle, like *considering*, etc.

An explanatory or causal particle: in view of the fact (that); considering; since; as, *seeing* you have come, I will settle it now.

SINCE

See the preposition SINCE under PREPOSITIONS.

Denoting sequence in time or in logical connection:

1. Of time: from and subsequently to the time when; during or within the time after that; in the interval between the present and (some designated time, act, or event); as, it is years *since* we met; we have both changed much *since* we parted.

> Yet know withal,
> *Since* thy original lapse, true liberty
> Is lost.   MILTON *Paradise Lost* bk. xii, l. 79.

Twelve years are past *since* we had tidings from him.
WORDSWORTH *The Brothers* st. 25.

If the men had been captured, it must have been *since* the captain's departure.   IRVING *Washington* vol. i, ch. 10, p. 96.

Fountains and wells, ever *since* the scriptural days, have been noted gossiping-places in hot climates.
IRVING *Alhambra, Moor's Legacy* p. 297.

2. Of cause or reason: because of the fact that; inasmuch as; seeing that; because; as, *since* you ask me, I will tell you.

Woman's faith must be strong indeed *since* thine has not yet failed.   HAWTHORNE *Mosses, Egotism* p. 308.

> For *since* he would sit on a Prophet's seat
> As a lord of the Human soul,
> We needs must scan him from head to feet,
> Were it but for a wart or a mole.
> TENNYSON *The Dead Prophet* st. 14.

Distinctions

Because—for—since: Compare BECAUSE; FOR.

SO

So is from the Anglo-Saxon *swā*, so, chiefly used as an adverb, but in certain cases having conjunctive force.

Denoting a concomitant or condition: provided_that; on condition that; as, he will be content so the debt is but paid.

> Appearances to save, his only care;
> *So* things seem right, no matter what they are.
> CHURCHILL *Rosciad* l. 299.

STILL

Still, from Anglo-Saxon *stille*, is an adverb often used with conjunctive force.

Noting a fixed opinion, choice, or decision maintained notwithstanding any argument, opposition, or doubt: in spite of anything to the contrary; after all; nevertheless; notwithstanding; as, I see your reasons, *still* I hold my opinion; though I know the danger, *still* I shall go.

Tacitus in fragments is *still* the colossal torso of history.
D'ISRAELI *Curios. of Lit., Lost Works* vol. i, p. 118.

THAN

Than, from Anglo-Saxon *thanne*, is by preeminence the particle of comparison.

After a comparative adjective or adverb, denoting the inferiority of that which follows to that which precedes: when compared with; as or if compared with; as, health is better *than* wealth; I had rather stay *than* go; I find it easier to work *than* to idle.

[NOTE.—*Than* is one of the most general of connectives, joining either single words, extended descriptions, clauses, or propositions; wherever one object, idea, or statement can be compared with another, *than* expresses the inferiority of the latter element to the former in the respect compared.

A pronoun after *than* is now commonly construed as the subject of a verb understood, and hence is put in the nominative case; as, he is richer *than* I [am]. The use of the objective (taller than *me*, etc.) common in the older English is now held to be incorrect. The single exception is the phrase *than whom*, which is accepted as correct. Compare Notes (*g*), (*h*) pp. 241–42.]

I were better to be eaten to death with rust, *than* to be scoured to nothing with perpetual motion.

         SHAKESPEARE *2 K. Henry IV.* act i, sc. 2, l. 218.

And ladies of the Hesperides, that seemed
Fairer *than* feign'd of old.

         MILTON *Paradise Regained* bk. ii, l. 357.

For age is opportunity no less
Than youth itself, though in another dress,
And as the evening twilight fades away
The sky is filled with stars, invisible by day.

         LONGFELLOW *Morituri Salutamus* l. 281.

The story . . . would fill a bigger folio volume, or a longer series of duodecimos, *than* could prudently be appropriated to the annals of all New England during a similar period.

         HAWTHORNE *House of Seven Gables* ch. 1, p. 10.

Not more the rose, the queen of flowers,
Outblushes all the bloom of bower,
Than she unrivall'd grace discloses;
The sweetest rose, where all are roses.

         MOORE *Odes of Anacreon* ode lxvi.

It is always much easier, however, to follow a pattern *than* a precept.   GEIKIE *Life of Christ* vol. ii, ch. 37, p. 81.

A chill sharper *than* that of the frosty air—a chill of fear— smote him.   LEW WALLACE *Ben-Hur* bk. i, ch. 11, p. 61.

No one has more to gain from a thorough system of civil service reform *than* the President. The present system makes a wire-puller of him.

         BRYCE *Am. Commonwealth* vol. i, pt. i, ch. 6, p. 61.

The Republic has no better citizens in peace and would have no braver soldiers in war *than* the men who twenty-five years ago wore the gray.   H. W. GRADY *New South* ch. 1, p. 147.

[NOTES.—(*a*) The comparative inferiority may be actual superiority. When the first element of the comparison is declared to be *less than*, *worse than*, or otherwise inferior, it is evident that the second element (following *than*) is greater, better, or superior: as, a foot is *less than* a yard; a fall is *worse than* a stumble.

Should possibilities be worse to bear *than* certainties ?
>> DICKENS *Old Curiosity Shop* ch. 15, p. 169.

Spend one penny less *than* thy clear gain.
>> B. FRANKLIN *Life and Essays, To Make Money Plenty* p. 182.

Taken as a whole the black race represents a lower, a more primitive state of society *than* the yellow race.
>> E. A. ALLEN *Hist. Civilization* vol. ii, ch. 1, p. 76.

(*b*) Not merely superiority but difference may be denoted by *than*, as in such phrases as *else than, other than.* We do not, however, say *different than*, much less *different to*, but *different from.*

> And he said with a smile, 'Our ship, I wis,
> Shall be of another form *than* this!'
>> LONGFELLOW *Building of the Ship* st. 8.

In many occupations industrial efficiency requires little else *than* physical vigour; that is, muscular strength, a good constitution and energetic habits. A. MARSHALL *Principles of Economics* vol. i, bk. iv, ch. 5, p. 250.

The Talmud informs us that Noah had no other light in the ark *than* that which came from precious stones.
>> J. T. FIELDS *Underbrush, Diamonds* p. 215.

Many a preacher becomes an author who has no other call to this vocation *than* the call of an admiring congregation for a volume of discourses. PORTER *Books and Reading* ch. 20, p. 327.

(*c*) Preference is commonly expressed by *rather—than, sooner—than*, or the like.

> Edward Strachey was . . . a man *rather* tacit *than* discursive.
>> CARLYLE *Reminiscences, Edward Irving* p. 175.

No *sooner* . . . did he show himself in Boston, *than* . . . measures were taken to arrest this cutpurse of the ocean.
>> IRVING *Traveller, Kidd the Pirate* p. 386.

(*d*) *Than* is often followed by a substantive clause containing an infinitive or beginning with *that*, etc., or by a relative as *that* or *that which* with no verb expressed.

I had *rather* be a doorkeeper in the house of my God *than* to dwell in the tents of wickedness.   *Ps.* lxxxiv, 10.

I had *rather* believe all the fables in the legends and the Talmud and the Alcoran, *than that* this universal frame is without a mind.   Bacon *Essays, Of Atheism.*

(*e*) Observe the *had rather* in the quotations above given from the Bible and from Bacon, and compare the *would sooner* of Guthrie in the quotation following, showing that either phrase is supported by good authority, though the *had rather* has the support of the greater number of eminent writers of the Elizabethan age.

I would a thousand times *sooner* believe, that man made himself what he is, *than* that God made him so.
       Guthrie *Gospel in Ezekiel* ser. iii, p. 41.

(*f*) The *to* of the infinitive or the relative in such construction is often omitted.

The desire of the law to effectuate *rather than* [to] defeat a contract, is wise, just, and beneficial.
       Parsons *Contracts* vol. ii, pt. ii, ch. 1, § 8, p. 18.

For there came a wind
Drowsier *than* [that which] blows o'er Malwa's fields of sleep.
       Edwin Arnold *Light of Asia* bk. iv, st. 25.

(*g*) *Than* is now classed by lexicographers and grammarians as a conjunction only, taking the same case after it as before, a verb being commonly understood as filling out the clause after *than*; as, he is older *than* I [am]; he likes her better *than* [he likes] me. This rule has the merit of absolute perspicuity, for "he likes her better *than* I" would be understood as meaning "better *than* I [like her]," while "he likes her better *than* me" would mean "better *than* [he likes] me"; the nominative case after *than* being always construed as the subject, and the objective as the object of a verb understood.

"*Than* has the same case (usually the nominative) after it as it has before it, in accordance with the syntactical rule that 'conjunctions connect . . . the same cases of nouns and pronouns': as, he is taller *than* I (am); I am richer *than* he (is); 'thrice fairer *than* (I) myself (am)' (*Shak.*, Venus and Adonis, 1, 7); they like you better *than* (they like) me." *Century Dictionary.*

16

(*h*) *Than whom*: The phrase *than whom* is an exception to this rule, and appears to be fixed in the language as such.

> Which when Beelzebub perceived, *than whom*,
> Satan except, none higher sat, with grave
> Aspect he rose.   Milton *Paradise Lost* bk. ii, l. 299.

For this phrase it seems impossible to suggest a substitute. We could not say *than who*, and the only alternative would seem to be to avoid the relative by changing the structure of the sentence, which would often be inconvenient.

"*Than whom*. A phrase objected to by some grammatical critics, in such locutions as "Cromwell, *than whom* no man was better skilled in artifice"; but shown to be "a quite classic expression." Formerly *than* was often but not always used as a preposition, and *than whom* is probably a survival of such usage. The habit of putting a pronoun that ends a sentence in the objective case strengthens the tendency to the prepositional employment of *than*, and hence the usage in such sentences as "He is older *than* me," "you are taller *than* him," so common in English literature before the 19th century. Nevertheless, this tendency has been resisted by grammarians, and in the 19th century such phraseology is considered bad English. "*Than whom*," however, is generally accepted as permissible—probably because the sentence where it occurs can not be mended without reconstruction, and it has abundant literary authority."
Standard Dictionary, Faulty Diction.

"How the expression, a quite classical one, . . . can be justified grammatically, except by calling its *than* a preposition, others may resolve at their leisure and pleasure." Fitzedward Hall *Recent Exemplifications of False Philology* p. 84.]

THAT

That, from Anglo-Saxon *thæt*, was originally a demonstrative pronoun, later used as a relative pronoun (see Relative Pronouns), and also as a conjunction.

The conjunction of the subordinate sentence, variously de noting fact, purpose, reason, result, etc.

[The conjunction *that* . . . is in English, in the most com prehensive sense, the conjunction of the subordinate sentence generally, so that it was once attached to almost all the conjunctions, as it still is or may be subjoined to some.

MAETZNER *English Grammar* vol. i, p. 421.]

[*That* is used primarily to connect the substantive sentence as a subordinate clause with its principal sentence. Beginning with the simple relation of fact or matter of fact, it takes in relations of purpose, reason, consequence, result, etc. . . . .

That as a conjunction retains much of its force as a demonstrative pronoun, and was considered by Horne Tooke, as it is by others, to be oftentimes nothing else. Thus the sentence, "I am told *that* you are miserable" may be transposed into, "You are miserable; I am told *that*." *Standard Dictionary*.]

[Confusion sometimes arises in our language from the triple meaning of '*that*,' which, with us, is a demonstrative pronoun, a relative pronoun, and a conjunction. It is possible to use six '*thats*' consecutively in the same sentence.

H. ALFORD *Plea for the Queen's English* § 101, p. 79.]

[NOTE.—*That* is a particle so ultimate and elementary that its various meanings can not be defined, but only described, since any other form of words will prove but an inadequate periphrasis unless it employs (as is often done) the very word *that*, which we wish to define, such repetition of course making no advance in thought, though the explanatory words added may have the effect of emphasizing or restricting the meaning. In the following arrangement the only attempt is to indicate by way of explanation the chief uses of this important conjunction.]

1. Introducing a fact in subordinate relation to the principal statement: the following fact, observation, statement, etc.; namely; as a fact; as, I am told *that* you are ill; it appears *that* he did not know; it is observed *that* great strength and good nature commonly go together.

One of these self-evident, necessary truths is *that* every change or new existence requires a cause.

MIVART *Nature and Thought* ch. 5, p. 180.

It is a trite remark, *that*, having the choicest tools, an unskilful artisan will botch his work.   SPENCER *Education* p. 115.

The great queen [Elizabeth] . . . was always too sagacious to doubt *that* the Dutch cause was her own—however disposed she might be to browbeat the Dutchmen.

MOTLEY *United Netherlands* vol. iv, ch. 41, p. 187.

It does not follow *that* I wish to be pickled in brine because I like a salt-water plunge at Nahant.

HOLMES *Autocrat* ch. 1, p. 10.

Nobody doubts now, or has doubted since the abolition of slavery, *that* the purchase of Louisiana was an act of sound statesmanship.   SYDNEY H. GAY *James Madison* ch. 16, p. 257.

To this general rule, *that* the burden of proof is on the party holding the affirmative, there are some exceptions.

GREENLEAF *On Evidence* vol. i, pt. ii, ch. 8, p. 105.

Let us have faith *that* right makes might, and in that faith let us, to the end, dare to do our duty as we understand it.

ABRAHAM LINCOLN *Address* Feb. 21, 1859.

2. Referring to or indicating time: at which time; when; as, it is time *that* we were starting; this is the day *that* the note falls due.

'Twas but a moment *that* he stood,
Then sped as if by death pursued.

BYRON *The Giaour* st. 8.

The February day *that* I stood on the Frankfort bridge the Main was sheeted with ice.   HOSMER *German Lit.* ch. 12, p. 334.

3. Denoting purpose, object, or tendency: having the following intention, aim, or tendency; for the following purpose; to the following effect; as, I send you to school *that* you may learn.

Love was given, . . . *That* self might be annulled.

WORDSWORTH *Laodamia* st. 22.

The law requires *that* our national cruisers shall be called after cities.   ELIZ. B. CUSTER *Following the Guidon* p. 4.

As denoting purpose the phrase *in order that* or *so that* (or formerly *to the end* or *intent that*) is often used; as, I wish to explain fully, *in order that* no mistake may be made; I gave him money, *so that* he could pay his fare.

4. Denoting or introducing a reason: inasmuch as; as; because; since; as, it is not *that* I wish this, but *that* I am forced to it.

The foreknowledge of God has then no influence upon either the freedom or the certainty of actions, for this plain reason, *that* it is knowledge, and not influence.

R. WATSON *Institutes* pt. ii, ch. 4, p. 880.

Shall I suspect myself of being ashamed *that* I am on such distant terms with my own country?

EDGAR FAWCETT *Gentleman of Leisure* ch. 4, p. 52.

5. Introducing a result, consequence, or effect, often as a correlative of *such* or *so* (see CORRELATIVE CONJUNCTIONS); as, what have I done *that* you desert me?

> Then get thee gone and dig my grave thyself,
> And bid the merry bells ring to thine ear
> *That* thou art crowned, not *that* I am dead.
> SHAKESPEARE *2 K. Henry IV.* act iv, sc. 4, l. 248.

He was so attentive in the choice of the passages in which words were authorised, *that* one may read page after page of his Dictionary with improvement and pleasure.

BOSWELL *Johnson, 1748* vol. i, p. 129.

Man cannot so far know the connection of causes and events as *that* he may venture to do wrong in order to do right.

JOHNSON *Rasselas* ch. 34, p. 159.

It is the uneven allotment of nature *that* the male bird alone has the tuft.   GEORGE ELIOT *Deronda* vol. i, ch. 9, p. 92.

Cellulose has the property of swelling when wet to such an extent *that* if perforated by a projectile it will rapidly close the aperture by its own action until water-tight.

New-York Times Nov. 28, 1890, p. 4, col. 4.

It was almost impossible *that* Sokrates could fail to discover the verbalism in which the Eleatic philosophers often involved themselves.   G. W. COX *Gen. Hist. Greece* bk. iv, ch. 2, p. 521.

6. Introducing an expression of wish, hope, aspiration, or regret, and usually preceded by *O* or *Oh*, *O that* [*Oh that*] being equivalent to *would that*; as, *O that* morning would come!

O that Ishmael might live before thee!   *Gen.* xvii, 18.

Oh that I might have my request!   *Job* vi, 8.

O that my ways were directed to keep thy statutes!

                                   Ps. cxix, 5.

7. In elliptical construction, expressing surprize, indignation, or other strong feeling, which naturally sweeps away the affirmative clause on which the conjunction depends; as, *that* he should fail me in this crisis! *i. e.,* (I am amazed, distrest, or the like) *that* he should, etc.

[Note.—*O, that* is often used in such phrase, but with a different meaning from the *O that* of def. 6.

              O, that deceit should dwell

         In such a gorgeous palace!

       Shakespeare *Romeo and Juliet* act iii, sc. 2, l. 84.]

8. Used at times, tho not so often as formerly, after a preposition, adverb, or conjunction, so that the whole expression has the effect of a compound conjunction; as, *after that* he had spoken, he departed; I do not doubt *but that* it is true.

[Note.—The phrase *but what* in such use is erroneous.]

     I neither can nor will deny *but that* I know them.

     Shakespeare *All's Well That Ends Well* act v, sc. 3, l. 167.

The Conjunction "That" Omitted

The conjunction *that* is often omitted where it may be readily supplied by the mind; as, I told him [*that*] the work was done; He promised [*that*] he would send it.

Words are grown so false [*that*] I am loath to prove reason with them.   Shakespeare *Twelfth Night,* act iii, sc. 1, l. 28.

THEN

Then, from Anglo-Saxon *thænne,* is primarily an adverb of time, becoming a conjunction by transference from the idea of succession in time to that of succession in thought.

Denoting a reason or consequence: for that reason; as a consequence or result; therefore; in that case; as, ''You have done the work? *Then* make your report"; if this is the fact, *then* our course is clear.

> If it were done when 'tis done, *then* 'twere well
> It were done quickly.
>
>   SHAKESPEARE *Macbeth* act i, sc. 7, l. 1.

>   And dar'st thou *then*
> To beard the lion in his den,
> The Douglas in his hall?
>
>   SCOTT *Marmion* can. 6, st. 14.

> Thy work is to hew down.   In God's name *then*
> Put nerve into thy task.   WHITTIER *To Ronge* l. 3.

Is reason *then* an affair of sex? No! But women are commonly in a state of dependence, and are not likely to exercise their reason with freedom.   COLERIDGE *Works, Friend* vol. ii, p. 181.

> Dear, tell them, that if eyes were made for seeing,
> *Then* beauty is its own excuse for being.
>
>   EMERSON *The Rhodora* l. 12

>   *Then* on! *then* on! where duty leads,
> My course be onward still.
>
>   HEBER *If Thou Wert by My Side* st. 7.

> I slept and dreamed that life was Beauty;
> I woke, and found that life was Duty:—
> Was thy dream *then* a shadowy lie?
>
>   ELLEN STURGIS HOOPER *Duty*.

[NOTE.—A sentence in which *then* might be used sometimes omits the connective, and gains force by its very abruptness.

The twilight of dubiety never falls upon him [a Scotchman]. Is he orthodox—he has no doubts. Is he an infidel—he has none either.   LAMB *Elia, Imperfect Sympathies* p. 89.

Each dash here might be replaced by *then*, but the expression would be weaker.]

THEREFORE

Therefore is a compound of *there* and *fore* or *for*.

Expressing a consequence and pointing to a preceding sufficient cause: for this or that reason; on that ground or account, consequently.

[NOTE.—*Therefore* has the distinction of being able to connect the thought of one sentence with that of another across a period, referring back to something previously stated even when that is embodied in a completed sentence, or in more than one such sentence preceding, thus often connecting in thought statements that are grammatically separate. *Therefore* is the conjunction especially used in formal and elaborate reasoning, and commonly introduces the conclusion of a syllogism or of a mathematical demonstration; as, A is equal to B. B is equal to C. *Therefore* A is equal to C.]

> *Therefore*, I pray you, lead me to the caskets,
> To try my fortune.
>> SHAKESPEARE *Merchant of Venice* act ii, sc. 1, l. 24.

The law whereby He worketh is eternal, and *therefore* can have no show or colour of mutability.
> HOOKER *Ecclesiastical Polity* bk. i, p. 64.

And *therefore* I do declare unto you that I do dissolve this Parliament.   CROMWELL *Letters and Speeches* p. 289.

No man will take counsel, but every man will take money: *therefore* money is better than counsel.
> SWIFT *Works, Thoughts* p. 520.

Friends are often chosen for similitude of manners, and *therefore* each palliates the other's failings because they are his own.   S. JOHNSON *Rambler* June 23, 1750.

Envy . . . is *therefore* the grudging sense of relative inferiority.   MARTINEAU *Types of Ethical Theory* vol. ii, p. 188.

Chartism means the bitter discontent grown fierce and mad, the wrong condition *therefore* or the wrong disposition, of the Working Classes of England.   CARLYLE *Chartism* ch. 1, p. 2.

We seem authorized to conclude, *therefore*, that the bowlders have been transported generally from the north.
> WINCHELL *Walks and Talks* ch. 2, p. 18.

THOUGH

Though, from Anglo-Saxon *theáh*, is simply and only a conjunction, unless we except a single use classed by some lexicographers as adverbial.

Though is preeminently the particle of concession. *Although* shares with it this office.

1. Introducing a clause expressing an actual fact: in spite of the fact that; notwithstanding; as, the road is passable, *though* it has been raining hard.

Though I bestow all my goods to feed the poor . . . and have not charity, it profiteth me nothing.   *1 Cor.* xiii, 8.

> But to my mind, *though* I am native here,
> And to the manner born, it is a custom
> More honour'd in the breach than the observance.
> > SHAKESPEARE *Hamlet* act i, sc. 4, l. 15.

> *Though* I look old, yet I am strong and lusty;
> For in my youth I never did apply
> Hot and rebellious liquors in my blood.
> > SHAKESPEARE *As You Like It* act ii, sc. 8, l. 47.

> I on the other side
> Us'd no ambition to commend my deeds ;
> The deeds themselves, *though* mute, spoke loud the doer.
> > MILTON *Samson Agonistes* l. 246.

> And with perpetual inroads to alarm,
> *Though* inaccessible, his fatal throne.
> > MILTON *Paradise Lost* bk. ii, l. 104.

Though a young man, I have ferreted out evidence, got up cases, and seen lots of life.   DICKENS *Bleak House* ch. 9, p. 162.

> Fear not, *though* I have woven countless snares,
> And tangled countless hearts.
> BICKERSTETH *Yesterday, To-day, and For Ever* bk. vii, l. 452.

Nature is always consistent, *though* she feigns to contravene her own laws.   EMERSON *Essays, Nature* in first series, p. 148.

2. Introducing a supposition or possibility: conceding that; granting that; admitting that; even on the supposition that; even if; as, let justice be done, *though* the heavens fall.

> I'll cross it *though* it blast me.
> > SHAKESPEARE *Hamlet* act i, sc. 1, l. 127.

Thrice is he arm'd that hath his quarrel just,
And he but naked, *though* lock'd up in steel,
Whose conscience with injustice is corrupted.
     SHAKESPEARE *2 K. Henry VI.* act iii, sc. 2, l. 232.

For this was all thy care,
To stand approved in sight of God, *though* worlds
Judged thee perverse.   MILTON *Paradise Lost* bk. vi, l. 36.

For blessings ever wait on virtuous deeds,
And *though* a late, a sure reward succeeds.
     CONGREVE *The Mourning Bride* act v, sc. 8.

The philosopher works upon the man in isolation, *though* he may for convenience assemble his pupils in classes.
     J. R. SEELEY *Ecce Homo* pt. i, ch. 9, p. 107.

Speak what you think now in hard words, and to-morrow speak what to-morrow thinks in hard words again, *though* it contradict everything you said to-day.
     EMERSON *Essays, Self-Reliance* in first series, p. 52.

3. Introducing a modification or limitation as an afterthought: and yet; still; however; except that; as, the weather is fine, *though* [it must be admitted to be] somewhat warm.

[NOTE. --*Though* in this sense is sometimes used alone at the end of a clause, when it is by some considered as an adverb. But the sentence above given would come into this form by simple transposition of words without change of meaning; as, the weather is fine—somewhat warm *though*. This would seem to show such usage to be truly conjunctive.

Your hands, than mine, are quicker for a fray;
My legs are longer *though*, to run away.
   SHAKESPEARE *Midsummer-Night's Dream* act iii, sc. 2.]

For some must follow, and some command,
Though all are made of clay!
          LONGFELLOW *Keramos* l. 6.

But she loved Enoch; *though* she knew it not,
And would if ask'd deny it.
     TENNYSON *Enoch Arden* st. 4.

I am pretty well, and take exercise regularly, *though*, as Parson Adams says, it must be of the vehicular kind.
SCOTT in Lockhart's *Walter Scott* vol. ii, ch. 46, p. 720.

We have two or three flowering air-plants in the Southern States, *though* they are not showy ones.
ASA GRAY *Field-Book of Botany* lesson v, p. 84.

In some of the crabs the footstalk of the eye remains, *though* the eye is gone. SPENCER *Biology* vol. i, pt. ii, p. 247.

The decrees of destiny according to the Homeric notion, can be put off by human agency, *though* they can never be finally averted. ANTHON *Homer's Iliad* bk. ii, p. 215, note.

[*As though* : *As* is often joined with *though*, the entire phrase signifying *as if*.

They brought him to the Watergate, Hard bound with hempen span,
As though they held a lion there, And not a fenceless man.
AYTOUN *Execution of Montrose* st. 4.

His face beamed *as though* his individual hand was striking slavery dead. LADY DUFFUS HARDY *Through Cities and Prairie Lands* ch. 2, p. 18.

It was indeed a grand portal, that same Gap, not fully fifty feet in width, and more than nine hundred in height — a mere fissure, in fact, as complete *as though* made by the stroke of a giant's scimitar. LEVER *Luttrell of Arran* ch. 12, p. 47.]

TILL (UNTIL)

For the etymology of these words, see TILL under PREPOSITIONS.

Till as a conjunction denotes expectancy or continuance to some definite point of time: up to the period when; up to such time as; till (prep.) the time when; as, wait *till* I return.

[*Until* is used interchangeably with *till*, with no appreciable difference of meaning.]

He shall not fail nor be discouraged, *till* he have set judgment in the earth. *Isa.* xlii, 4.

So may'st thou live, *till* like ripe fruit thou drop
Into thy mother's lap, or be with ease
Gather'd, not harshly pluck'd, for death mature.
MILTON *Paradise Lost* bk. xi, l. 535.

Like birds, whose beauties languish half concealed,
Till, mounted on the wing, their glossy plumes
Expanded, shine with azure, green and gold;
How blessings brighten as they take their flight.
YOUNG *Night Thoughts, Night ii* l. 589.

Scientific results grow out of facts, but not *till* they have been fertilized by thought.   AGASSIZ *Methods of Study* ch. 18, p. 202.

The shot of the assassin cut short their [Lincoln's and Garfield's] martyr lives, but not *until* their work was done.
FARRAR *Lectures, Thoughts on Am.* p. 85.

Until the Indian is a citizen, subject to the same privileges and penalties as are other men in this country, we may expect war.
G. T. KERCHEVAL in *North American Review* Feb., 1891, p. 253.

Climate, sky, soil, occupation, physical environment, have acted upon generation after generation of Englishmen *until* a distinct type of man has been produced.
H. W. MABIE *Short Studies in Lit.* ch. 10, p. 49.

He waited a few minutes, *until* the wine had comforted his epigastrium.   HOLMES *Guardian Angel* p. 296.

She is not fair to outward view
  As many maidens be;
Her loveliness I never knew
  Until she smiled on me:
Oh! then I saw her eye was bright
A well of love, a spring of light.
HARTLEY COLERIDGE *Song.*

There the thrushes
Sing *till* latest sunlight flushes
In the west.
CHRISTINA G. ROSSETTI *Sound Sleep* st. 2

Till their own dreams at length deceive 'em
And oft repeating, they believe 'em.
PRIOR *Alma* can. iii, l. 13

UNLESS

Unless, formerly written *onlesse,* is derived from *on* plus *less,* and is analogous in meaning to the phrase *at least.* Compare LEST.

Like the conjunction *lest,* including an implied negative: if it be not a fact that; in the event that . . . not; in case . . . not; supposing that . . . not; if . . . not; as, we shall go *unless* it rains; I shall believe it *unless* you can prove the contrary.

[NOTE.—By the omission of an implied verb, *unless* often approaches the meaning of *except;* as, he never stammers, *unless* [it be] when he is angry.

> *Unless* the old adage must be verified,
> That beggars mounted, run their horse to death.
> SHAKESPEARE *3 K. Henry VI.* act i, sc. 4, l. 126.

> Here nothing breeds,
> *Unless* the nightly owl, or fatal raven.
> SHAKESPEARE *Titus Andronicus* act ii, sc. 3, l. 97.]

Grievances cannot be redressed *unless* they are known; and they cannot be known but through complaints and petitions.
> B. FRANKLIN *Autobiography* vol. ii, ch. 7, p. 198.

No man securely rejoiceth, *unless* he have within him the testimony of a good conscience.
> THOMAS À KEMPIS *Imitation of Christ* bk. i, ch. 20, p. 49.

Burke rarely shows all his powers *unless* where he is in a passion.   COLERIDGE *Table Talk* Jan. 4, 1828.

The horse . . . felt that his rider was in a great stew of terror; and he would not have been a horse, *unless* he shared it.
> BLACKMORE *Christowell* vol. ii, ch. 25, p. 266.

The range of a bee, *unless* urged by hunger, is about two miles.   N. EAMES in *American Agriculturist* June, 1891, p. 331.

A body will never change its place *unless* moved, and if once started will move forever *unless* stopped.
> J. D. STEELE *Natural Philosophy* ch. i, p. 25

UNTIL

See TILL.

WHEN

See WHEN under ADVERBS. The use of *when* as a conjunction is an extension of its use as an interrogative adverb in a dependent sentence, and the word is by some lexicographers classed only as an adverb with conjunctive uses. Since, however, *when* is paralleled with *then*, it would seem reasonable to treat it, like *then*, as a true conjunction.

1. Of time: at which or what time; as, I slept till daylight, *when* I awoke with a start.

> I will go wash;
> And *when* my face is fair, you shall perceive
> Whether I blush or no.
> > SHAKESPEARE *Coriolanus* act i, sc. 9, l. 68.

> But, thou know'st this,
> 'Tis time to fear *when* tyrants seem to kiss.
> > SHAKESPEARE *Pericles* act i, sc. 2, l. 78.

> Sweet is the trance, the tremor sweet,
> *When* all we love is all our own.
> > CAMPBELL *Stanzas to Painting* st. 4.

In books lies the soul of the whole Past Time; the articulate audible voice of the Past, *when* the body and material substance of it has altogether vanished like a dream. CARLYLE *Heroes and Hero Worship, The Hero as a Man of Letters.*

Women and winds are only understood *when* fairly in motion.
> COOPER *Water-Witch* ch. 6, p. 56.

When the sun of that day went down, the event of Independence was no longer doubtful.
> WEBSTER *Works, Bunker Hill Monument* in vol. i, p. 91.

The pick, stone-saw, wedge, chisel, and other tools were already in use *when* the pyramids were built.
> RAWLINSON *Herodotus* vol. ii, bk. ii, p. 198, note 4.

We crave the astonishing, the exciting, the far away, and do not know the highways of the gods *when* we see them.
> BURROUGHS *Winter Sunshine* subject ii, p. 86.

The only revolutions which have happened in this land [England] have been *when* Heaven was the only court of appeal.
> ERSKINE *Speeches, Council of Madras* in vol. iv, p. 88

> O thrush, your song is passing sweet,
>> But never a song that you have sung
> Is half so sweet as thrushes sang
>> *When* my dear love and I were young.
>>> Wm. Morris *Other Days*

When hands clasped hands, and lips to lips were pressed,
And the heart's secret was at once confessed.
>>> Abraham Coles *Man, the Microcosm* p. 25.

2. Of connection in thought, introducing a clause expressing condition or contrariety: at the very time that; although; whereas; seeing that; on condition that; provided; while on the contrary; as, do not ask for charity *when* you might work; he remained passive *when* every thing called for action.

When they will not give a doit to relieve a lame beggar, they will lay out ten to see a dead Indian.
>>> Shakespeare *Tempest* act ii, sc. 2, l. 32.

> Who shall decide *when* doctors disagree,
> And soundest casuists doubt, like you and me ?
>>> Pope *Moral Essays* ep. iii.

By a Fallacy is commonly understood, any unsound mode of arguing, which appears to demand our conviction, and to be decisive of the question in hand, *when* in fairness it is not.
>>> Whately *Logic* bk. iii, intro., p. 148.

She was ready to sacrifice holocausts of feelings, *when* the feelings were other people's.
>>> H. James, Jr. *Tragic Muse* vol. i, ch. 19, p. 374.

How it happens that we see things right side up *when* the picture that is formed in the eye by which we see them is upside down, is a mystery.   Jacob Abbott *Light* ch. 27, p. 253.

Distinctions

When—while: *When* refers to a point of time, *while* to continuous duration. Used of logical connection by contrast or antithesis, it will be found that *when* is, as a rule, more sharply adversative than *while*. *While* is always concessive, giving some consideration to the contrasted thought; as, "*While* I am opposed to such action on general principles, I am willing to make an exception in this case," *while* having nearly the force of *although*. The use of *when* would make the opposition the controlling factor; as, "*When* I am opposed to such action on general principles, how can I make this case an exception?" It will be seen that *when* as compared with *while* implies a more irreconcilable contrast.

WHENCE

See WHENCE under ADVERBS.

Whence has conjunctive use as signifying:

1. From what or which place, origin, or source; as, we knew not *whence* he came.

> Childe Harold was he hight:—but *whence* his name
> And lineage long, it suits me not to say.
> > BYRON *Childe Harold* can. 1, st. 3.

> And, when a damp
> Fell round the path of Milton, in his hand
> The Thing became a trumpet, *whence* he blew
> Soul-animating strains—alas, too few!
> > WORDSWORTH *Scorn Not the Sonnet* l. 13.

> Leave to the nightingale her shady wood;
> A privacy of glorious light is thine:
> *Whence* thou dost pour upon the world a flood
> Of harmony, with instinct more divine;
> Type of the wise, who soar, but never roam—
> True to the kindred points of Heaven and Home!
> > WORDSWORTH *To a Skylark* st. 3.

> Even a lowly cottage *whence* we see,
> Stretch'd wide and wild the waste enormous marsh.
> > TENNYSON *Ode to Memory* st. 5

2. From what or which cause; for which reason; wherefore; therefore; as, this is credibly related, *whence* I conclude that it is true.

WHERE

Where, from Anglo-Saxon *hwær*, from *hwā*, who, primarily an interrogative adverb, is used like *when* with conjunctive force, in which case it is variously treated as an adverb used conjunctively and as a true conjunction. It accords with the plan of this book to treat this word as a conjunction like *when, whence*, etc. Compare WHERE under RELATIVE OR CONJUNCTIVE ADVERBS.

I. Of place:

1. At or in which or what place; at the place in which; wherever; as, you are likely to find it *where* you left it.

> See *where* she comes, apparell'd like the spring.
> > SHAKESPEARE *Pericles* act i, sc. 1, l. 12.

> The ribbèd sand is full of hollow gulfs,
> *Where* monsters from the waters come and lie.
> > R. H. STODDARD *The Witch's Whelp* st. 1.

> *Where* deep and misty shadows float
> In forest's depths is heard thy note.
> Like a lost spirit, earthbound still,
> Art thou, mysterious whip-poor-will.
> > MARIE LE BARON *The Whip-Poor-Will.*

> Hast thou not glimpses, in the twilight here,
> Of mountains *where* immortal morn prevails?
> > BRYANT *Return of Youth* st. 5.

> It seem'd a place *where* Gholes might come.
> > MOORE *Lalla Rookh, Fire-Worshippers* pt. ii, st. 10.

The house *where* Shakspeare was born . . . is a small, mean-looking edifice of wood and plaster, a true nestling-place of genius.   IRVING *Sketch-Book, Stratford-on-Avon* p. 318.

> The chamber *where* the good man meets his fate.
> > YOUNG *Night Thoughts* ii, l. 681.

> Alas! how little can a moment show
> Of an eye *where* feeling plays
> In ten thousand dewy rays;
> A face o'er which a thousand shadows go!
> > WORDSWORTH *The Triad.*

2. To which or what place; to a place in which; whither; as, no one knows *where* he went.

> He paused, and led *where* Douglas stood,
> And with stern eye the pageant view'd.
> <div align="right">Scott <i>Marmion</i> can. 5, st. 14.</div>

Answer me, burning stars of night!   *Where* is the spirit gone?
Felicia D. Hemans Invocation st. 1.

II. Metaphorically, of the course of events, situation of affairs, processes of thought, etc.:

1. In which or what event, situation, or set of circumstances; in which case; according to which fact, rule, arrangement, etc.; as, to seek happiness in selfish enjoyment, *where* it can never be found.

> The azure gloom
> Of an Italian night, *where* the deep skies assume
> Hues which have words, and speak to ye of heaven.
> <div align="right">Byron <i>Childe Harold</i> can. 4, st. 128.</div>

> With silence only as their benediction,
>   God's angels come
> *Where* in the shadow of a great affliction,
>   The soul sits dumb!
> <div align="right">Whittier <i>To my Friend on the Death of his Sister</i>.</div>

The dews of blessing heaviest fall   *Where* care falls too.
Jean Ingelow The Letter L pt. i, st. 49.

Active fortitude is demanded *where* evils are to be encountered and overcome. It comprehends resolution or constancy, and intrepidity or courage. . . . Passive fortitude is demanded *where* evils are to be met and endured [and includes] . . . patience, . . . humility, . . . meekness.
D. S. Gregory Christian Ethics pt. ii, div. 1, ch. 8, p. 214.

There is a mode of letting lands, not unusual in the country, *where* the tenant is to cultivate them, and share the crops with his landlord.
E. Washburn Am. Law of Real Property vol. i, p. 864.

> *Where* none admire, 'tis useless to excel;
> *Where* none are beaux, 'tis vain to be a belle.
> <div align="right">Lord Lyttleton <i>Soliloquy of a Beauty in the Country</i> l. 11.</div>

> There is a silence *where* hath been no sound,
> There is a silence *where* no sound may be.
> HOOD *Sonnet, Silence* l. 1.

2. To which or what situation, end, or conclusion; whither, as, observe *where* this reasoning will lead us.

> You have the Pyrrhic dance as yet,
>   *Where* is the Pyrrhic phalanx gone?
> Of two such lessons, why forget
>   The nobler and the manlier one?
> BYRON *Don Juan* can iii, st. 86, l. 10.

[NOTE.—*Where* was formerly at some times used in the sense of *whereas,* as by Shakespeare and others of the older writers.]

Compounds of "Where"

Where is compounded with various particles as *for, in, of, to, ever,* and *with,* to produce relative adverbs and relative conjunctions, the same word being often used both as adverb and conjunction. (Compare RELATIVE ADVERBS.) With the exception of *wherever,* these words have passed almost wholly out of use, except in formal or legal phraseology. Their conjunctive meanings and uses are the following:

WHEREAS

1. Noting or introducing a prologue, preamble, or the reason on which a conclusion is based, and often correlative with *therefore* (see CORRELATIVE CONJUNCTIONS): since the facts are such; in view of existing circumstances; in view of the fact that; seeing that; as, *whereas* our president has tendered his resignation, *therefore* be it resolved, etc.

2. Implying opposition to or contradiction of a previous statement: the fact or the matter being; when on the contrary; when in truth; as, he assured me that this was a genuine diamond, *whereas* it is only paste.

> And, *whereas* I was black and swart before,
> With those clear rays, which she infus'd on me,
> That beauty am I bless'd with, which you see.
> SHAKESPEARE *1 K. Henry VI.* act i, sc. 2, l. 84.

> For by my mother I derived am
> From Lionel, Duke of Clarence, the third son
> To King Edward the Third; *whereas* he
> From John of Gaunt doth bring his pedigree.
> > SHAKESPEARE *2 K. Henry VI.* act ii, sc. 5, l. 76.

Emotion is often weakened by association with thought, *whereas* thoughts are always strengthened by emotion.
> H. R. HAWEIS *Music and Morals* § 6, p. 24.

WHEREAT

At which: now little used except in formal or legal phraseology.

> *Whereat* his horse did snort, as he
> Had heard a lion roar. COWPER *John Gilpin* st. 52.

WHEREBY

By means of which; by or through which; near which; as, we see the result, but not the means *whereby* it is accomplished.

They [the Saxons] invented the words 'humbug,' 'cant,' 'sham,' 'gag,' 'soft-sodder,' 'flap doodle,' and other disenchanting formulas *whereby* the devil of falsehood and unreality gets his effectual apage Satana!
> LOWELL *My Study Windows, Chaucer* p. 349.

Our dragoman . . . washed his dishes in the sand, *whereby* they were not only cleansed but scoured.
> H. M. FIELD *On the Desert* ch. 8, p. 49.

WHEREFOR, WHEREFORE

For which; for which reason.

There came a dwarf . . . and found the dead bodies, *wherefore* he made great dole.
> SIDNEY LANIER *Boy's King Arthur* bk. i, ch. 14, p. 92.

WHEREIN

1. Definitely· in which or what.

> This wide and universal theatre
> Presents more woful pageants than the scene
> *Wherein* we play in.
> > SHAKESPEARE *As You Like It* act ii, sc. 7, l. 137.

> I built my soul a lordly pleasure-house
> *Wherein* at ease for aye to dwell.
> TENNYSON *Palace of Art* st. 1.

High Air-castles are cunningly built of Words, the Words well bedded also in good Logic-mortar; *wherein*, however, no Knowledge will come to lodge.　CARLYLE *Sartor Resartus* bk. i, ch. 8.

In the poorest cottage are books: is one Book, *wherein* for several thousands of years the spirit of man has found light, and nourishment, and an interpreting response to whatever is deepest in him.　　　　　　　CARLYLE *Essays, Corn-Law Rhymes.*

2. Indefinitely: in whatever.

> Dark night, that from the eye his function takes,
> The ear more quick of apprehension makes;
> *Wherein* it doth impair the seeing sense,
> It pays the hearing double recompense.
> SHAKESPEARE *Midsummer-Night's Dream* act iii, sc. 2, l. 179.

WHEREINSOEVER

Emphasizing the distributive or indefinite meaning of *wherein* now found only in old writings or style: in whatever place, point, or respect; as, *whereinsoever* we have offended.

Howbeit, *whereinsoever* any is bold, (I speak foolishly,) I am bold also.　　　　　　　　　　　　　　　*2 Cor.* xi, 21.

WHEREINTO

Into which; as, the gulf *whereinto* he sailed.

There was no other boat there, save that one *whereinto* his disciples were entered.　　　　　　　　　　*John* vi, 22.

WHEREOF

Of which; of whom.

Neither can they prove the things *whereof* they now accuse me.　　　　　　　　　　　　　　　　*Acts* xxiv, 13.

WHERETO

To which; to whom; to which place; whither.

Nevertheless, *whereto* we have already attained, let us walk by the same rule.　　　　　　　　　　　*Phil.* iii, 16.

WHEREUPON

Upon which; upon whom; after which; in consequence of which.

Whereupon he promised with an oath to give her whatsoever she would ask.   *Matt.* xiv, 7.

Whereupon, O King Agrippa, I was not disobedient unto the heavenly vision.   *Acts* xxvi, 19.

WHEREVER (WHERE'ER)

In or at whatever place; as, find him, *wherever* he may be. *Where'er* is a shortened form used chiefly in poetry.

> *Where'er* ye fling the carrion, the raven's croak is loud.
>   MACAULAY *Virginia* st. 2.

> *Where'er* I came   I brought calamity.
>   TENNYSON *Dream of Fair Women* st. 24.

Wherever man is . . . there is religion—hopes that look forward and upward—the belief in an unending existence, and a land of separate souls.   HUGH MILLER in Wilson's *Tales of the Borders, Recollections of Burns* in vol. ii, p. 85.

Wherever the mean man sits is the foot of the table.
          J. F CLARKE *Every-Day Religion* ch. 12, p. 185.

In brief, Baal seems to have been *wherever* his cultus was established, a development or form of the old sun-worship.
          MACKEY *Encyc. Freemasonry, Baal* p. 98.

Wherever there is an ascendant class, a large portion of the morality of the country emanates from its class interests.
          MILL *On Liberty* ch. 1, p. 17.

WHEREWITH, WHEREWITHAL

With which.

O, my lord, *wherewith* shall I save Israel?   *Judges* vi, 15.

What shall we eat? or, What shall we drink? or, *Wherewithal* shall we be clothed?   *Matt.* vi, 31.

WHETHER

Whether is from the Anglo-Saxon *hwœther*, which is derived from *hwá*, who.

As a conjunction, involving an implied question:

1. Introducing the first of two (or more) alternatives, and commonly correlative to a following *or* or *or whether* (see COR-RELATIVE CONJUNCTIONS). in case; if; as, it is decided, *whether* for better *or* worse; it is hard to tell *whether* to go *or* stay.

It was a toss-up *whether* they turned out well *or* ill.
T. HUGHES *Tom Brown at Rugby* pt. i, ch. 9, p. 215.

For she loved him — loved him so!   *Whether* he was good *or* no.
DINAH M. CRAIK *The Little Comforter* st. 8.

2. Introducing a single indirect question, with the alternative and correlative omitted but understood: if; as, I do not know *whether* he will consent [*or* not].

[NOTE.—There are those who would insist that the correlative phrase with *or* must always be added.   But its omission is in accord with the genius of our language, ever seeking to be concise and compendious, and it is in accord with the usage of the best writers.

It is doubted by the ablest judges, *whether*, except in the introduction of new names for new things, English has made any solid improvement for two centuries and a half.
G. P. MARSH *Lect. on Eng. Lang.* lect. i, p. 17.]

WHILE

While, from Anglo-Saxon *hwîl*, in conjunctive or adverbial use is an abbreviation of a phrase employing the noun *while*, *the while* [*i. e.*, the time] *that.*

1. During the time that; in or within the time that; as long as; *while* he slept the fire went out; you are safe *while* I am here.

> *While* the cock with lively din
> Scatters the rear of darkness thin,
> And to the stack or the barn door
> Stoutly struts his dames before.
> MILTON *L'Allegro* l. 49.

> And, *while* a merry catch I troll,
> Let each the buxom chorus bear.
> SCOTT *Lady of the Lake* can. 6, st. 4.

Thus the lungs of the tadpole are developed *while* it is yet a breather of water.   Winchell *Doctrine of Evolution* pref., p. 9.

While the horns are covered with velvet, which lasts with the red-deer for about twelve weeks, they are extremely sensitive to a blow.   Darwin *Descent of Man* vol. ii, ch. 17, p. 248.

While the first drizzling shower is borne aslope.
Swift *A City Shower* l. 18.

While the border-tale's told and the canteen flits round.
Lowell *Growth of the Legend* st. 5.

There never can be prosperity in any country *while* all the numerous cultivators of the soil are permanently depressed and injured.   John Bright *Speeches, Mar. 26, '45* p. 448.

2. At the same time that; notwithstanding the fact that; though; although; as, *while* he was severe, he was also just. Compare when.

While the hunger of the populace was thus appeased, its passion for amusement was at the same time pampered by shows in the theatre and circus.   Chas. Merivale *Rome* ch. 26, p. 186.

Their steps were graves; o'er prostrate realms they trod.
They worshipped Mammon *while* they vowed to God.
Montgomery *West Indies* pt. i, st. 11.

He shivered absolutism, *while* making himself the most absolute prince.   Paxton Hood *Cromwell* ch. 17, p. 348.

Profound thinkers are often helpless in society, *while* shallow men have nimble and ready minds.
Mathews *Great Conversers* essay i, p. 24.

While stone and marble have perished, the stucco of these [the Caracalla] vaults still remains, and is as impressive as any other relic of ancient Rome.
James Fergusson *Hist Arch.* vol. i, bk. iv, ch. 4, p. 334.

We know not why riches are often given to the churl, *while* persons of a liberal and bountiful spirit have their hands chained up with poverty.   Watson *Sermons* vol. ii, p. 55.

WHITHER, WHITHERSOEVER

See WHITHER under RELATIVE OR CONJUNCTIVE ADVERBS.

1. To which or what; to which or what place; as, the city *whither* they were going was far distant.

They drew nigh unto the village *whither* they went.
Luke xxiv, 28.

The temple *whither* the Jews always resort.   *John* xviii, 20.

Marry, as I take it, to Rousillon;
Whither I am going.
SHAKESPEARE *All's Well That Ends Well* act. v, sc. 1, l. 29.

2. To any place whatever; as, you may go *whither* you will: in this sense often *whithersoever*.

Then *whither* he goes, thither let me go.
SHAKESPEARE *K. Rich. II.* act. v, sc. 1, l. 85.

I will follow thee *whithersoever* thou goest.   *Matt.* viii, 29.

WHY

See WHY under RELATIVE OR CONJUNCTIVE ADVERBS.

1. As a simple relative: because or by reason of which; for which; as, this is the reason *why* that was done.

I could draft a report that would give theological reasons *why* his appointment as a professor should be vetoed.
New-York Tribune May 29, 1891, p. 2, col. 8.

Indeed, the reason of our own decimal notation, *why* we reckon by tens instead of the more convenient twelves, appears to be that our forefathers got from their own fingers the habit of counting by tens which has been since kept up, an unchanged relic of primitive man.   E. B. TYLOR *Anthropology* ch. 1, p. 18.

2. As a compound relative: the reason or cause for which; the thing or reason on account of which; that for which; as, I will tell you *why* I would not; you will now see *why* [*i. e.,* the reason *why*] we can not do it.

Tell me, Laertes,   *Why* thou art thus incens'd.
SHAKESPEARE *Hamlet* act. iv, sc. 5, l. 124.

And if, after the unmerited success of that translation, any one will wonder *why* I would enterprise the Odyssey, . . . Homer himself did the same.   POPE *Homer's Odyssey* postscript, p. 488.

[NOTE.—The use of *why* in introducing a sentence must not be confounded with its use as a conjunction, since it has lost all connection with the idea of cause or reason in such use, and has become simply an interjection; as, *why*, that is odd!

An old miser kept a tame jackdaw that used to steal pieces of money, and hide them in a hole, which a cat observing, asked, 'Why he would hoard up those round shining things that he could make no use of?' '*Why*,' said the jackdaw, 'my master has a whole chestful, and makes no more use of them than I do.'   SWIFT *Thoughts on Various Subjects*.]

WITHOUT

See WITHOUT under PREPOSITIONS.

Unless; except; as, it never rains *without* it pours.

[Introducing a substantive clause, and conjunctive by ellipsis of *that*: in disuse by careful writers.   *Standard Dictionary.*

He may stay him; marry, not *without* the prince be willing.
    SHAKESPEARE *Much Ado about Nothing* act iii, sc. 8, l. 86.]

YET

Yet, from Anglo-Saxon *git*, now, is used chiefly as an adverb, but to a certain extent as a conjunction.

1. Denoting something in opposition or contradiction: nevertheless; notwithstanding; as, I come as a friend, *yet* you treat me as a stranger.

     Yet from those flames
No light, but rather darkness visible.
      MILTON *Paradise Lost* bk. i, l. 62.

I knew the foul enchanter, though disguised,
Enter'd the very lime-twigs of his spells,
And *yet* came off.   MILTON *Comus* l. 647.

Forced by hunger to work for the most niggardly pay, he [Samuel Johnson] was *yet* not to be insulted with impunity.
    H. CURWEN *Booksellers, Of Olden Times* p. 58.

Though they abominate all language purely bitter or sour, *yet* they can relish discourse having in it a pleasant tartness.

> BARROW *Works, Sermon, Eph. v, 4* in vol. i, p. 182.

2. Denoting contrast or unlikeness: but at the same time; but; as, he is aged *yet* active and enterprising.

> Here in the body pent,
> Absent from Him I roam,
> *Yet* nightly pitch my moving tent,
> A day's march nearer home.
>> MONTGOMERY *Anticipations of Heaven* st. 2.

With unassured *yet* graceful step advancing.
> MARIA BROOKS *Zophiël* can. 2, st. 47.

> There my life, a silent stream,
> Glid along, *yet* seem'd at rest.
>> MONTGOMERY *Wanderer of Switzerland* pt. ii, st. 8.

3. Denoting concession: although; though; as, he is not here, *yet* he promised to meet me.

> And rank for her meant duty, various,
> *Yet* equal in its worth, done worthily.
> Command was service; humblest service done
> By willing and discerning souls was glory.
>> GEORGE ELIOT *Agatha.*

Correlative or Paired Conjunctions

Correlative conjunctions are those which are used in pairs or series in clauses that succeed each other in the same sentence and neither of which makes complete sense without the other or others. The principal correlative conjunctions are the following:

Although—yet (see THOUGH); *as—as; as—so; both—and; either—or; if—then; neither—nor; no—nor; not—nor; now—then; so—as; though—yet; whether—or; whither—thither.*

[NOTE.—Some words other than conjunctions are included in this enumeration, an adjective or adverb often forming part of a correlation of which the other part is a conjunction, and being conveniently treated with it.]

[Some conjunctions are apt to go in pairs, the principal of which are: as—as, if—then, whether—or, as—so, either—or, though—yet, both—and, neither—nor. One member of the pair can generally be dispensed with. It is a question, fortunately not an important one, whether one of these pairs is one conjunction or two. We have seen that adverbial and prepositional phrases may be made up of two or more words, and the same is true of conjunctions. We have such compound expressions as, *and yet, if however, as soon as, inasmuch as, now therefore, on the other hand*. Of however many words such an expression may consist, it performs the work of a single conjunction, and so does one of the pairs under consideration.

RAMSEY *English Language* ch. 8, p. 494.]

ALTHOUGH—YET

See THOUGH—YET.

AS—AS

Example: The wind is *as* favorable *as* possible. In this case the first *as* is classed as a conjunctive adverb; it might be changed, somewhat clumsily to be sure, to an adverbial expression; as, the wind is *so far* favorable *as* [is] possible. The advantage of the *as* is that it binds the two clauses together, pointing the mind on to the concluding expression. We sometimes hear colloquially the unfinished phrase; as, "he was just *as* kind," where the speaker despairs of finding an adequate term of comparison, while yet the mind waits in suspense for the expected completion, the *as* thus showing itself a true connective.

AS—SO

Example: *As* he lived, *so* he died. While the *so* here is an adverb, yet the correlatives have conjunctive force, binding each clause to the other, each needing the other to complete the thought which the whole sentence is designed to express.

BOTH—AND

Example: Food and lodging for *both* man *and* beast. *Both* indicates the completeness of the enumeration, and also draws attention individually to the elements composing it. "*Both* man *and* beast" is more emphatic than simply "man *and* beast," pausing, as it were, upon the items, and showing that neither has been omitted or neglected.

EITHER — OR

Example: *Either* it will rain *or* it will not. This correlation presents to the mind a pair of alternatives, of which one or the other, but not both, may be accepted or found to be true. The enumeration may be extended to a greater number of terms by the addition of successive clauses beginning with *or*; as, it will *either* rain *or* hail *or* snow. *Or* may be omitted at each point of transition except the last, and a comma substituted; as, *either* rain, hail, *or* snow. *Either* may be omitted in simple and unemphatic combinations, the alternation being sufficiently expressed by *or*; as, it will rain, hail, *or* snow. Modern swiftness of expression tends constantly to such omissions, where the meaning is not made less clear.

Or is sometimes in poetic usage substituted for *either*; as, *or* love *or* hate, *or* life *or* death.

IF — THEN

Example: *If* this note was in answer to mine, *then* it must have been written at a later date.

If, denoting a condition or supposition, points onward to a conclusion; *then*, denoting an inference or a conclusion, points back to a condition or supposition, on which it depends. *Then* in such case may be omitted, making the connection closer, but calling less attention to the separate steps of the reasoning.

NEITHER — NOR

The negative of *either—or*, used in the same way and subject to the same conditions. Any number of alternatives with *nor* may follow *neither*.

As in the case of *or* after *either*, *nor* may be omitted after *neither*, and a comma substituted at each transition except the last, as in the old New England saying, " *Neither* fish, flesh, *nor* good red herring."

Nor may, in poetic or highly rhetorical utterance, be substituted for *neither*; as, *nor* threats *nor* promises could move him.

NO—NOR

The negative adjective *no* may take *nor* as a correlative equivalent to *and no;* as, I have *no* gold *nor* silver. For the use of *or* in such connection, see under NOT—NOR.

NOT—NOR; NOT—OR

The negative adverb *not* may take as a correlative the conjunction *nor* equivalent to *and not;* as, you must *not* move *nor* speak.

In such correlation, either with *no* or *not, or* may be used instead of *nor,* but with difference of emphasis. *Or* groups the alternatives as members of a single class, spreading the meaning of the introductory negative over all together; *nor* takes each item separately, assigning to it its own individual negative. Thus, "I want *no* notes *nor* promises; I want money" treats the rejected items separately, so that we might say, "I want *no* notes, *nor* promises [either]," etc.

But if one says, "I want *no* notes *or* promises; I want money," he groups notes and promises together, and discards them collectively. *Nor* emphasizes and individualizes the items which *or* groups in one total with slighter discrimination of parts. *Nor* is therefore the more emphatic particle in such correlation. The same is true of *or* and *nor* after *not.* "You must *not* move *nor* speak" treats the moving and the speaking as separate activities to be individually repressed; "You must *not* move *or* speak" groups moving and speaking together in opposition to perfect stillness, without concentrating attention upon either one.

In such a statement as "I will *not* do it, *nor* consider it," *nor* is the necessary correlative, since the latter clause is emphatic in its own nature, being added to make the refusal more absolute; the meaning might be given more fully by saying, "I will *not* do it, *nor even* consider it."

SO—AS

So is more emphatic than *as* in introducing a balanced comparison, and has a suggestion of weight and solemnity; as, *so* long *as* time shall last, his memory shall endure. This is a stronger and more impressive statement than "*As* long *as* time shall last," etc. Also, after a negative *so* is preferred to *as* as the first of two correlatives. We say, "He is *as* tall *as* I am," but, negatively, on the contrary, "He is *not so* tall *as* I am."

SUCH—AS; SUCH—THAT

The adjective *such* indicating comparison takes as its correlative *as* or *that*.

[*Such* is essentially a term of comparison, and to complete its force that with which comparison is made requires to be expressed, implied, or understood. When expressed, *as* or *that* is used before the subject of the comparison as the correlative of *such*; as, *such* a voice *as* hers is unusual; the averment was *such that* it could not be gainsaid.   *Standard Dictionary*.]

THOUGH—YET; ALTHOUGH—YET

Example: *Though* (or *although*) I believe the contrary, *yet* I am open to conviction. These correlatives are at the same time disjunctives, setting their respective clauses in sharp opposition while combining the contrasted thoughts in a single affirmation.

WHETHER—OR

Example: I am in doubt *whether* to buy *or* sell.

This correlation always expresses uncertainty or hesitation looking toward decision or choice.

Where the concluding phrase is a simple negative, all but the negative and correlative may be omitted, the rest being understood from what goes before; as, he can not decide *whether* to go *or not*, *i. e.*, *whether* to go *or not* [to go].

No is often substituted for *not*, forming the idiomatic phrase *whether or no*; as, he is going *whether or no*; *i. e.*, whether his going is approved, permitted, safe, etc., or not.

Still further, the entire concluding phrase may be omitted, especially in familiar speech, leaving *whether* to stand without correlative; as, let me know *whether* to expect you [*or not*]

PART III

Relative Pronouns Defined and Illustrated

The relative pronouns are *who*, *which*, *what*, *that*, and *as*, with the inflections of *who*, viz.: the objective *whom* and the possessive *whose*, and the compounds in *-ever*, *-so*, and *-soever*, as, *whoever*, *whoso*, *whosoever*, *whomever*, *whomsoever*, *whosesoever*, *whichever*, *whichsoever*, *whatever*, and *whatsoever*.

[NOTE.—In the list as given above, the words are placed in the order commonly adopted by grammarians, which is probably due to the fact that *who* is used of persons, giving it the place of dignity, while *which* and *what* are naturally associated with *who*. In the separate treatment of the words, however, the alphabetical order, used elsewhere throughout this book, will be followed.]

Who, *which*, and *what* are used also as interrogative pronouns, and *that* as a demonstrative pronoun; but as when so used they are not properly connectives, those uses will not be here considered.

AS

As is most frequently used as an adverb or as a conjunction. (See under CONJUNCTIONS.) It is, however, also used with the force of a pronoun. In some such uses in the older writers it would be possible to substitute *that* without appreciable change of meaning; as:

> I have not from your eyes that gentleness,
> And show of love, *as* I was wont to have.
>> SHAKESPEARE *Julius Cæsar* act i, sc. 2, l. 68.

Here we might say:

> "... that gentleness,
> And show of love, *that* I was wont to have."

In the *Tatler* (conducted by Addison and Steele, 1709) we read of "a body of men *as* [that] lay in wait."

This usage would now be considered incorrect or inelegant. But after the correlatives *as* (adv.), *same*, *so*, and *such*, *as* is used with pronominal force. In many such cases it would be very difficult to treat it either as an adverb or as a conjunction. Its meaning as a pronoun can not be directly defined, because no other word or set of words will take its place with the same correlative force. But its pronominal import will appear from the fact that *who*, *which*, or *that* might in many cases be substituted by a slight change in the form of the sentence, especially of the verb. Thus:

By breadth is meant such a massing of the quantities, . . . *as* shall enable the eye to pass without obstruction . . . from one to another, so that it shall appear to take in the whole at a glance.
W. ALLSTON *Lectures on Art, Composition* p. 154.

Here we might substitute *that*, except that the latter word lacks the correlative force. By omitting "such" from the first clause, *that* may be readily substituted in the second; thus, "a massing of the quantities *that* shall enable the eye," etc.

Again:

On the sides of the cave were fan-like ivory tracings, such *as* the frost leaves upon a pane.
HAGGARD *King Solomon's Mines* ch. 16, p. 225.

The reference here is not to manner or mere sequence of thought. It is not "*as* the frost leaves a pane." The reference is to *something* traced upon the pane, and we might give the meaning precisely by substituting for "such as" the words "like those which," "like those" carrying the meaning of "such" and "which" of "as"; thus, "fan-like ivory tracings *like those which* the frost leaves upon a pane." There are many cases in which the exact part of speech represented by *as* is admittedly difficult to assign, and as to which grammarians would not agree. A safe rule would be, that where *as* can not be readily explained as a conjunction or as an adverb, it should be classed as a relative pronoun. The very untranslatableness of *as* makes it one of the closest of all connectives. It seems to have a meaning belonging in part to the clause preceding, and in part to the clause containing it, while the two references are so indissolubly entwined that it is impossible to separate them; and of the two clauses so connected neither is complete without the other.

For in those days shall be affliction such *as* was not from the beginning of the creation. *Mark* xiii, 19.

Those *as* sleep and think not on their sins.
Shakespeare *Merry Wives of Windsor* act v, sc. 5, l. 57.

[Note.—Such usage as in the quotation from Shakespeare given above would now be classed as illiterate and incorrect.]

> If thou tak'st more,
> Or less, than a just pound,—be it but so much
> *As* makes it light or heavy in the substance,
> Or the division of the twentieth part
> Of one poor scruple . . .
> Thou diest.
> Shakespeare *Merchant of Venice* act iv, sc. 1, l. 328.

> It eats and sleeps, and hath such senses
> *As* we have, such.
> Shakespeare *Tempest* act i, sc. 2, l. 413.

His coursers are of such immortal strain *as* were the coursers of Achilles. A. B. Edwards *Up the Nile* ch. 16, p. 298.

The viceroy still further enlarged his resources by the sequestration of the revenues belonging to such ecclesiastics *as* resided in Rome. Prescott *Philip II.* vol. i, bk. i, ch. 6, p. 171.

There was no class of human beings so low *as* to be beneath his sympathy. Channing *Works, Char. of Christ* p. 309.

THAT

For its etymology, see THAT in place under Conjunctions.

That is the most general of the relative pronouns, being used indiscriminately for persons or things. Like *as*, *that* is almost insusceptible of definition; it may be imperfectly rendered as "the one"; thus, "the man *that* I saw" may be converted into "the man; *the one* I saw"; the latter phrase retains the general sense, but loses the connective force of the phrase employing "*that*." In the expression "the man *that* I saw," "*that*" is the object of the following verb, "saw," while at the same time it points back to the preceding noun "man" as its antecedent, thus welding the preceding and following words into a single whole.

That, though older than *who* or *which*, was at one time almost displaced by these last-cited relatives. It has recovered its position, but an attempt is now being made to assign it separate territory from *who* and *which*. See DISTINCTIONS under WHO.

[*That* came in during the twelfth century to supply the place of the indeclinable relative *the*, and in the fourteenth century it is the ordinary relative. In the sixteenth century, *which* often supplies its place; in the seventeenth century, *who* replaces it. About Addison's time, *that* had again come into fashion, and had almost driven *which* and *who* out of use.   *Century Dictionary*.]

[Steele, in the *Spectator*, with the ignorance of English philology so common in that age, presents the "Humble Petition of *Who* and *Which* against the upstart Jack Sprat, *That*, now trying to supplant them." The truth was, they were supplanting *That*. Perhaps he was not acquainted with the English Psalter of 1380:

"Blesse thou, my soule, to the Lord! and wile thou not forzete all the zeldingus of him.

That hath mercy to alle thi wickednessis; *that* helith alle thin infirmyties.

That azen-bieth fro deth thi lif; *that* crowneth thee in mercy and mercy-doingis.

That fulfilleth in goode thingus thy deseyr."

In all ages of the English tongue *that* has been the standard relative of the body of the people, and to this day *which* is stiff and formal, suggestive of the student's lamp or the pedagogue's birch. Here is an excellent example:

"This is the cock *that* crew in the morn,
    Unto the farmer sowing his corn,
    That met the priest with his pen and ink-horn,
    That married the man so tattered and torn,

> *That* kissed the maiden all forlorn,
> *That* milked the cow with the crumpled horn,
> *That* tossed the dog, *that* worried the cat,
> *That* killed the rat, *that* ate the malt,
> *That* lay in the house, *that* Jack built."

This familiar word occurs here eleven times; and to replace it by *which* and *who* would destroy the rippling rhythm that has delighted the young ears of so many generations.
> Ramsey *English Language* pt. ii, ch. 4, p. 882.]

That is subject to certain differences in grammatical construction from *who* or *which*. See Distinctions under who.

[*That* in this use [as a relative pronoun] is never used with a preposition preceding it, but may be so used when the preposition is transposed to the end of the clause; thus, the man *of whom* I spoke, the book *from which* I read, the spot *near which* he stood, the pay *for which* he works; but not the man *of that* I spoke, etc., though one may say, the man *that* I spoke *of*, the book *that* I read *from*, the place *that* he stood *near*, the pay *that* he works *for*, and so on.   *Century Dictionary.*]

[The relatives *that* and *as* have this peculiarity; that, unlike *whom* and *which*, they never follow the word on which their case depends: nor indeed can any simple relative be so placed, except it be governed by a preposition or an infinitive. Thus, it is said (John, xiii, 29th), "Buy those things *that* we have need *of*;" so we may say, "Buy such things *as* we have need of." But we cannot say, "Buy those things *of that* we have need;" or, "Buy such things *of as* we have need." Though we may say, "Buy those things *of which* we have need," as well as, "Buy those things *which* we have need *of*;" or, "Admit those persons *of whom* we have need," as well as, "Admit those persons *whom* we have need *of*." By this it appears that *that* and *as* have a closer connexion with their antecedents than the other relatives require: a circumstance worthy to have been better remembered by some critics. Goold Brown *Grammar of English Grammars* pt. ii, ch. 5, p. 304.]

> He *that* is strucken blind cannot forget
> The precious treasure of his eyesight lost.
> Shakespeare *Romeo and Juliet* act i, sc. 1, l. 238.

Her cap of velvet could not hold
The tresses of her hair of gold,
That flowed and floated like the stream,
And fell in masses down her neck.

    LONGFELLOW *Christus* pt. vi, l. 375.

Rapt into still communion *that* transcends
The imperfect offices of prayer and praise.

    WORDSWORTH *The Excursion* bk. i, st. 9.

Our choices are our destiny. Nothing is ours *that* our choices have not made ours.

    A. BRONSON ALCOTT *Table-Talk* bk. ii, p. 157.

Cheerless night *that* knows no morrow.

    BURNS *Raving Winds* st. 1.

What thought so wild, what airy dream so light
That will not prompt a theorist to write?

    CRABBE *The Library* l. 383.

There are certain books *that* are read to be laid aside, and there are certain other books *that* are laid aside to be read.

    J. T. FIELDS *Underbrush, Paul and Virginia* p. 253.

A fellow-feeling *that* is sure To make the outcast bless his door.

    LOWELL *The Heritage* st. 6.

No, Freedom has a thousand charms to show
That slaves, howe'er contented, never know.

    COWPER *Table-Talk* l. 260.

Domestic Happiness, thou only bliss
Of Paradise, *that* has survived the fall !

    COWPER *The Task* bk. iii, l. 41.

The Relative "That" Omitted

The relative *that* is often omitted—a usage which some criticize as colloquial, but which has high literary authority, and is often forcible by compactness and elegant by seeming simplicity.

In the following quotations *that* is supplied in brackets—[*that*]—as indicating where the meaning if fully expressed would require it, but not as indicating that such expression is necessary, or would in every case be desirable.

> While I deduce,
> From the first note [*that*] the hollow cuckoo sings,
> The symphony of spring.
>   THOMSON *The Seasons, Spring* l. 576.

> Wouldst thou be famed? have those high acts in view,
> [*That*] brave men would act though scandal would ensue.
>   YOUNG *Love of Fame* satire vii, l. 175.

> Circumstances try the metal [*that*] a man is really made of.
>   WILKIE COLLINS *Moonstone, The Story* period i, ch. 11, p. 98.

> Mr. Lecky has justly remarked that the only charge [*that*] utilitarians can bring against vice is that of imprudence.
>   W. S. LILLY *On Right and Wrong* ch. 2, p. 48.

> Complaint is the largest tribute [*that*] heaven receives, and the sincerest part of our devotion.
>   SWIFT *Works, Thoughts on Various Subjects* p. 517.

> It was one of the propositions [*that*] Jefferson often talked about in private, that the high places of Europe were filled with imbeciles, the result of consanguineous marriages.
>   JOSEPH COOK *Heredity* lect. x, p. 268.]

WHAT

For its etymology see WHAT under CONJUNCTIONS.

What as a pronoun is both interrogative and relative, the interrogative use coming first in order of time.

[*What, who,* and *which* were all originally interrogatives only, and their interrogative and relative senses often mingle and pass into each other, so as not to be easily distinguished.
    Standard Dictionary.]

The connective uses of *what* are the following:

1. As a relative:

(a) A Simple Relative

Formerly as a simple relative, equivalent to *that, which,* or *who.* This use, always limited, has long been accounted a vulgarism; as, "If I had a donkey *what* wouldn't go." *What* is never so used by good writers or speakers of the present day.

(b) A Double Relative

What has the peculiarity of being a double relative equivalent to a demonstrative followed by a simple relative, and correctly defined as *that which*; as, I know *what* [that which] he told me; I will see *what* [that which] is in the room; I do not know *what* [that which] he has done.

> For *what* I will, I will, and there an end.
> > SHAKESPEARE *Two Gentlemen of Verona* act i, sc. 8, l. 65.

> *What* man dare, I dare.
> > SHAKESPEARE *Macbeth* act iii, sc. 4, l. 95.

> Omission to do *what* is necessary
> Seals a commission to a blank of danger.
> SHAKESPEARE *Troilus and Cressida* act iii, sc. 8, l. 280.

> Approve the best and follow *what* I approve.
> > MILTON *Paradise Lost* bk. viii, l. 611.

> Think not I am *what* I appear.
> > BYRON *The Bride of Abydos* can. i, st. 12.

> And *what* he greatly thought, he nobly dared.
> > HOMER *The Odyssey* Pope's transl., bk. ii, l. 312.

> The other day I was *what* you would call floored by a Jew.
> > COLERIDGE *Table Talk* July 8, 1830.

> Everywhere in life, the true question is not *what* we gain, but *what* we do. CARLYLE *Essays Goethe's Helena* ¶ 6, l. 31.

> No one will give anything for *what* can be obtained gratis.
> > MILL *Political Economy* bk. i, ch. 1, p. 54.

> That idea of duty . . . which is to the moral life *what* the addition of a great central ganglion is to animal life.
> > GEORGE ELIOT *Janet's Repentance* ch. 10, p. 255.

> *What* ardently we wish, we soon believe.
> > YOUNG *Night Thoughts* night vii, pt. ii, l. 1811.

> And *what* they dare to dream of, dare to do.
> LOWELL *Ode Recited at the Harvard Commemoration* July 21, 1865, st. 8.

2. As an interrogative in a dependent sentence, having the force of a relative: when the question "*what* was that?" passes

into the form "he asked me *what* that was," *what* becomes a true connective, and scarcely distinguishable from a relative.

For prevision — the perception of *what* is to turn up hereafter — is an apprehension of phenomena.　　MARTINEAU *Essays* p. 27.

They [women] ought to know *what* is fact and *what* is fol-de-rol.　　GAIL HAMILTON in *Atlantic Monthly* Apr., 1863, p. 419.

'Every man,' said Imlac, 'may by examining his own mind guess *what* passes in the minds of others.'
　　　　　　　　　　JOHNSON *Rasselas* ch. 16, p. 76.

If you would be better satisfied *what* the beatifical vision means, my request is, that you live holily and go and see.
　　　　　　　　BUNYAN *Works, Joys of Heaven* p. 81.

[There is still another use of *what* in which some authorities (as the *Standard Dictionary*) class it as an adjective, while others (as the *Century Dictionary*) treat it as a pronoun used adjectivally; as, "*What* flag is that?" or "He asked me *what* flag that was."]

What poet of her own sex, except Sappho, could she [Mrs. Browning] herself find worthy a place among the forty immortals grouped in the hemicycle of her own 'Vision of Poets.'
　　　　　　　E. C. STEDMAN *Victorian Poets* ch. 4, p. 115.

There is no estimating or believing, till we come into a position to know it, *what* foolery lurks latent in the breast of very sensible people.　　　　HAWTHORNE *Our Old Home* p. 25.

WHICH

Which is from Anglo-Saxon *hwilc*, from *hwā*, who, plus *-lic*, *-ly*. *Which* is both an interrogative and a relative pronoun. The two uses shade into one another so as to be often difficult to discriminate. See note under WHAT. As in the case of *what*, it will be desirable here to give a certain amount of consideration to both uses of the pronoun *which*.

Which is both singular and plural; the objective is the same in form as the nominative; *whose* is used as the possessive. See WHOSE. As to the use of *which* with reference to persons, see DISTINCTIONS under WHICH.

Which as an interrogative asks, what one of a certain number, class, or group, implying that the number, class, or group is known, the only question being the selection of one or more from among the others.

It is as a relative that *which* has connective use in the significations following:

[NOTE.—*Which* as a relative is not now used of persons. See DISTINCTIONS.]

1. Simply descriptive or restrictive, with such reference to an antecedent object as binds the two clauses in close connection: the one that; that; such as; as, this is the paper *which* I referred to; that is the matter to *which* we must give our attention.

[NOTE.—If *that* were substituted in the second example given above, it would be necessary to reverse the order of the words, putting the preposition at the end of the clause; as, that is the matter *that* we must give our attention *to*.]

I have found the piece *which* I had lost.   *Luke* xv, 9.

> That in the captain's but a choleric word,
> *Which* in the soldier is flat blasphemy.
> SHAKESPEARE *Measure for Measure* act ii, sc. 2, l. 130.

> Vain, very vain, my weary search to find
> That bliss *which* only centres in the mind.
> GOLDSMITH *The Traveller* l. 423.

The burlesquing spirit *which* ranges to and fro and up and down on the earth, seeing no reason . . . why it should not appropriate every sacred, heroic, and pathetic theme.
GEORGE ELIOT *Theophrastus Such* ch. 10, p. 76.

2. Resumptive or explanatory, referring to an antecedent in such a way as sharply to distinguish what is said of it in the preceding from what is said of it in the following clause, so that a phrase involving a conjunction, as *and* or *since*, might be substituted for *which :* and it; and that; and this; namely; viz.; as, it was something to eat, *which* [and that] was all we asked for ; here is the boat, *which* [and it] is stanch and seaworthy; this document, *which* [since it; as it] is brief and clear, will answer every purpose.

[NOTE.—In some such cases a participial phrase might be substituted for *which* with its accompanying word. Thus in the last sentence given above we might say, "this document *being* brief and clear," etc.]

> The other keeps his dreadful day-book open
> Till sunset, that we may repent; *which* doing,
> The record of the action fades away.
>   LONGFELLOW *Christus* pt. vi, l. 228.

Books are the legacies that a great genius leaves to mankind, *which* are delivered down from generation to generation, as presents to the posterity of those who are yet unborn.
     ADDISON *The Spectator* No. 166, l. 24.

And after this comes the bush proper, the growth of a few years *which* admits no ingress whatever within its shade.
     STANLEY *In Darkest Africa* vol. ii, ch. 28, p. 79.

> It is the secret sympathy,
> The silver link, the silken tie,
> *Which* heart to heart, and mind to mind,
> In body and in soul can bind.
>   SCOTT *Lay of the Last Minstrel* can. v, st. 13.

3. In indirect question, where the interrogative and relative significations intermingle, used substantively or adjectivally: what one (of a number or class referred to); as, please tell me *which* you prefer; I must know *which* you decide upon; did you see *which* way he went?

[NOTE.—The use of *which* merely to introduce a relative clause containing another word that is the true object of the verb is now discountenanced as illiterate, though it was once approved; as, I order you to leave, *which* if you don't do it, I shall take measures to make you.

Which I wish to remark, and my language is plain.
  BRET HARTE *Plain Language from Truthful James* st. 1.]

Distinctions

What—which—who: *Which*, as already stated, refers to some one or more among a class or group of objects definitely known or clearly referred to. *What* is unlimited in range of reference. "*What* book would you like?" opens the way to selection from among all books ever made. "*Which* book would you like?" restricts the thought to some known group of books, as those in one's hands, on a table, in a room, library, store, or elsewhere. "Ask *what* you will" is boundless permission; "Ask *which* you will" restricts the choice to one of certain alternatives.

What, either as interrogative or as relative, though it may be used with reference to persons, is used chiefly of animals, inanimate objects, abstractions, etc. It is possible to say "*What* man is that?" though more usual to ask "*Who* is that?" or "*Who* is that man?" As used with reference to persons, *what* applies to origin, character, or office; as, an emergency will show *what* a man is. One remarks, "That man is not the President," and the question is asked in response, "*What* is he then?" that is, "*What* office does he hold?" In speaking directly to the person concerned, the latter form would be the more courteous. "*What* are you?" unless in familiar conversation would seem rude, and might be asked in such a tone as to be absolutely insulting.

Which as interrogative may refer either to persons or things; as, to *which* person do you refer? *which* is the man? To ask "*Who* is the man?" would leave the question open to all mankind and be equivalent to "*Which* one of all the men in the world?" or to "Is there any man who?" etc. But in the question "*Which* is the man?" "*which*" carries its distributive force, and asks "*What one* [of these especially referred to, as in a group or line] is the man?"

Which as a relative formerly referred to persons as well as to things, and is often so used in the Scriptures; as, Our Father *which* art in heaven. It is now, however, used only of animals and of inanimate objects, abstractions, etc., often referring to an entire clause or preceding statement or fact expressed or implied. *Who* is now used exclusively of persons. See WHO. *That* may take the place of either *who* or *which*. See DISTINCTIONS under WHO.

WHO

Who, from Anglo-Saxon *hwā*, is both an interrogative and a relative pronoun. Though used of persons, it is not classed as a personal pronoun, because it does not specify what person is intended, as is done by *I, thou, he,* etc., but applies indefinitely to either of the three persons as its antecedent may determine; as, I am the one *who* built the house [first person]; you are the friend *who* helped me [second person]; he is the one *who* hindered me [third person]. *Who* is both singular and plural, and may refer to an antecedent of any number or gender.

[*Who* is always used substantively, and as referring to one or more persons. In number, it is uninflected, being singular or plural as required by its antecedent. In case, it has *whose* for its possessive and *whom* for its objective.   *Standard Dictionary.*]

As the objective *whom* presents no special difficulty, it will be considered in connection with its nominative, *who;* but since the possessive *whose* is used also as the possessive of *which*, it will receive special and separate treatment. See WHOSE.

As an interrogative, *who* asks for the identification of some person or persons, as for the name of a person answering to a certain description, or for the doer of a certain act: which or what person; as, *who* did this? *who* was the greatest of poets? *who* was Charlemagne?

Who has connective force as a relative, introducing a dependent clause, and identifying the subject or object in a relative clause with that of the principal clause: in such use not admitting of definition by any other word or words, though often interchangeable with *that* (see DISTINCTIONS); as, this is the man *who* brought the message; have you met the lady *who* lives here? there are the guests *who* came yesterday; I will lead you to the man *whom* you seek.

> Thou *who* hast
> The fatal gift of beauty.
>   BYRON *Childe Harold* can. iv, st. 42.

Telling tales of the fairy *who* travelled like steam
In a pumpkin-shell coach, with two rats for her team !
            WHITTIER *The Pumpkin* st. 4.

     And critics have no partial views,
     Except they know *whom* they abuse.
     And since you ne'er provoke their spite,
     Depend upon't their judgment's right.
            SWIFT *On Poetry* l. 129.

         He ne'er is crowned
With immortality, *who* fears to follow
Where airy voices lead.
            KEATS *Endymion* bk. ii, l. 212.

Errors, like straws, upon the surface flow ;
He *who* would search for pearls, must dive below.
            DRYDEN *All for Love* prologue.

Thou knowest the maiden *who* ventures to kiss a sleeping man,
wins of him a pair of gloves.
         SCOTT *Fair Maid of Perth* ch. 5, l. 444.

Some positive persisting fops we know,
Who, if once wrong, will needs be always so.
         POPE *Essay on Criticism* pt. iii, l. 9.

A man *whom* it is proper to praise cannot be flattered, and a
man *who* can be flattered ought not to be praised.
         HOLLAND *Lessons in Life* lesson xix, p. 273.

A fundamental mistake to call vehemence and rigidity
strength ! A man is not strong *who* takes convulsion-fits ; though
six men cannot hold him then.
         CARLYLE *Heroes and Hero-Worship* lect. v, p. 170.

[NOTE.—By ellipsis or omission of its antecedent, *who* may be
used with the force of a double relative, equivalent to *he that,*
they that, the one or *ones that,* etc.; as, *whom* the gods would
destroy they first make mad. With the exception of some old
proverbial sayings, this usage is now confined to poetry.

         Nor think thou with wind
Of aery threats to awe *whom* yet with deeds
Thou canst not.   MILTON *Paradise Lost* bk. vi, l. 282

Who best   Bear his mild yoke, they serve Him best.
         MILTON *Sonnet, On His Blindness* l. 10.

Who never walks save where he sees men's tracks
Makes no discoveries.   HOLLAND *Kathrina, Labor* st. 88.

    To get thine ends, lay bashfulnesse aside ;
    Who feares to aske, doth teach to be deny'd.
        HERRICK *Hesperides, No Bashfuleness in Begging.*

Who builds a church to God, and not to Fame,
Will never mark the marble with his name.
         POPE *Moral Essays* ep. iii, l. 285.]

Distinctions

That—which—who : Reference has been made to the difference between the restrictive and the resumptive use of the relatives. In the *restrictive* use, the clause introduced by the relative
simply limits the antecedent to a certain class, number, or the
like, indicated by the relative clause ; as, "This is the book *that* I
refer to." This sentence might be changed to a participial form
with no change of meaning ; as, "This is the book *referred to* by
me." The latter rendering of the thought shows that the relative
clause in the restrictive sense has really adjectival force, so that
the *restrictive* use has been by some termed *explanatory*, and by
others *definitive*. The *restrictive* use thus simply brings out
something supposed to be contained in the antecedent, or limits
the antecedent to one of many possible meanings.

In the *resumptive* use, on the contrary, something is really
added by the relative clause ; as, "I will tell you the story, *which*
I have come to believe to be true." Here the clause with *which*
adds something to the thought of the principal sentence, so that a
conjunction and pronoun might be substituted for *which ;* as,
"This is the story, *and* I have come to believe *it* to be true."
This *resumptive* use is also termed *coordinating* or *descriptive*.
That, which, and *who* have been for the most part used indiscriminately in the *restrictive* sense, it being possible to say either
"The man *who* was ill has recovered," or "The man *that* was
ill," etc.; "This is the book *that* [or *which*] I brought with me."

19

That is rarely, if ever, used resumptively, *who* or *which* being employed in that sense. But the use of *who* or *which* in both the *restrictive* and the *resumptive* sense leads to a certain possible ambiguity. Thus, "I have seen the man *who* promised to meet us" may mean either "the man [the one that] promised" or "the man, [and he] promised to meet us." This ambiguity is often avoided by the use of a comma, "the man *who* promised" being understood as *restrictive*, and "the man, *who* promised" as *resumptive* or *coordinating*. But punctuation is a dubious expedient. Hence many would use *that* in all cases where the relative is *restrictive* or *explanatory*, and *who* or *which* where it is *resumptive* or *coordinating*. Thus, "This is the house *that* [*i. e.*, the particular one that] I built for my own use" would be *restrictive*, but "This is the house, *which* I built for my own use" [*i. e.*, *and* I built *it* for my own use] would be *resumptive*; "I have seen the man *that* [the particular one that] brought me the despatches" being *restrictive*, but "I have seen the man, *who* [*and he*] brought me the despatches" being *resumptive*.

Such a distinction would be convenient, but many reasons operate against its uniform enforcement.

That being impersonal, its use would seem in many cases to depersonalize its antecedent. "Washington *that* gave us so grand an example of patriotism" would be an undesirable expression, seeming to treat the great historic man as a mere item or quantity. *Who* is needed in such a sentence for the expression of personality.

[*That*, in modern use, rarely introduces, being simply demonstrative and restrictive, and often preceded by the definite article. Thus we say: Washington, *who* was the first President, is often called Father of his country. *The* Washington *that* emigrated to this country was his ancestor. In the first sentence *that* could have been used formerly, but is never so used now; in the second, however, *who* may be used, though many object to its use as confusing.   *Standard Dictionary.*]

The present tendency seems to be to the use of *who* as the relative in all direct reference to a person or persons.

Where the antecedent is something other than a person, as one of the lower animals, an inanimate object, or an abstraction, it would seem to be a simple matter to use *that* as the *restrictive* and *which* as the *resumptive* relative. But here a serious difficulty intervenes. *That* can not be governed by a preceding preposition, but must put its governing preposition at the end of the clause.

[*Who, which,* and *that* agree in being relatives, and are more or less interchangeable as such; but *who* is used chiefly of persons (though also often of the higher animals), *which* almost only of animals and things (in old English also of persons), and *that* indifferently of either, except after a preposition, where only *who* or *which* can stand. Some recent authorities teach that only *that* should be used when the relative clause is limiting or defining: as, the man *that* runs fastest wins the race; but *who* or *which*, when it is descriptive or coordinating: as, this man, *who* ran fastest, won the race; but, though present usage is perhaps tending in the direction of such a distinction, it neither has been nor is a rule of English speech, nor is it likely to become one, especially on account of the impossibility of setting *that* after a preposition; for to turn all relative clauses into the form "the house *that* Jack lived *in*" (instead of "the house *in which* Jack lived") would be intolerable. In good punctuation the defining relative is distinguished (as in the examples above) by never taking a comma before it, whether it be *who* or *which* or *that*.

Century Dictionary.]

Thus, the sentence "He has a diamond for *which* he paid a thousand dollars" would become, "He has a diamond *that* he paid a thousand dollars for"—a correct, but at times clumsy or undignified, construction. See PREPOSITION ENDING SENTENCE, p. 4.

"Who," "Which" or "That" Omitted

The omission of *which* closely parallels the omission of *that* (explained p. 246); as, This is the book [*that* or *which*] I referred to; He showed me a letter [*that* or *which*] he had just received. *Who* may be similarly omitted, especially in the objective case; as, This is the man [*whom*] I met at the door; the omission of the nominative *who* generally involves an ellipsis of the accompanying verb; as, Notify every man [*who* is, or *who* may be] there.

WHOSE

Whose, the possessive of *who*, requires no comment when so used. But *whose* is also used as the possessive of *which*, and this usage has been strenuously objected to by many grammarians. As to this usage, it should be observed that we greatly need a possessive for the pronoun *which*, the prepositional phrase *of which* being often clumsy and inconvenient. To supply this need, the possessive *whose* has been employed by many eminent writers.

[The pronoun *who* is usually applied only to persons. Its application to brutes or to things is improper, unless we mean to personify them. But *whose*, the possessive case of this relative, is sometimes used to supply the place of the possessive case, otherwise wanting, to the relative *which*. Examples: 'The mutes are those consonants *whose* sounds cannot be protracted.'—*Murray's Gram.*, p. 9. 'Philosophy, *whose* end is, to instruct us in the knowledge of nature.'—*Ib.*, p. 54; *Campbell's Rhet.*, p. 431. 'Those adverbs are compared *whose* primitives are obsolete.'—*Adam's Latin Gram.*, p. 150. 'After a sentence *whose* sense is complete in itself, a period is used.'—*Nutting's Gram.*, p. 124. 'We remember best those things *whose* parts are methodically disposed, and mutually connected.'—*Beattie's Moral Science*, i, 59. 'Is there any other doctrine *whose* followers are punished?'—Addison: *Murray's Gram.*, p. 54; *Lowth's*, p. 25.

> 'The question, *whose* solution I require,
> Is, what the sex of women most desire.'—DRYDEN.
>
> *Lowth*, p. 25.

Buchanan, as well as Lowth, condemns the foregoing use of *whose*, except in grave poetry, saying, 'This manner of *personification* adds an air of dignity to the higher and more solemn kind of poetry, but it is highly improper in the lower kind, or in prose.'—*Buchanan's English Syntax*, p. 78. And, of the last two examples above quoted, he says, 'It ought to be *of which*, in both places: i. e. The followers *of which*; the solution *of which*.'—*Ib.*, p. 78. The truth is, that no personification is here intended. Hence it may be better to avoid, if we can, this use of *whose*, as seeming to imply what we do not mean. But Buchanan himself (stealing the text of an older author) has furnished at least one example as objectionable as any of the foregoing: 'Prepositions are naturally placed betwixt the Words *whose* Relation and Dependence each of them is to express.'—*English Syntax*, p. 90; *British Gram.*, p. 201. I dislike this construction, and yet sometimes adopt it, for want of another as good. It is too much, to say with Churchill, that 'this practice is now discountenanced by all correct writers.'—*New Gram.*, p. 226. Grammarians would perhaps differ less, if they would read more. Dr. Campbell commends the use of *whose* for *of which*, as an improvement suggested by good taste, and established by abundant authority. See *Philosophy of Rhetoric*, p. 420. '*Whose*, the possessive or genitive case of *who* or *which;* applied to persons or things.'—*Webster's Octavo Dict.* '*Whose* is well authorized by good usage, as the possessive of *which*.'—*Sanborn's Gram.*, p. 69. 'Nor is any language complete, *whose* verbs have not tenses.'—*Harris's Hermes.*

> ———' Past and future, are the wings,
> On *whose* support, harmoniously conjoined,
> Moves the great spirit of human knowledge.'—MS.
>   *Wordsworth's Preface to his Poems,* p. xviii.
> Goold Brown *Grammar of English Grammars* pt. ii, ch. 5, p. 399.]

The personal use of *whose* is so clear as scarcely to need illustration :

> His house was known to all the vagrant train,
> He chid their wanderings but reliev'd their pain ;
> The long-remembered beggar was his guest,
> *Whose* beard descending swept his aged breast.
>   Goldsmith *Deserted Village* l. 149.

> Ye mariners of England
>   Who guard our native seas,
> *Whose* flag has braved, a thousand years,
>   The battle and the breeze !
>   Campbell *Mariners of England* st. 1.

The use of *whose* with reference to animals, abstractions, or inanimate objects is common among authors of foremost eminence, as the following, among many illustrations, will abundantly show :

> 'Tis beauty truly blent, *whose* red and white
> Nature's own sweet and cunning hand laid on.
>   Shakespeare *Twelfth Night* act i, sc. 5, l. 257.

Beauty is a witch,
Against *whose* charms faith melteth into blood.
SHAKESPEARE *Much Ado About Nothing* act ii, sc. 1, l. 186.

A hornèd stag, *whose* side a shaft hath pierc'd.
HOMER *Iliad* tr. by F. W. Newman, bk. xi, l. 476.

No stone is fitted in yon marble girth
Whose echo shall not tongue thy glorious doom.
TENNYSON *Tiresias* st. 10.

His 'lady' glares with gems *whose* vulgar blaze
The poor man through his heightened taxes pays.
LOWELL *Tempora Mutantur* l. 68.

Some slow water-rat, *whose* sinuous glide
Wavers the sedge's emerald shade from side to side.
LOWELL *Summer Storm* st. 1.

Ye lakes, *whose* vessels catch the busy gale.
GOLDSMITH *Traveller* l. 47.

Spires *whose* 'silent finger points to heaven.'
WORDSWORTH *The Excursion* bk. vi, l. 19.

[That Shandon bell],
Whose sounds so wild would,
In the days of childhood,
Fling round his cradle
Its magic spell.
BLANCHARD JERROLD *Final Reliques of Father Prout* p. 86.

'Twas not the fading charms of face
That riveted Love's golden chain;
It was the high celestial grace
Of goodness, that doth never wane—
Whose are the sweets that never pall,
Delicious. pure, and crowning all.
ABRAHAM COLES *Prayer in Affliction* can. 2, st. 8.

Mere facts . . . are the stones heaped about the mouth of the well in *whose* depth truth reflects the sky.
E. C. STEDMAN *Nature and Elements of Poetry* ch. 6, p. 196.

It was essentially a buccaneering expedition, *whose* naked object was plunder and murder. E. P. WHIPPLE *Essays and Reviews, Prescott's Peru* in vol. ii, p. 195.

At last the ancient inn appears, . . .
Whose flapping sign these fifty years
Has seesawed to and fro.
HOLMES *Agnes* pt. ii, st. 9.

The country *whose* exports are not sufficient to pay for her imports offers them on cheaper terms, until she succeeds in forcing the necessary demand.   MILL *Polit. Econ.* bk. iii, ch. 17, p. 431.

Relative Compounds in "-ever," "-so," "-soever"

Who, which, and *what* add the suffixes *-ever* and *·soever* with distributive effect, to denote universality. Thus, *whoever* or *whosoever* applies to any one of all humanity, or even of all intelligent beings, without limitation. *Whoso* is equivalent to *whosoever*, but is now archaic. The possessive *whosesoever*, once in good use, has also been found too cumbrous for modern speech to retain. *Whichever* and *whichsoever* apply to any one of some class designated or had in mind (see WHICH), with express denial of all limitation within that class. *Whatever* and *whatsoever* emphasize the unlimited meaning of *what*, directly expressing that which the pronoun *what* of itself implies. Thus, "Take *what* you will" applies to any object or any number of objects that may fall within one's choice; "Take *whatever* you will" says the same thing, only more explicitly and emphatically. *Whoever, whichever*. and *whatever* are in common use, but modern language. with its tendency to brevity and simplicity, has dropped the forms in *-soever*, which are now found only in the older literature or in a style modeled upon the archaic.

Whatsoever things are true, *whatsoever* things are honest, . . . if there be any praise, think on these things.   *Phil.* iv, 8.

Whosoever has seen a person of powerful character and happy genius will have remarked how easily . . . nature became ancillary to a man.   EMERSON *Nature* ch. 3, p. 27.

Whate'er betide, we'll turn aside   And see the Braes of Yarrow.
WORDSWORTH *Yarrow Unvisited* st. 1.

Whatever comes from the brain carries the hue of the place it came from.   HOLMES *Professor* ch. 6, p. 185.

Whatever in books or reading weakens the conscience or corrupts the moral feelings, should be rejected as evil.

> PORTER *Books and Reading* ch. 9, p. 101.

Whatever shows that a greater happiness is to be found in immaterial things tends to stifle the utilitarianism which is the cause of the growing paralysis of American life.

> W. J. STILLMAN in *Atlantic Monthly* Nov., 1891, p. 694.

Whatever be the means of preserving and transmitting properties, the primitive types have remained permanent and unchanged.

> AGASSIZ in Mrs. Agassiz's *Louis Agassiz* vol. ii, ch. 25, p. 780.

Whoever strives to do his duty faithfully is fulfilling the purpose for which he was created.   SMILES *Character* ch. 1, p. 15.

By the 5th and 6th of Edward VI., chap. 14, it was enacted, that *whoever* should buy any corn or grain with intent to sell it again, should be reputed an unlawful engrosser.

> ADAM SMITH *Wealth of Nations* vol. ii, bk. iv, ch. 5, p. 104.

He assumed that *whatever* belonged to the cardinal family belonged to him; perhaps he even thought she went with the house.   OLIVE T. MILLER *In Nesting Time* ch. 12, p. 202.

PART IV

Relative or Conjunctive Adverbs Defined and Illustrated

There are certain adverbs which besides their use in denoting place, manner, time, or the like serve also to join a subordinate to a principal clause, and are hence called *relative* or *conjunctive adverbs*.

The principal adverbs so used are the following: *hence, henceforth, henceforward, how, however, now, so, then, thence, thenceforth, thenceforward, when, whence, whencesoever, when ever, whensoever, where, whither, why.*

HENCE

Hence, from Anglo-Saxon *heonan*, is primarily an adverb of place, signifying away from this place; it is then, by natural ex tension, applied to time, in the sense of onward from this time, in the future; it is finally used of cause or reason, origin or source, and in this use becomes a connective, requiring a knowledge of what precedes for the understanding of that which follows. Compare THENCE and WHENCE.

1. Of cause or reason: because of this or that (thing, event, fact, circumstance, or state of affairs mentioned or referred to); consequently; therefore; as, his means are limited: *hence* he is compelled to economize.

2. Of origin or source: as a result of; proceeding from; as, the word "guilt" has been variously understood: *hence* have arisen endless disputes about sin, responsibility, etc.

And here we wander in illusions:
Some blessed power deliver us from *hence!*
SHAKESPEARE *Comedy of Errors* act iv, sc. 8, l. 42.

(308)

HENCEFORTH, HENCEFORWARD

Henceforth and *henceforward*, self-explaining compounds, convey emphatically the meaning of *hence* with reference to time: from this time forth, onward, or forward; in all the future.

> Pardon me, wife. *Henceforth* do what thou wilt.
> SHAKESPEARE *Merry Wives of Windsor* act iv, sc. 4, l. 7.

> All manner of men, assembled here in arms this day, against God's peace, and the king's, we charge and command you, in his highness' name, to repair to your several dwelling-places; and not to wear, handle, or use, any sword, weapon, or dagger, *henceforward*, upon pain of death.
> SHAKESPEARE *1 K. Henry VI.* act i, sc. 3, l. 79.

HOW

How, from Anglo-Saxon *hû*, is closely akin to the Anglo-Saxon *hwy*, *hwî*, why, and is primarily an interrogative. When the direct question becomes indirect or dependent, the interrogative has the force of a relative; thus, in the question, "*How* did he do it?" the "how" is independent of anything that may precede; but in the sentence, "Tell me *how* he did it," neither clause is complete without the other, and this latter "how" is the connective that binds the two clauses into one sentence, having the force of a relative. Hence the interrogative readily passed into relative use, with the following meanings:

1. In what way or manner; as, tell me *how* it was done.

> *How* he gormandizes, that jolly miller! rasher after rasher, *how* they pass away frizzling hot and smoking from the gridiron down the immense grinning gulf of a mouth!
> THACKERAY in F. G. Stephens's *George Cruikshank* p. 88.

> There must be discussion, to show *how* experience is to be interpreted.
> MILL *On Liberty* ch. 2, p. 40.

> Hear *how* the birds, on ev'ry blooming spray,
> With joyous musick wake the dawning day!
> POPE *Pastorals, Spring* l. 28.

[NOTE.—After words of caution, as *take care, beware,* etc., *how* is almost equal to *of* with a participle, or to *that not.*

Let a man beware *how* he keepeth company with choleric and quarrelsome persons.   BACON *Essays, Of Travel* in vol. i, p. 62.

The meaning here evidently is, "beware *of* keeping company," etc., or "beware *that* he does *not* keep company," etc., but *how* expresses the warning with delicate yet forcible indirectness.]

2. By what means, process, or agency; as, it is a question *how* the ore can be separated from the rock.

> In the beginning, *how* the heav'ns and earth
> Rose out of chaos.   MILTON *Paradise Lost* bk. i, l. 10.

Upon the wall of rock was placed a second wall of snow, which dwindled to a pure knife-edge at the top. . . . *How* to pass this snow catenary I knew not.
>   TYNDALL *Hours of Exercise* ch. 9, p. 99.

3. To what degree, extent, or amount; by what number, measure, or quantity; in what proportion; as, let me know *how* much is due; I wish to find *how* high that building is.

Jesu! Jesu! the mad days that I have spent! and to see *how* many of mine old acquaintance are dead!
>   SHAKESPEARE *2 K. Henry IV.* act iii, sc. 2, l. 34.

> And underneath is written,
>   In letters all of gold,
> *How* valiantly he kept the bridge
>   In the brave days of old.
>   MACAULAY *Horatius* st. 50.

> Those evening bells! those evening bells!
> *How* many a tale their music tells,
> Of youth, and home, and that sweet time
> When last I heard their soothing chime!
>   MOORE *Those Evening Bells* st. 1.

It is incalculable *how* much that royal bigwig cost Germany.
>   THACKERAY *Four Georges, George I.* p. 278.

> *How* purely true, how deeply warm,
> The inly-breathed appeal may be.
> ELIZA COOK *Prayer* st. 1.

4. In what condition or state; as, let us see *how* the account stands.

> *How* would you be,
> If He, which is the top of judgment, should
> But judge you as you are?
> SHAKESPEARE *Measure for Measure* act ii, sc. 2, l. 76.

5. At what price; for what sum; as, I inquired *how* the stock sold.

> *Shallow.* . . . *How* a good yoke of bullocks at Stamford fair?
> *Silence.* Truly, cousin, I was not there.
>
> *   *   *   *   *   *   *
>
> *Shallow.* . . . *How* a score of ewes now?
> *Silence.* Thereafter as they be; a score of good ewes may be worth ten pounds.
> SHAKESPEARE *2 K. Henry IV.* act iii, sc. 2, l. 39.

6. By what name or designation; as, find *how* he is called by his own people.

7. For what reason; why; as, I can not understand *how* he came to do it.

> *Ford.*   And sped you, sir?
> *Falstaff.*   Very ill-favouredly, Master Brook.
> *Ford.*   *How* so, sir? Did she change her determination?
> SHAKESPEARE *Merry Wives of Windsor* act iii, sc. 5, l. 65.

If we ask *how* out of the state of innocence man can ever have fallen into evil, we can find no answer; the origin of evil is unsearchable. CAIRD *Kant* vol. ii, bk. iv, ch. 1, p. 568.

8. Denoting at once manner and result, after *relate, report, say, tell,* and the like: nearly equivalent to the conjunction *that;* formerly *how that;* as, he told me *how* he was reduced to poverty.

Guermonprez described lately *how* a person had remained three days in hypnosis, nobody being able to wake him.   •
ALBERT MOLL *Hypnotism* ch. 2, p. 87.

How without anxiety or care the flower woke into loveliness.
DRUMMOND *Natural Law, Growth* p. 123.

HOWEVER

See HOWEVER under CONJUNCTIONS.

In whatever manner, way, or state; by whatever means; to whatever amount or degree; as, the work must be done, *however* difficult it may be.

> And yet I knew that every wrong
> *However* old, *however* strong,
> But waited God's avenging hour.
> WHITTIER *Astræa at the Capitol* st. 7.

Every station in life, *however* great or *however* prosperous, has its drawbacks, its checks, its limits. •
A. P. STANLEY *Thoughts that Breathe* § 74, p. 128.

Glacier ice, *however* hard and brittle it may appear, is really a viscous substance, resembling treacle, or honey, or tar, or lava.
TYNDALL *Forms of Water* ¶ 390, p. 155.

Truth is the same, *however* different . . . the quantity apprehended by us.   HOLLIS READ *God in Hist.* ch. 10, p. 184.

However I may err in future, I will never be disingenuous in acknowledging my errors.
FRANCES BURNEY *Evelina* letter lx, p. 281.

No people ever lived by cursing their fathers, *however* great a curse their fathers might have been to them.
THOREAU *Cape Cod* ch. 2, p. 19.

NOW

Now, from Anglo-Saxon *nû*, an adverb of time, referring to the immediate present, has in certain uses the force of a connective.

1. In the way of logical inference, a conjunctive use: in view of the facts stated; things being so; in such circumstances; as, "That is the situation.   *Now*, what shall we do?"

> Being mad before, how doth she *now* for wits?
> SHAKESPEARE *Venus and Adonis* l. 249.

How *now* shall this be compassed?

SHAKESPEARE *The Tempest* act iii, sc. 2, l. 59.

[NOTE.—*Now* in this sense is often used almost as an expletive, having reference to facts not mentioned, but mutually understood; as, *now*, no trifling.

Now in this sense is also used elliptically, with the force of *now that*; as, *now* I am in need, my friends desert me.]

2. As a correlative, followed by another *now* or by *then*: at one time (contrasted with another time).

Now . . . *now*, *now* . . . *then*, at one time . . . at another time; as, he is *now* talkative, *now* taciturn; he was *now* timid, *then* rash.

> And *now* he feels the bottom;
> * *Now* on dry earth he stands;
> *Now* round him throng the Fathers
> To press his gory hands;
> And *now* with shouts and clapping,
> And noise of weeping loud,
> He enters through the River-Gate,
> Borne by the joyous crowd.
>
> MACAULAY *Horatius* st. 48.

> The bells themselves are the best of preachers,
> Their brazen lips are learned teachers,
> From their pulpits of stone, in the upper air,
> Sounding aloft, without crack or flaw,
> Shriller than trumpets under the Law,
> * *Now* a sermon and *now* a prayer.
>
> LONGFELLOW *The Golden Legend* pt. iii, st. 88.

Now . . . *then*: See THEN.

The political needle was . . . pointing *now* to one set of men as the coming Government and *then* to another.

TROLLOPE *Phineas Finn* ch. 85, p. 262.

SO

See SO under CONJUNCTIONS. See also CORRELATIVE CONJUNCTIONS. *So*, as an adverb, has relative and connective force, by reference to a standard of comparison elsewhere expressed

or implied. When the standard of comparison is neither expressed nor implied in language, but understood from mutual
knowledge of facts, *so* is simply an adverb and not a connective;
as, it is a mistake to wait *so* long [*i. e.*, as we both know you
are doing].

1. To this or that or such a degree; to this or that extent; in
the same degree, quantity, or proportion: followed or preceded
by a dependent clause introduced by *as*, *that*, or (after a negative)
but; as, he was *so* unlucky *as* to fall; *as* they were commanded,
so they did; they are not *so* weak *but* they can fight.

[NOTE.—In many cases it is difficult to decide whether *so* in
such use is a conjunction or an adverb in conjunctive use.
Compare CORRELATIVE CONJUNCTIONS, p. 270.]

> My circumstances
> Being *so* near the truth *as* I will make them,
> Must first induce you to believe.
> > SHAKESPEARE *Cymbeline* act ii, sc. 4, l. 62.

> I know a falcon swift and peerless
> > As e'er was cradled in the pine;
> No bird had ever eye *so* fearless,
> > Or wing *so* strong *as* this of mine.
> > > LOWELL *The Falcon.*

By adroit movements, detachments of the American army
so intercepted Clinton's march, *as* to compel him to change his
course.   LOSSING *United States* fifth period, ch. 5, p. 287.

There is no audience *so* hard to face *as* one of school-children.
> EGGLESTON *Hoosier School-Master* ch. 1, p. 20.

Who would hold the order of the almanac *so* fast but for the
ding-dong 'Thirty days hath September,' etc.
> EMERSON *Letters and Social Aims, Poetry* p. 48.

Factions do not *so* soon give up either their vengeance or
their hopes.   GUIZOT *France* tr. by Black, vol. ii, ch. 28, p. 290.

> Men drop *so* fast, ere life's mid stage we tread,
> Few know *so* many friends alive, *as* dead.
> > YOUNG *Love of Fame* l. 97.

So far from being stationary and fixed, as it were, in a hollow glass globe, at nearly equal distances from us, they [the stars] are all in rapid motion, and their distances vary enormously.

J. N. LOCKYER *Elements of Astron.* int., art. viii, p. 11.

'Tis pity a man should be *so* weak and languishing, *that* he can't even wish. MONTAIGNE *Works* tr. by Hazlitt *Of Experience* in vol. iii, bk. iii, ch. 18, p. 429.

So universal is the action of capillarity, *that* solids and liquids cannot touch one another without producing a change in the form of the surface of the liquid.

MARY SOMERVILLE *Connection of Phys. Sciences* § 14, p. 110.

> *Such* dupes are men to custom, and *so* prone
> To rev'rence what is ancient, and can plead
> A course of long observance for its use,
> *That* even servitude, the worst of ills,
> Because deliver'd down from sire to son,
> Is kept and guarded as a sacred thing !
>
> COWPER *Task* bk. v, l. 298.

2. In this, that, or such a manner (as stated or implied): often following a clause beginning with *as*, or preceding a clause beginning with *that*; as, so act *that* the event will justify it; *as* it had been predicted, *so* it came to pass.

> And being fed by us you used us *so*
> As that ungentle gull, the cuckoo's bird,
> Useth the sparrow.
>
> SHAKESPEARE *1 K. Henry IV.* act v, sc. 1, l. 59.

So shows a snowy dove trooping with crows.

SHAKESPEARE *Romeo and Juliet* act i, sc. 5, l. 50.

> O, such a day,
> *So* fought, *so* follow'd and *so* fairly won.
>
> SHAKESPEARE *2 K. Henry IV.* act i, sc. 1, l. 20.

So the struck eagle, stretched upon the plain,
No more through rolling clouds to soar again,
Viewed his own feather on the fatal dart,
And wing'd the shaft that quivered in his heart.

BYRON *English Bards and Scotch Reviewers* l. 826.

So let the hills of doubt divide,
So bridge with faith the sunless tide!
> Whittier *The River Path* st. 19.

Curses, like chickens, come home to roost; and *so* do Falsities!   Geikie *Entering on Life, Character* p. 55.

All the columns [in the Doric order] slope slightly inward, *so as* to give an idea of strength and support to the whole.
> James Fergusson *Hist. Arch.* vol. i, pt. i, bk. iii, ch. 2, p. 251.

3. Just as said, implied, or directed; according to a fact or facts stated or implied; accordingly; as, he asked me to give him a receipt, and I did *so*; is it really *so?*

I was ever a fighter, *so*—one fight more, the best and the last!
> Browning *Prospice* l. 18.

So warned by the wolf in his own fold this shepherd of souls tried to keep his flock from harm.
> Louisa M. Alcott *Silver Pitchers* ch. 6, p. 40.

4. For this or that reason; consequently; therefore: often preceded by *and*; as, the business did not pay, *so* he gave it up.

People did not understand him; *so* they said he was a doubtful sort of a man and passed by on the other side.
> Kipling *Plain Tales, Miss Youghal's Sais* p. 30.

5. According to the truth of what is sworn to or affirmed: a limiting clause introduced by *as* being often expressed or implied; as, *so* help me God (*i. e.*, May God *so* help me *as* what I speak is true).

So help me every spirit sanctified,
As I have spoken for you all my best,
And stood within the blank of his displeasure,
For my free speech.
> Shakespeare *Othello* act iii, sc. 4, l. 180.

THEN

See **then** under Conjunctions.

1. At that time (expressed or implied); as, if I am here next year, how will it be *then?*

> *Then* none was for a party—
> *Then* all were for the state;
> *Then* the great man helped the poor,
> And the poor man loved the great;
> *Then* lands were fairly portioned!
> *Then* spoils were fairly sold:
> The Romans were like brothers
> In the brave days of old.
>
> MACAULAY *Horatius* st. 32.

2. Next or immediately afterward; later; next; afterward: often with indication of result or consequence (compare THEN, conjunction); as, first came the police, *then* the military; he neglected his work, and *then* lost his place.

> Go *then* merrily to Heaven.
>
> BURTON *Anatomy of Melancholy* pt. ii, sec. 3, memb. 1.

> Work first, and *then* rest.
>
> RUSKIN *Seven Lamps of Architecture, The Lamp of Beauty.*

> You bring up your girls as if they were meant for sideboard ornaments, and *then* complain of their frivolity.
>
> RUSKIN *Sesame and Lilies, Of Queens' Gardens* p. 108.

> We let our blessings get mouldy, and *then* call them curses.
>
> H. W. BEECHER in *Life Thoughts* p. 25.

3. At another time: used as a correlative, following *now, at first, at one time*, etc.; as, *now* one was ahead, *then* the other. Compare CORRELATIVE CONJUNCTIONS.

> Sometime like apes, that moe and chatter at me,
> And after, bite me; *then* like hedge-hogs, which
> Lie tumbling in my bare-foot way.
>
> SHAKESPEARE *The Tempest* act ii, sc. 2, l. 10.

THENCE

Thence, from Middle English *thennes*, Anglo-Saxon *thanan*, primarily an adverb of place, has connective force by referring to some place, time, source, reason, etc., expressed or implied in the immediate context. Compare HENCE and WHENCE.

1. Of place: from that place; as, he went to the market, and *thence* to the office.

> Sitting on a bank,
> Weeping again the king my father's wreck,
> This music crept by me upon the waters,
> Allaying both my fury and their passion,
> With its sweet air: *thence* I have follow'd it,
> Or it hath drawn me rather.
>
>   Shakespeare *The Tempest* act i, sc. 2, l. 394.

2. Of time: from that time; after that time; thereafter: a usage that is now somewhat rare; as, "this continued till the fall of the Roman Empire: *thence* many centuries elapsed," etc.

3. Of origin, source, reason, etc.: from the circumstance, fact, or cause that; by reason of that; on that ground; therefore; as, all the shutters were closed—*thence* I inferred that the house was unoccupied.

[Note.—Since *thence* includes the meaning of *from*, the expression *from thence* is pleonastic, though used by good writers.]

The poet is poet only because he is more finely strung than other men, and *thence* more capable of the heart's music.
     G. H. Calvert *Goethe* p. 140.

THENCEFORTH, THENCEFORWARD

Thenceforth and *thenceforward*, self-explaining compounds, are emphatic extensions of *thence*; *thenceforth* applying only to time, *thenceforward* referring both to place and time.

WHEN

When, from Anglo-Saxon *hwænne*, is primarily an interrogative adverb, asking the question "at what time?" as, *when* will you come? By changing the question to the indirect form, the adverb *when* acts as a relative with connective force; as, please inform me *when* [*i. e.*, at what time] you will come. See also When under Conjunctions.

Who gave thee, O Beauty,
  The keys of this breast,—
Too credulous lover
  Of blest and unblest?
Say, *when* in lapsed ages
  Thee knew I of old?
Or what was the service
  For which I was sold?

EMERSON *Ode to Beauty* st. 1.

We must know *when* to spare and *when* to spend.
JULIA McN. WRIGHT *Complete Home* ch. 14, p. 406.

WHENCE

Whence, from Middle English *whennes*, adverbial genitive of *whenne*, when, is primarily an interrogative adverb of place, correlative in meaning to the demonstrative *thence*. (Compare HENCE and THENCE.) Like other interrogative adverbs, *whence* acquires relative and conjunctive uses through its employment as an interrogative in indirect questions, "*Whence* did you come?" being converted into "Tell me *whence* you came."

1. In interrogative, passing into relative or conjunctive use: from what or which place, origin, or source; as, no one knew *whence* he came; it is uncertain *whence* the word is derived

The boy stood on the burning deck,
  Whence all but he had fled;
The flame that lit the battle's wreck
  Shone round him o'er the dead.

MRS. HEMANS *Casabianca.*

Whence is yonder flower so strangely bright?
  Would the sunset's last reflected shine
Flame so red from that dead flush of light?
  Dark with passion is its lifted line,
Hot, alive, amid the falling night.

DORA READ GOODALE *Cardinal Flower*

2. Of logical connection: for which cause or reason; wherefore; therefore; as, these are the facts, *whence* I conclude, etc.

[NOTE.—*From whence* is pleonastic, since the meaning of *from* is included in *whence*, yet the expression *from whence* is used by good writers, including Shakespeare and Milton.

More should I question thee . . . *from whence* thou camest.
SHAKESPEARE *All's Well That Ends Well* act ii, sc. 1, l. 210.]

WHENCESOEVER

Whencesoever, with distributive force, signifying from whatever place, source, or cause, is in approved use, but, like all cumbrous forms, is now becoming rare.

> It is my son, young Harry Percy,
> Sent from my brother Worcester, *whencesoever*.
> SHAKESPEARE *K. Richard II.* act ii, sc. 3, l. 22.

WHENEVER (WHENE'ER)

Whenever, a self-explaining compound, extends distributively the meaning of *when*, signifying at whatever time; as, I retire early *whenever* I can. *Whene'er* is an abbreviated and poetic form of *whenever*.

It seems that it was no part of Hannibal's plan to engage the Romans *whenever* he might meet with them.
CHAS. MERIVALE *Rome* ch. 20, p. 158.

WHENSOEVER

Whensoever, an extended form of *whenever*, with practically the same meaning, has now passed almost out of use, giving place to the shorter form. The Standard Dictionary terms this expression "formal and slightly emphatic."

Blandishments will not fascinate us, nor will threats of a 'halter' intimidate. For, under God, we are determined that wheresoever, *whensoever*, or howsoever we shall be called to make our exit, we will die free men.
JOSIAH QUINCY *Observations on the Boston Port Bill* 1774.

WHERE

See WHERE under CONJUNCTIONS.

Where as an interrogative in direct questions is not a connective, but when the question is made indirect or dependent, the interrogative is used as a connective with relative force.

1. At or in what place, relation, or situation; as, do you know *where* your hat is?

> Tell me *where* is fancy bred,
> Or in the heart or in the head?
> How begot, how nourished?
>   Reply, reply.
> It is engender'd in the eyes,
> With gazing fed; and fancy dies
> In the cradle where it lies.
> SHAKESPEARE *Merchant of Venice* act iii, sc. 2, l. 63.

'*Where* Liberty is, there is my Country,' was the sentiment of that great Apostle of Freedom, Benjamin Franklin, uttered during the trials of the Revolution.

> SUMNER *Works, Speech, Nov. 2, '55* in vol. iv, p. 80.

2. To what or which place or end; whither; as, tell me *where* you are going.

> He is in heaven, *where* thou shalt never come.
> SHAKESPEARE *K. Richard III.* act i. sc. 2, l. 106.

She stooped *where* the cool spring bubbled up.
> WHITTIER *Maud Muller* st. 10.

> Go *where* glory waits thee;
> But while fame elates thee,
> Oh! still remember me.
>   MOORE *Go Where Glory Waits Thee.*

I go . . . *where* wild men howl around
Their blood-stained altars — to uplift th' unknown
Unawful Crucifix.
> H. H. MILMAN *Anne Boleyn* sc. 3, st. 21.

3. From what place; whence; as, I wish to know *where* he got that money.

Dieu de battailes! *where* have they this mettle?
SHAKESPEARE *K. Henry V.* act jii, sc. 5, l. 15.

[NOTE.—*Where* has taken the meanings of *whence* and *whither*, words once common, but which have now practically disappeared from ordinary use, being found only in the literary style.

The meanings of *at* and *to* are included in *where*, so that the expressions " *Where* is he *at?* " and " *Where* are you going *to?* " are inelegant. While the meaning of *from* is sometimes included in *where* (as in definition 8, above), yet such inclusion is neither uniform nor certain, so that the question " *Where* do you come? " would not be understood as meaning " *Whence* [from what place] do you come? " Hence it is both common and allowable to use *from* with *where*, and we may ask, " *Where* do you come *from?* "]

For compounds of *where* see CONJUNCTIONS.

WHITHER

Whither, from Anglo-Saxon *hwider*, is primarily an interrogative, signifying to which or what place. Thence it comes to have the force of a relative, the direct question, " *Whither* are you going? " passing into the indirect, " Tell me *whither* you are going." The excellent word *whither* is unfortunately in modern popular usage almost completely displaced by *where*.

And they drew nigh unto the village *whither* they went.
Luke xxiv, 28.

Whither gains distributive force in the extended form *whithersoever*, meaning to whatever place, direction, etc., but this latter form is altogether archaic.

WHY

Why, from Anglo-Saxon *hwi*, as an interrogative adverb, asking for a reason, becomes a connective in a dependent question, " *Why* did you do it? " passing into " Tell me *why* you did it." See WHY under CONJUNCTIONS.

ADDENDA

Introductory Particles

It—There

The pronoun and the adverb here associated are used quite apart from their ordinary meaning in introducing a clause or sentence. When we say, "*It* is a fine day," we do not think of any special antecedent of the pronoun "it," and when we say, "*There* is money enough in the bank," we do not think of the particular location of that "money." The "it" and "there" are used in such cases like the algebraic x or y simply to fill the place of some quantity not exactly specified, but to be supplied later. In such expressions as "*It* is pleasant weather," "*It* is I," the "it" simply holds the thought in expectancy for the coming predicate. In such expressions as "*It* is time to go," "*It* rains," the "it" serves the same purpose.

In the phrase "*there* is," the word "there" is so independent of local suggestion that a local adverb, as "here" or another "there," may be added to give the local meaning which the introductory "there" fails to express, and we may say, "*There* is material *here*," or "*There* is a gate *there*," the final adverb keeping the local meaning which the introductory adverb has lost. The introductory "there" is more slightly pronounced than "there" denoting location.

There is a lad *here*, which hath five barley loaves and two small fishes.   *John* vi, 9.

In interrogations the sentence may be inverted, so that the "it" or "there" will follow its verb, just as a subject noun might do, but yet keep the same essential relation as when used in introducing the clause or sentence; as, "Does *it* rain?" "Is *there* time?"

> Breathes *there* the man, with soul so dead,
> Who never to himself hath said,
>   This is my own, my native land!
>   SCOTT *Lay of Last Minstrel* can. 6, st. 1.

Sometimes the introductory "it" stands as the equivalent of a whole clause or phrase, as an infinitive with its adjuncts or the like; as, "When . . . *it* becomes necessary for one people to sever the bonds which have bound them to another," etc.; that is, "When . . . to sever the bonds," etc., "becomes necessary," etc. But the latter expression seems stiff and forced, while that with the introductory "it" is flowing and easy, the "it" serving as an usher to direct the mind to the principal thought. These two introductory particles, "it" and "there," have much to do with the coherence and ease of English speech.

INDEX

Lightning Source UK Ltd.
Milton Keynes UK
UKOW05f1202120917
309040UK00006B/153/P